Preserving the Seasons

A Guide to Canned, Jammed, Frozen, Dehydrated, Freeze-Dried, Quick-Pickled, *and* Infused Produce, Herbs, and Flowers

Preserving the Seasons

HOLLY CAPELLE

Photography by Michael Shay and Jeremy Dunham
of Polara Studio

SIMON ELEMENT

New York · Amsterdam/Antwerp · London · Toronto · Sydney/Melbourne · New Delhi

To my kids,
Katlyn, Cole, Jack, Ryan, Sidnee, and Violet,
this book is for you.

Contents

9
Introduction

PART ONE
SAVING THE SEASONS

14 • CHAPTER 1
Freeze It!

44 • CHAPTER 2
No-Can Jams & Quick Pickles

62 • CHAPTER 3
Boiling Water Canning

86 • CHAPTER 4
Dry It!

114 • CHAPTER 5
Dehydrate It!

138 • CHAPTER 6
Freeze-Dry It!

PART TWO
SAVORING THE SEASONS WITH INFUSIONS

160 • CHAPTER 7
Water Infusions

182 • CHAPTER 8
Savory Infusions

210 • CHAPTER 9
Sweet Infusions

PART THREE
SERVING THE SEASONS

236
I'll Cheers to That!

242
Snack Shack

248
Off to a Good Start

262
Soups & Sandwiches

274
Salad Bar

284
Dinner Menu

303
Hit the Sauce

305
The Bread Box

318
Sweet Tooth

342
Acknowledgments

344
Journal Pages

346
Index

Introduction

For as long as I can remember, my husband, Kevin, and I have been playing house. A benefit of marrying young, I have had my fella by my side for over thirty years. We have grown up and are growing old together, always creating a life from scratch. We fill our home with love, laughter, and lots of little feet—twelve, to be exact. We have six kids, including two sets of twins, who range in age from thirteen to twenty-eight as I write this. Being their mom has taught me a lot of things, including how to be imaginative, frugal, and resourceful, and how to live a grateful life.

As our family grew, so did the grocery bill. The once-small garden that Kevin and I tended took on new meaning. More than just a garden, it became our together project and a living classroom for our children. It became a source of peace and a way to provide organic, seed-to-table food for our big family. With every new season, our harvests got bigger, so I began to learn to preserve, infuse, and flavor our abundance, creating custom ingredients for my cooking, or "kitchen playtime," as I like to call it. As I deepened my preserving knowledge and learned to make the most of seasonal produce, I saved more than just our garden harvests: I took advantage of leftovers, food scraps, coupon days, super sales, bulk stores, and those farm stands along the road that always make my heart skip a beat.

Our large suburban lot just outside Portland, Oregon, is now a mini hobby homestead. With a coop of egg-laying chickens and several vegetable, fruit, herb, and edible flower gardens throughout, we're able to provide quite a bit for ourselves.

Don't get me wrong; we grocery shop often and love pizza delivery. But that's the beauty of preserving your own food: You don't need to be all in. Doing what works for your family, whatever that may be, is just right.

My tiny 1960s kitchen is the heart of our home and my social media. It still has the original cupboards and counters, spiffed up with a few coats and paint and some thrift store decor. The open shelves are lined with jars of preserved garden bounty. Just around the corner is an old coat closet we converted into a pantry.

My intention in the kitchen is to enjoy the experience. To create and to learn. To use and preserve what I grow and buy in various ways to feed our family. Home cooking for me is a way to be an artist, a provider, and a source of comfort. It's how I show my love.

But in between my winning culinary creations, I burn things, I forget ingredients, and sometimes I just make mistakes. A chef I am not. But you don't need to be a professional to love being in the kitchen.

Just as cooking isn't just for chefs, home food preservation isn't just for homesteaders. Whether your bounty comes from the backyard garden, farmers' markets, or bulk sales at the grocery store, preserving your own food is healthy and cost effective. Some of my favorite ways to preserve are boiling water canning, dehydrating, infusing, drying, freezing, quick pickling, and now I can't get enough of freeze-drying!

Preserving the Seasons is a gift to my family. It's how I can inspire my kids, Katlyn, Cole, Jack, Ryan, Sidnee, and Violet, and our family's generations to come, to cook, create, connect with their food, and be more self-sufficient. A true blessing. For Kevin and me, it's been an unforgettable chapter in our love story that continues to grow in ways I never imagined. This book is also my way of hanging out with you and cheering you on while you preserve and cook.

Holly Capelle

How to Use This Book

Preserving the Seasons is organized into three parts.

Parts One and Two show you how to build a pantry of preserved kitchen staples. "Saving the Seasons" (page 13) is a deep dive into **freezing, pickling, boiling water canning, drying, dehydrating, and freeze-drying**. These chapters include everything you need to know about those techniques. They include charts, lists, and tips that will show you exactly how to preserve many of your favorite foods. Do you want to can peaches or dehydrate apples? It's in there! I also provide basic recipes to illustrate key points of the technique in each chapter. "Savoring the Seasons with Infusions" (page 159) walks you through **infusions, both savory and sweet**, and stars vinegar, oil, butter, salt, sugar, honey, and yes, even water. You'll find charts and lists to inspire you to make your own tisanes, herb blends, flavored syrups, and so much more.

Part Three is about incorporating these ingredients into your everyday cooking. "Serving the Seasons" is a collection of recipes that I make for my family and that I hope you will put into rotation at your house, too.

Throughout the book, I've scattered tidbits for two subjects close to my heart, "ZERO WASTE ALERT!" and "A LITTLE ME TIME." **The first shows you how to repurpose food scraps in ways you may not have considered. The second is a guide on making your own beauty and health-care products with botanical infusions.** It's my friendly reminder as you work hard in the kitchen to take time for self-care in simple ways.

Almost as important as the recipes is my desire to inspire you to come up with your own ideas for how to use what you've preserved. What you make will depend on what you grow or what is available where you live. I give lots of options in the recipes so that you can mix and match what you have on hand or what you like. Finally, the journal pages at the end of the book are for you—a place to put your recipes, ideas, and notes. This is your book as much as it is mine. It is *our* book.

So, are you ready? Get out the canning jars, prep the freezer, or plug in your dehydrator or freeze-dryer. It's kitchen playtime!

Saving the Seasons

PART ONE

---

14 • CHAPTER 1
Freeze It!

44 • CHAPTER 2
No-Can Jams & Quick Pickles

62 • CHAPTER 3
Boiling Water Canning

86 • CHAPTER 4
Dry It!

114 • CHAPTER 5
Dehydrate It!

138 • CHAPTER 6
Freeze-Dry It!

CHAPTER 1
Freeze It!

17
Get Set Up for Freezing

26
Freezing Fresh Vegetables, Herbs, and Flowers

21
Freezing Fresh Fruit

Freezing may be the easiest, most accessible method of preserving food. It is a budget-friendly way to savor the seasons (or those bulk sales) all year long. In addition to maintaining color and flavor, freezing retains most nutrients and stunts the growth of microorganisms that causes food to spoil.

37
Troubleshooting Home Freezing

38
Ice Box Treats
Garden Yogurt Pops 38
Strawberry Patch Ice Cream 39
Strawberry Rose Sorbet 39
Berry Good Freezer Smoothie Cubes 41
Fresh Mint Chocolate Chip Ice Cream 43

Get Set Up for Freezing

Get it good and cold: Whether you're using an upright or chest freezer, or the freezer compartment of a refrigerator, you want to set the temperature at or below 0°F. This is essential. A freezer thermometer, used to double-check this crucial temperature, is a good investment.

Good freezing is all about the storage: Sealing or wrapping food well to keep air and moisture at bay is important. Proper storage prevents freezer burn, which can ruin flavor and cause oxidation, resulting in a change of color. Here are the tools I recommend:

- **Aluminum foil:** Foil is ideal for wrapping meat and baked goods. I use heavy-duty foil for maximum protection. For best storage, place foil-wrapped food inside freezer bags.

- **Freezer bags:** Made of durable plastic, freezer bags provide extra protection against air and moisture. Regular plastic bags are comparatively flimsy. *Always press or suck the excess air from the bag before closing.* Resealable freezer bags are great for dry-packed fruits and vegetables as well as soft foods and liquids. Seal the bags, lay them flat in the freezer, unstacked, until frozen (2 to 6 hours), then stack them up to save space. Vacuum-sealed freezer bags, which require the use of a vacuum sealer, can double or triple shelf life. Follow the manufacturer's instructions for filling and sealing. Reusable freezer bags are also readily available online.

- **Freezer wrap:** Thicker than the plastic wrap you may have on hand, freezer wrap stretches to enclose the food in a tighter wrap, keeping out the air that causes freezer burn. This storage option works well for cookie dough, pasta, and baked goods. For added protection, place wrapped food in freezer bags or wrap them in foil.

- **Freezer paper:** This thick paper has a plastic- or wax-coated side and is mainly used for meat. *Make sure that the coated side touches the food.* Secure tightly wrapped foods with specially designed freezer tape.

- **Ice trays or silicone molds:** These are used for freezing small batches of pureed foods or chopped herbs mixed with water or oil.

- **Rigid plastic or glass containers, plastic freezer jars, freezer-safe wide-mouth jars, or tapered freezer-safe jars:** Any of these can be used for freezing soft, liquid, or semiliquid foods.

Prep Steps

Turn it down: Twenty-four hours before you want to start freezing, turn the freezer temperature down to –10°F. This helps maintain a temperature of 0°F once the prepared food is added and absorbs some of the cold air.

Know your freezer capacity: For every cubic foot of freezer space, you can freeze two to three pounds of food at one time.

Use high-quality, fully ripe, unblemished fruits and vegetables, and make sure to give everything a good rinse.

Additional steps, depending on what you're freezing:

Flash freezing: Also known as pre-freezing, **this extra step is ideal for small ingredients like berries or peas to keep them from clumping**. It also allows you to use just the amount of food you need each time, instead of thawing out an entire container.

To flash freeze, line a rimmed baking sheet with wax or parchment paper. Spread the food on the prepared baking sheet. Freeze for 1 to 4 hours, or until frozen solid. Transfer to airtight containers for longer storage.

Pretreating fruit: Fruits like apples and pears, which oxidize and brown quickly, can benefit from a protective layer of natural acid such as ascorbic acid. This extra step also preserves the flavor and retains nutrients.

- Ascorbic Acid: Mix 1 tablespoon with 1 quart water.
- Citric Acid: Mix $\frac{1}{4}$ teaspoon with 1 quart water.
- Lemon/Lime Juice: Mix 1 cup fresh or bottled with 1 quart water.

- Fresh Fruit Protector: Often sold at supermarkets in the canning section, this product is usually a mix of ascorbic and citric acid. Follow the directions on the packaging.

In a large bowl, stir together the acid of choice and water until completely dissolved. Add the produce, making sure it is completely submerged (mix more solution as needed). Let stand for 3 to 5 minutes. Drain well in a colander. The pretreatment solution can be used twice before discarding.

Blanching: This two-step process involves quick, intense heat followed by an ice bath. Blanching prevents the chemical reactions that cause food to lose flavor and color. It also breaks down the cellulose in vegetables that would otherwise trap water in the produce, making it soggy after defrosting. And with stone fruits and tomatoes, it helps loosens their thin skins for easier peeling.

You can blanch in boiling water or by steam. Although both methods are effective, steam blanching, which takes a little longer, preserves texture and flavor better and retains more vitamins and minerals. Steaming is my preferred way to prep leafy greens for the freezer. Water blanching, however, does the best job of maintaining vibrant color and flavor and is the preferred method for freezing in most cases.

Altitude note: *Add 1 minute to blanching time if you're 5,000 feet or higher above sea level.*

Whether you're boiling or steaming, make sure to have an ice bath (a large bowl filled with cold water and plenty of ice cubes) ready to go. It must be large enough to shock and cool down your produce. When working in batches, be sure to change the water and ice frequently to keep it very cold.

To water blanch:

- Work in batches of 1 pound of vegetables at a time. Bring 1 gallon of water to a full boil in a large pot set over high heat. Add the produce directly to the water or into a steamer basket and return to a boil. (If the water doesn't return to a boil after 1 minute, it is a sign that the batch is too large. Remove some of the produce.)

- Blanch for the time directed in the individual freezing recipes, maintaining high heat and a rapid boil for the entire time. Underblanching can activate enzymes, making spoilage occur faster. Overblanching results in loss of color and flavor and diminishes the food's nutrient value.

- Drain the produce into a colander in the sink. (Or, if working in batches, keep the water boiling and use a slotted spoon, tongs, or a small wire sieve to transfer the produce to the ice bath.) Working quickly, transfer the produce to an ice bath. Let cool for the same amount of time the produce was blanched.

To steam blanch:

- Set a steamer basket or heatproof colander inside a large pot with a tight-fitting lid, making sure it is 3 to 4 inches above the floor of the pot.

- Add 2 to 3 inches of water and bring to a full boil, making sure that the bottom of the basket and the water are not touching.

- Arrange the produce in a single layer in the basket, cover the pot, and immediately start the recommended blanching time. Remove the basket from the heat and transfer the produce to an ice bath to stop the cooking.

Blanching for peeling fruit: Bring a large pot of water to a boil. Using a sharp paring knife, score the round end of stone fruit or tomatoes with an X. Drop the fruit into the boiling water and boil for 30 to 60 seconds, or until the skins split. Using a slotted spoon or tongs, immediately transfer to the ice bath. Use the knife to peel away the loosened skin. Be sure to save the skins for dehydrating into a powder (see page 113).

Freezer Packing

There are a few options for packing produce destined for the freezer. The packing method you choose will depend on how you plan to use the food after thawing.

Dry/unsweetened packs: This method is for produce packed without liquid. It can be used for all vegetables and some fruits—it's my go-to method for my berry harvests. Dry packs offer options for sweet and savory dishes.

Liquid packs:

- **Sugar:** Coating fruit with granulated sugar is a way to both sweeten and preserve. It's ideal for baking as well as using in smoothies and sauces.

- **Syrup:** Packing fruit in syrup is the sweetest of all the liquid pack options. Ideal for baking pies, cobblers, and crisps, a syrup pack also helps maintain the color, flavor, texture, and shape of the fruit.

- **Juice or water:** For a less sweet option, you can cover fruit with unsweetened apple or white grape juice. For a no-sugar option, pack in water.

Headspace

This is a term you'll see peppered throughout all the preservation chapters. It refers to the space between the food inside a container (even if it's a freezer bag) and that container's opening or point of entry. When freezing, headspace is important because some foods expand. Using insufficient headspace may cause the storage container to rupture and the food to spoil. Use the following headspace measurements below for freezing:

Headspace for dry pack

- Pint or quart containers: ½ inch
- Freezer-safe bags: no headspace for dry packs
- Wrapped: none
- Vacuum-sealed plastic bags: 3 inches (refer to manufacturer's directions on headspace and sealing)

Headspace for liquid pack (includes syrup, water, juice, purees, and sugar packs)

- Rigid containers, pint: ½ inch; quart: 1 inch
- Wide-mouth glass jars, pint: ¾ inch; quart: 1½ inches

Last but Not Least: Label It!

Labeling and dating your frozen foods will save you from the guessing game months down the road. Adding details such as measurement or weight may also be useful. Be sure to use a waterproof marker that can withstand cold temperatures without fading or smudging. Pens designed for the freezer are ideal, but a good old Sharpie works, too.

Syrups for Liquid Packs

Use light syrups to freeze sweet fruit and heavier syrups for fruit that is tart. For every 2 cups of fruit, you need about ⅔ cup of chilled syrup. Up to one-fourth of the sugar may be replaced by corn syrup or honey. The water should be warm so that the sugar dissolves. Chill the syrup before using.

Syrup Type	% of Sugar	Water	Sugar	Yield
Extra-light	10	4 cups	½ cup	4½ cups
Light	20	4 cups	1 cup	4¾ cups
Medium	30	4 cups	1¾ cups	5 cups
Heavy	40	4 cups	2¾ cups	5⅓ cups
Extra-heavy	50	4 cups	4 cups	6 cups

Freezing Fresh Fruit

Freezing fruit when it's in season or on sale will provide options for sweet and savory cooking. Be sure to refer to the checklist below before you get started.

Apples Select crisp, firm apples.

Prep Rinse. Peel (keep the peels for dehydrating into powder; see page 113), core, and cut into ½-inch slices.

Dry Pack Pretreat: In a small bowl, mix ½ teaspoon (1,500 mg) ascorbic acid in 3 tablespoons cold water. Place the apples in a large bowl and drizzle the mixture on top, stirring until evenly coated. Arrange the fruit, not touching, on a wax or parchment paper–lined rimmed baking sheet. Flash freeze for 1 to 3 hours, or until frozen solid. Pack into a freezer-safe container or bag, leaving the proper headspace.

Sugar Pack Pretreat as for *Dry Pack*. In a freezer-safe container or bag, layer 1 quart fruit with ½ cup sugar. Press the fruit down to pack, leaving the proper headspace.

Syrup Pack Make a heavy or medium syrup and chill. Add ½ teaspoon (1,500 mg) ascorbic acid to each quart of chilled syrup. Pack the fruit into a freezer-safe container or bag, then ladle in ½ cup syrup. Push down to submerge the fruit, then top with additional syrup to cover, leaving the proper headspace.

Storage Freeze for 8 to 12 months.

Apricots Choose evenly colored, firm, ripe apricots.

Prep Rinse. Using a sharp paring knife, score the bottom of each fruit with an X. Blanch in boiling water until the skins begin to split, 30 to 60 seconds. Transfer the apricots to an ice bath for 30 to 60 seconds. If desired, remove the skins (keep for dehydrating into powder; see page 113). Halve and pit.

Dry Pack Pretreat: In a small bowl, mix ¼ teaspoon (750 mg) ascorbic acid in 3 tablespoons cold water. Place the apricots in a large bowl and drizzle the mixture on top, stirring until evenly coated. Arrange the fruit, not touching, on a wax or parchment paper–lined rimmed baking sheet. Flash freeze for 2 to 4 hours, or until frozen solid. Pack into a freezer-safe container or bag, leaving the proper headspace.

Sugar Pack Pretreat as for *Dry Pack*. In a freezer-safe container or bag, layer 1 quart fruit with ½ cup sugar. Press the fruit down to pack, leaving the proper headspace.

Syrup Pack Make a medium or heavy syrup and chill.

FREEZING CHECKLIST

- ☐ Refer to page 19 for liquid pack syrup guidelines.
- ☐ Refer to page 19 for proper headspace.
- ☐ Remove as much air as possible from freezer bags before freezing.
- ☐ Label and date the packaging.
- ☐ Lay freezer bags flat to start. Once fully frozen, bags can be stacked to save space.
- ☐ Store similar foods together with the most recent additions placed at the bottom or in the back, allowing for older frozen foods to be consumed first.
- ☐ Storage times are estimates. For best quality, use the shorter storage times listed. Food after the period noted is still safe to consume but will begin to diminish in overall quality.

Add ¾ teaspoon (2,250 mg) ascorbic acid to each quart of chilled syrup. Pack the fruit into a freezer-safe container or bag, then ladle in ½ cup syrup. Push down to submerge the fruit, then top with additional syrup to cover, leaving the proper headspace.

Storage Freeze for 8 to 12 months.

Bananas Dry packing works best for bananas. They work wonders in muffins, pancakes, and quick breads, such as my Banana Bread (page 311). Pack in 1-cup measurements and note the amount on the labels for easy baking. Estimate 1½ fresh bananas to yield 1 cup dry-packed bananas. The pretreatment step, which slows browning, is optional, especially if you plan to use the bananas in a batter.

Prep Peel. Cut in half or into 1- to 2-inch chunks.

Dry Pack Pretreat (optional): In a small bowl, mix ½ teaspoon (1,500 mg) ascorbic acid in 3 tablespoons cold water. Place the banana pieces in a large bowl bowl and drizzle the mixture on top, stirring until evenly coated. Arrange the fruit, not touching, on a wax or parchment paper–lined rimmed baking sheet. Flash freeze for 2 to 4 hours, or until frozen solid. Pack into a freezer-safe container or bag, leaving the proper headspace.

Storage Freeze for 3 months.

Berries without skins (blackberries, boysenberries, loganberries, and raspberries) These berries all freeze wonderfully using any of the packing options. Frozen berries are great right out of the freezer for smoothies, beverages, and sorbets. Thaw for baked goods, sweet sauces, and infusions.

Prep Rinse and pat dry. Remove stems and caps as needed.

Dry Pack Arrange the fruit, not touching, on a wax or parchment paper–lined rimmed baking sheet. Flash freeze for 2 to 3 hours, or until frozen solid. Pack into a freezer-safe container or bag, leaving the proper headspace.

Sugar Pack Stir together ¾ cup sugar and 1 quart berries until evenly coated. Let stand for 10 minutes. Pack into a freezer-safe container or bag, leaving the proper headspace.

Syrup Pack Make a light or extra-light syrup and chill. Pack the fruit into a freezer-safe container or bag, then ladle in ½ cup chilled syrup. Push down to submerge the fruit, then top with additional syrup to cover, leaving the proper headspace.

Storage Freeze for 8 to 12 months.

Berries with skins (blueberries and huckleberries) Dry pack for best results.

Prep Prerinsing can change the texture of the skins, making them tough. Be sure to mark the label with "Rinse before using."

Dry Pack Arrange the fruit, not touching, on a wax or parchment paper–lined rimmed baking sheet. Flash freeze for 2 to 3 hours, or until frozen solid. Pack into a freezer-safe container or bag, leaving proper headspace.

Storage Freeze for 8 to 12 months.

Cherries, sour Use a sugar pack or syrup pack for the best results.

Prep Rinse and pat dry. Remove stems and pits.

Sugar Pack Stir together ¾ cup sugar and 1 quart cherries until evenly coated. Let sit for 10 minutes. Pack into a freezer-safe container or bag, leaving the proper headspace.

Syrup Pack Make a heavy syrup and chill. Pack the fruit into a freezer-safe container or bag, then ladle in ½ cup chilled syrup. Push down to submerge the fruit, then top with additional syrup to cover, leaving the proper headspace.

Cherries, sweet Sweet cherries benefit from a dry pack or syrup pack when freezing. The pretreatment step, which slows browning, is optional, especially if you plan to use the cherries for baking.

Prep Rinse and pat dry. Remove stems and pits.

Dry Pack Pretreat (optional): In a small bowl, mix ¼ teaspoon (750 mg) ascorbic acid in 3 tablespoons cold water. Place the cherries in a large bowl and drizzle the mixture on top, stirring until evenly coated. Arrange the fruit, not touching, on a wax or parchment paper–lined rimmed baking sheet. Flash freeze for 2 to 3 hours, or until frozen solid. Pack into a freezer-safe container or bag, leaving the proper headspace.

Syrup Pack Make a medium or light syrup and chill. Pretreat (optional): Add ½ teaspoon (1,500 mg) ascorbic acid to each quart of syrup. Pack the fruit into a freezer-safe container or bag, then ladle in ½ cup chilled syrup. Push down to submerge the fruit, then top with additional syrup to cover, leaving the proper headspace.

Storage Freeze for 8 to 12 months.

Cranberries These holiday staples aren't easy to find outside their late fall season. The good news is that cranberries are easy to freeze and ready to add to baked goods or turn into sauce.

Prep Rinse and pat dry. Remove stems. Discard any cranberries with blemishes.

Dry Pack Arrange the fruit, not touching, on a wax or parchment paper–lined rimmed baking sheet. Flash freeze for 2 to 3 hours, or until frozen solid. Pack into a freezer-safe container or bag, leaving the proper headspace.

Syrup Pack Make a heavy syrup and chill. Pack the fruit into a freezer-safe container or bag, then ladle in ½ cup chilled syrup. Push down to submerge the fruit, then top with additional syrup to cover, leaving the proper headspace.

Storage Freeze for 8 to 12 months.

Figs Here's another seasonal treat that takes well to freezing.

Prep Rinse. Remove stems. Leave whole or cut into quarters.

Dry Pack Pretreat: In a small bowl, mix ¾ teaspoon (2,250 mg) ascorbic acid in 3 tablespoons cold water. Place the figs in a large bowl and drizzle the mixture on top, stirring until evenly coated. Flash freeze for 1 to 4 hours, or until frozen solid. Pack in a freezer-safe container or bag, leaving the proper headspace.

Syrup Pack Make a medium or heavy syrup and chill. Add ½ cup bottled lemon juice to 1 quart chilled syrup. Pack the fruit into a freezer-safe container or bag, then ladle in ½ cup chilled syrup. Push down to submerge the fruit, then top with additional syrup to cover, leaving the proper headspace.

Storage Freeze for 8 to 12 months.

Grapes, seedless When stored using the dry pack method and eaten frozen, these are tasty snacks!

Prep Rinse and pat dry. Remove stems.

Dry Pack Arrange the grapes, not touching, on a wax or parchment paper–lined rimmed baking sheet and flash freeze for 2 to 3 hours, or until frozen solid. Pack into a freezer-safe container or bag, leaving proper headspace.

Syrup Pack Make a light or medium syrup and chill. Pack the fruit into a freezer-safe container or bag, then ladle in ½ cup chilled syrup. Push down to submerge the fruit, then top with additional syrup to cover, leaving the proper headspace.

Storage Freeze for 3 months.

Mangoes Frozen mangoes are excellent in smoothies and sorbet. I also like to use them to make fruit leathers and chips. Be sure the mangoes are ripe and sweet before freezing. Mangoes can also be pureed (with or without sugar added) and frozen in molds, then transferred to freezer-safe bags.

Prep Rinse. Peel, pit, and slice.

Dry Pack Arrange the fruit, not touching, on a wax or parchment paper–lined baking sheet. Flash freeze for 2 to 3 hours, or until frozen solid. Pack into a freezer-safe container or bag, leaving the proper headspace.

Syrup Pack Make a light syrup and chill. Pack the fruit into a freezer-safe container or bag, then ladle in ½ cup chilled syrup. Push down to submerge the fruit, then top with additional syrup to cover, leaving the proper headspace.

Storage Freeze for 8 to 12 months.

Oranges and grapefruit Frozen citrus sections are a delightful addition to your summer beverages. Use in place of ice cubes and to make Garden Coolers (page 162). Choose firm, ripe, heavy fruit without blemishes.

Prep Rinse. Peel (save the peels to dehydrate; see page 120) and divide into sections or cut in half. Remove seeds and membranes.

Dry Pack Arrange the fruit, not touching, on a wax or parchment paper–lined baking sheet. Flash freeze for 2 to 3 hours, or until frozen solid. Pack into a freezer-safe container or bag, leaving the proper headspace.

Syrup Pack Make an extra light or light syrup and chill. Pack the fruit into a freezer-safe container or bag, then ladle in ½ cup chilled syrup. Push down to submerge the fruit, then top with additional syrup to cover, leaving the proper headspace.

Storage Freeze for 3 to 4 months (dry pack) or 6 to 8 months (syrup pack).

Peaches From cobblers and muffins to smoothies and fruit chips, frozen peaches are a staple in my kitchen. I love them in Peach Slab Pie (page 339). Select well-ripened, unbruised fruit.

Prep Rinse. Using a sharp paring knife, score the bottom of each fruit with an X. Blanch in boiling water until the skins begin to split, 30 to 60 seconds. Transfer the peaches to an ice bath for 30 to 60 seconds. Remove the skins (keep for dehydrating into powder; see page 113). Halve and pit. Leave in halves or slice.

Dry Pack Pretreat: In a small bowl, mix ¼ teaspoon (750 mg) ascorbic acid in 3 tablespoons cold water. Place the fruit in a large bowl and drizzle the mixture on top, stirring until evenly coated. Arrange the fruit, not touching, on a wax or parchment paper–lined rimmed baking sheet. Flash freeze for 2 to 4 hours, or until frozen solid. Pack into a freezer-safe container or bag, leaving the proper headspace.

Sugar Pack Pretreat as for *Dry Pack*. Combine ¾ cup sugar with 1 quart fruit, stirring to coat evenly. Let stand for 10 minutes. Pack into a freezer-safe container or bag, leaving the proper headspace.

Syrup Pack Make a medium or heavy syrup and chill. Add ½ teaspoon ascorbic acid to each quart of syrup. Pack the fruit into a freezer-safe container or bag, then ladle in ½ cup chilled syrup. Push down to submerge the fruit, then top with additional syrup to cover, leaving the proper headspace.

Storage Freeze for 8 to 12 months.

Pears A syrup pack is best for freezing pears to avoid oxidation and help retain flavor. Thaw and use in cobblers, crisps, muffins, and more. Select crisp fruit, avoiding overripe or mushy pears.

Prep Rinse. Peel, halve, and core. Cut into ½-inch slices.

Syrup Pack Make a medium or heavy syrup. Bring the syrup to a boil in a large saucepan. Add the fruit and cook for 2 minutes. Drain, reserving the syrup, and let the fruit cool. Refrigerate the syrup until chilled. Pack the cooled fruit into a freezer-safe container or bag and cover with the chilled syrup, leaving the proper headspace. (Use any leftover syrup to make yourself a mocktail with sparkling water or a cocktail with spirits—you deserve it!)

Storage Freeze for 8 to 12 months.

Plums This stone fruit makes excellent cobblers, crisps, and pies. Look for the dark and meaty Italian prune plums that appear at the end of the season.

Prep Rinse. Using a sharp paring knife, score the bottom of each fruit with an X. Blanch in boiling water until the skins begin to split, 30 to 60 seconds. Transfer to an ice bath for 30 to 60 seconds. Remove the skins, if desired (keep for dehydrating into powder; see page 113). Halve and pit. Leave halved, or cut into quarters or thick slices.

Dry Pack Pretreat: In a small bowl, mix ¼ teaspoon (750 mg) ascorbic acid with 3 tablespoons cold water. Place the fruit in a large bowl and drizzle the mixture on top, stirring until evenly coated. Arrange the fruit, not touching, on a wax or parchment paper–lined rimmed baking sheet. Flash freeze for 2 to 3 hours, or until frozen solid. Pack into a freezer-safe container or bag, leaving the proper headspace.

Sugar Pack Pretreat as for *Dry Pack*. Combine ¾ cup sugar with 1 quart fruit, stirring to coat evenly. Let stand for 10 minutes. Pack into a freezer-safe container or bag, leaving the proper headspace.

Syrup Pack Make a heavy syrup and chill. Add ½ teaspoon ascorbic acid to each quart of chilled syrup. Pack the fruit into a freezer-safe container or bag, then ladle in ½ cup chilled syrup. Push down to submerge the fruit, then top with additional syrup to cover, leaving the proper headspace.

Storage Freeze for 8 to 12 months.

Rhubarb I love to dry pack rhubarb and use it to make simple syrup (see simple syrup soak on page 116). But a syrup pack is also a great way to go, especially for crisps, cobblers, and other baked goods.

Prep Remove leaves and trim ends. Rinse. Cut into ½- to 1-inch pieces.

Dry Pack Pack the rhubarb tightly into a freezer-safe container or bag, leaving the proper headspace.

Syrup Pack Make a heavy syrup and chill. Pack the fruit into a freezer-safe container or bag, then ladle in ½ cup chilled syrup. Push down to submerge the fruit, then top with additional syrup to cover, leaving the proper headspace.

Storage Freeze for 8 to 12 months.

Strawberries Frozen strawberries can be used in multiple ways, and a dry pack will allow you flexibility with uses.

Prep Rinse and pat dry. Hull. Leave berries whole, cut in half, or slice.

Storage Freeze for 8 to 12 months.

ZERO WASTE ALERT!
Save the discarded hulls to make Strawberry Thyme Simple Syrup (page 230).

Dry Pack Place the berries, not touching, on a wax or parchment paper–lined rimmed baking sheet. Flash freeze for 2 to 4 hours, or until frozen solid. Transfer to a freezer-safe container or bag, leaving the proper headspace.

Freezing Fresh Vegetables, Herbs, and Flowers

When it comes to preparing meals for my big, busy family, a freezer full of vegetables makes cooking so much easier. Although I usually serve them as a side dish, frozen vegetables can also be put to good use for vegetarian main courses, soups, and omelets. The freezer can also be home to dry packed and pureed herbs and floral ice cubes.

Artichokes thrive in Oregon's cool climate. Our Green Globe plant is a main attraction in our garden. It's over a decade old and provides several artichokes every year! Freeze the hearts for casseroles and pastas, or use as a pizza topping.

Prep Choose compact globes with tight leaves. Remove the leaves and the silks in the center, leaving just the heart. Cut the stem right below the heart. Rinse. Blanch in boiling water for 7 minutes. Transfer immediately to an ice bath for an equal amount of time. Drain and pat dry.

Dry Pack Pack in a freezer-safe container or bag, leaving the proper headspace.

Storage Freeze for 8 to 12 months.

Asparagus This is a handy vegetable to have in the freezer—there's no need to thaw before grilling or roasting whole spears. Cut spears are delicious in quiches and omelets.

Prep Rinse and scrape off the scales. Remove the woody ends. Rinse again. Cut into 1-inch lengths or leave whole. Sort by thickness for blanching. Blanch in boiling water for 1½ minutes for cut pieces or 2 to 4 minutes for whole spears, depending on the thickness. Transfer immediately to an ice bath for an equal amount of time. Drain and pat dry.

Dry Pack Pack in a freezer-safe container or bag, leaving the proper headspace.

Storage Freeze for 8 to 12 months.

Beans, green (wax and snap) When I was a kid my favorite thing to eat straight from my parents' and grandparents' gardens were the fresh green beans. Today, we grow a variety of beans in our garden, and I still look forward to a handful in my pocket for summer snacking. When we can't enjoy them fresh, frozen is the next best thing!

Prep Rinse. Remove ends and strings. Leave whole or cut into 2- to 3-inch pieces. Blanch in boiling water for 2 to 4 minutes, depending on size, or steam blanch for 4 to 5 minutes. Transfer immediately to an ice bath for an equal amount of time. Drain and pat dry.

Dry Pack Pack in a freezer-safe container or bag, leaving the proper headspace.

Storage Freeze for 8 to 12 months.

Beets Beets require cooking before freezing.

Prep Rinse. Trim leaves and straggly roots, leaving a small amount of the root and stem ends intact so that the beets don't bleed color. Cook unpeeled in boiling water until tender when pierced with a small knife, 25 to 30 minutes for small beets or 45 to 50 minutes for large. Drain and cool until easy to handle. Peel, remove the root and stem ends, and cut into slices or chunks.

Dry Pack Arrange the beets, not touching, on a wax or parchment paper–lined rimmed baking sheet and flash freeze for 2 to 4 hours, or until frozen solid. Transfer to a freezer-safe container or bag, leaving the proper headspace.

Storage Freeze for 3 months.

Broccoli You can roast, sauté, or microwave broccoli straight from the freezer; there is no need to thaw!

Prep Remove leaves. Separate florets and stalks from the stem base. Discard the stem base. To remove hiding insects, in a large bowl, whisk 4 teaspoons salt in 1 gallon of water to dissolve. Add the broccoli and soak for 30 minutes. Drain and rinse well. Blanch in boiling water for 3 minutes, or steam blanch for 5 minutes. Transfer immediately to an ice bath for an equal amount of time. Drain and pat dry.

Dry Pack Arrange the broccoli pieces, not touching, on a wax or parchment paper–lined rimmed baking sheet. Flash freeze for 2 to 3 hours, or until frozen solid. Pack into a freezer-safe container or bag, leaving the proper headspace.

Storage Freeze for 8 to 12 months.

Brussels sprouts These go straight from the freezer to pan, oven, air fryer, or microwave. Oh, the possibilities!

Prep Trim off outer leaves. Rinse. Blanch in boiling water for 3 to 5 minutes, depending on size. Transfer immediately to an ice bath for an equal amount of time. Drain and pat dry.

Dry Pack Arrange the sprouts, not touching, on a wax or parchment paper–lined rimmed baking sheet. Flash freeze for 2 to 3 hours, or until frozen solid. Pack in a freezer-safe container or bag, leaving the proper headspace.

Storage Freeze for 8 to 12 months.

Carrots Carrots are a must-have in the home freezer collection. I use frozen carrot sticks to make Glazed Carrots (page 288).

Prep Remove green tops and root ends. Rinse, peel, and rinse again. Slice, dice, cut into spears, or leave small carrots whole. Blanch in boiling water for 2 minutes for cut carrots or 5 minutes for whole. Transfer immediately to an ice bath for an equal amount of time. Drain and pat dry.

Dry Pack Arrange the carrots, not touching, on a wax or parchment paper–lined rimmed baking sheet. Flash freeze for 2 to 3 hours, or until frozen solid. Pack in a freezer-safe container or bag, leaving the proper headspace.

Storage Freeze for 8 to 12 months.

Cauliflower For best flavor, choose compact white heads.

Prep Remove leaves. Separate florets and stalks from the stem base. Discard the stem base. To remove hiding insects, in a large bowl, whisk 4 teaspoons salt in 1 gallon of water to dissolve. Add the cauliflower and soak for 30 minutes. Drain and rinse well. Blanch in boiling water for 3 minutes, or steam blanch for 5 minutes. Transfer immediately to an ice bath for an equal amount of time. Drain and pat dry.

Dry Pack Pack in a freezer-safe container or bag, leaving the proper headspace.

Storage Freeze for 8 to 12 months.

Corn, whole kernel Freshly harvested, tender corn is best for freezing.

Prep Remove the husks and silks from the ears of corn. Rinse. Blanch the ears in boiling water for 4 to 5 minutes. Transfer immediately to an ice bath for an equal amount of time. Drain and pat dry. Use a knife to remove the kernels from the cobs.

Dry Pack Pack in a freezer-safe container or bag, leaving the proper headspace.

Storage Freeze for 8 to 12 months.

Corn on the cob Cooling the corn quickly in the ice bath will keep the cobs from developing an off flavor.

Prep Remove the husks and silks from the ears of corn. Rinse. Blanch in boiling water for 7 to 11 minutes, depending on size, or steam blanch for 10 to 16 minutes. Transfer immediately to an ice bath for an equal amount of time. Drain and pat dry.

Dry Pack Wrap ears of corn individually in freezer wrap, freezer paper, or aluminum foil and pack into freezer bags, removing as much air as possible and leaving no headspace.

Storage Freeze for 8 to 12 months.

Edible flowers Freezing edible flowers as a method of preservation is not something I recommend. When thawed, flowers become limp and can darken in color. But! Frozen flowers suspended in ice cubes, are not only beautiful but also an easy way to enjoy springtime blooms year-round. See the chapter on Water Infusions for directions on making your own floral ice cubes (see Variation on page 169).

Eggplant Choose evenly colored, firm eggplants. If you're harvesting, pick before the seeds mature.

Prep Rinse. Peel and slice the eggplants into ⅓-inch-thick rounds or 1-inch chunks. Bring 1 gallon water and ¼ cup bottled lemon juice to a boil in a large pot. Add the eggplants, in a steamer basket if desired, and blanch for 4 minutes. Immediately transfer to an ice bath for an equal amount of time. Drain and pat dry.

Dry Pack Pack in a freezer-safe container or bag, adding freezer wrap between layers for extra protection, removing as much air as possible, and leave proper headspace.

Storage Freeze for 8 to 12 months.

Herbs Thawed herbs, regardless of packing choice, become limp and no longer suitable to use as garnish or decoration. But those limp herbs still pack a flavorful punch when used for cooking or for tea.

Prep Rinse and pat dry. Leave herbs whole or chop the leaves.

Dry Pack (whole herbs) Spread sprigs on a wax or parchment-lined rimmed baking sheet and flash freeze for 45 minutes. Wrap a handful of the frozen herbs in freezer-safe plastic wrap. For added protection, place the wrapped herbs in a freezer bag, removing as much air as possible and leaving the proper headspace.

Liquid Pack (chopped leaves) Place leaves in ice cube trays, filling each cell or mold. Top each section with water or oil—figure about 1 tablespoon herbs to 2 tablespoons liquid. Freeze for 2 to 6 hours, or until frozen solid. Transfer the frozen cubes to freezer bags, removing as much air as possible and leaving no headspace.

Storage Freeze for 8 to 12 months.

Kohlrabi Select fully grown, tender stems.

Prep Remove tops and root ends, peel, and rinse. Leave whole or cut into ½-inch chunks. Blanch in boiling water for 3 minutes for whole kohlrabi or 1 minute for chunk. Transfer immediately to an ice bath for an equal amount of time. Drain and pat dry.

Dry Pack Pack in a freezer-safe container or bag, leaving the proper headspace.

Storage Freeze for 8 to 12 months.

Leafy greens (spinach, kale, collards, and chard) Leafy greens become limp after thawing. Use them in cooked dishes like soups and stews or add them to smoothies and ice pops. For the best results, partially thaw greens before cooking.

Prep Rinse, remove stems and veins, and chop leaves. Steam blanch for 3 minutes (add 1 minute for collard greens). Transfer immediately to an ice bath for an equal amount of time. Drain and pat dry.

Dry Pack Pack in a freezer-safe container or bag, leaving the proper headspace. Or pack into ice cube trays, filling each cell or mold. Top each section with water—figure about 1 tablespoon greens to 2 tablespoons water. Freeze for 2 to 4 hours, or until frozen solid. Transfer the frozen cubes to freezer bags, removing as much air as possible, leaving no headspace.

Storage Freeze for 8 to 12 months.

Onions, green (scallions) No extra steps are needed, but keep in mind that their texture changes after thawing, so it is best to use in soups and sauces rather than in fresh dishes.

Prep Rinse and pat dry. Cut into ½-inch pieces.

Dry Pack Arrange the onion pieces, not touching, on a wax or parchment paper–lined rimmed baking sheet and flash freeze for 2 to 3 hours, or until frozen solid. Pack in a freezer-safe container or bag, leaving the proper headspace.

Storage Freeze for 3 months.

Onions, white, red, and yellow Onions are easy to freeze but have a shorter freezer life than many other items. But having them on hand to grab from the freezer will save you time with weekday dinner prep.

Prep Peel, cut ends, and cut into ¼- to ½-inch pieces.

Dry Pack Arrange the onion pieces, not touching, on a wax or parchment paper–lined rimmed baking sheet and flash freeze for 2 to 3 hours, or until frozen solid. Pack in a freezer-safe container or bag, leaving the proper headspace.

Storage Freeze for 3 months.

Peas with edible pods (snow, sugar, and sugar snap) I have so many memories of my kids eating peas as fast as they could pick them in the spring garden. I love to use them fresh to make Fresh Pea Soup (page 264), but frozen peas can also be used.

Prep Rinse. Remove stems, blossom ends, and strings. Blanch in boiling water for 90 seconds for small pods or 2 minutes for larger pods. Transfer immediately to an ice bath for the same amount of time. Drain and pat dry.

Dry Pack Arrange the peas, not touching, on a wax or parchment paper–lined rimmed baking sheet and flash freeze for 2 to 3 hours, or until frozen solid. Pack in a freezer-safe container or bag, leaving the proper headspace.

Storage Freeze for 8 to 12 months.

Peas, shelled (green and English) I save and freeze the pods after shelling peas. The pods add delicious flavor to homemade Zero-Waste Vegetable Broth (page 163).

Prep Rinse. Shell the peas. Rinse again. Reserve the pods for stock or soup. Blanch in boiling water for 90 seconds. Transfer immediately to an ice bath for the same amount of time. Drain and pat dry.

Dry Pack Spread the peas, not touching, on a wax or parchment paper–lined rimmed baking sheet. Flash freeze for 2 to 3 hours, or until frozen solid. Pack in a freezer-safe container or bag, leaving the proper headspace.

Storage Freeze for 8 to 12 months.

Peppers, hot (chiles) Be sure to wear food-safe gloves (and not touch your face) when working with hot peppers. Things can get spicy!

Prep Rinse and pat dry. Remove stems.

Dry Pack Pack in a freezer-safe container or bag, leaving the proper headspace.

Storage 8 to 12 months.

Peppers, sweet/bell I freeze lots of bell peppers every year. I often dice them so they are ready to use in dishes like Ham and Cheese Garden Quiche (page 254).

Prep Rinse. Cut in half. Remove stem and seeds. Cut into strips, chunks, or dice.

Dry Pack Pack in a freezer-safe container, leaving the proper headspace.

Storage Freeze for 8 to 12 months.

Potatoes, sweet (yams) Medium to large sweet potatoes are best for freezer storage. Cook until they are nearly tender before freezing. Thaw in the refrigerator before using in baked dishes, roasting, cooking, or microwaving.

Prep Rinse and pat dry. Cook unpeeled in simmering hot water until tender when pierced with a small knife, 20 to 30 minutes. Drain and cool until easy to handle. Peel and cut into slices or chunks, or mash. For every quart of mash, mix in 2 tablespoons of bottled lemon juice to keep them from discoloring. For slices or chunks, dip them in a mixture of ½ cup lemon juice and 1 quart water for 5 seconds.

Dry Pack Pack completely cooled mashed sweet potatoes in a freezer-safe container or bag, leaving the proper headspace. Flash freeze cut pieces on a wax or parchment paper–lined rimmed baking sheet for 2 to 4 hours, or until frozen solid. Transfer to a freezer-safe container or bag, leaving the proper headspace.

Storage Freeze for 8 to 10 months.

Potatoes, white, red, and russet Select firm, unblemished potatoes. If harvesting from the garden, young new potatoes are best. Knowing how you'll use them after freezing will determine what prep is needed.

Prep Rinse, peel (if desired), and rinse again. Leave new potatoes whole or cut in half. Cut larger potatoes into 1-inch chunks. For french fries, cut into ¼-inch-wide strips. For mashed potatoes, peel before cutting into chunks. In a large bowl, mix ½ cup bottled lemon juice with 1 quart of water. As you cut the potatoes, drop into the water until you're ready to blanch. Drain. Blanch in boiling water for 3 to 5 minutes for smaller chunks or 4 to 7 minutes for larger strips. Transfer immediately to an ice bath for the same amount of time. Drain and pat dry.

Dry Pack Pack in a freezer-safe container or bag, leaving the proper headspace.

Storage Freeze for 3 months.

Spinach cubes (see also Leafy greens, page 30) Spinach frozen in cubes comes in handy for smoothies, soups, and stews.

Prep Rinse. Puree 2 cups packed spinach leaves and stems and ½ cup water in a blender. Pour the puree into ice cube tray cells. Freeze for 4 to 6 hours, or until frozen solid. Transfer the frozen cubes to freezer bags, leaving the proper headspace.

Storage Freeze for 8 months.

Squash, summer (crookneck, pattypan/scallop, straightneck, and zucchini) Homegrown summer squash are known for being prolific, and freezing is a great way to preserve your excess. After thawing shredded squash, remove the excess moisture before adding to your recipes.

Prep Rinse and pat dry. Cut into ½- to 1-inch slices or cubes, or shred. Steam blanch shredded squash for 90 seconds or slices or cubes for 2 minutes. Transfer immediately to an ice bath for the same amount of time. Drain and pat dry slices or cubes; air-dry shredded squash on paper towels for several hours before packaging. Arrange slices or cubes on a wax or parchment paper–lined rimmed baking sheet and flash freeze for 1 to 3 hours, or until frozen solid.

Dry Pack Pack cut pieces in a freezer-safe container or bag, leaving the proper headspace. Pack the shredded squash in measured amounts in freezer bags, pressing out as much air as possible and leaving the proper headspace; once frozen, store flat and stacked to maximize storage space.

Storage Freeze for 10 months.

Squash, winter (acorn, butternut, and pumpkin) puree This is my favorite way to preserve pumpkin. The cooked puree can be thawed, strained as needed, and then used in baked goods like my Pumpkin Spice Pancakes (page 250). Proper headspace is important, as the puree will expand in the freezer. You can substitute winter squash puree in your favorite recipes.

Prep Rinse well. Cut in half. Remove the seeds and stringy pulp. Fill a large pot with a few inches of water and bring it to a boil. Place the squash in a steamer basket and set it in the pot. Cover and cook until the squash is fork-tender, about 20 to 30 minutes. Alternatively, place the squash, flesh side down, in a shallow baking pan and add ¼ cup water. Bake in 375°F oven until fork-tender, about 45 to 55 minutes. Cool until easy to handle. Scoop out the flesh. Puree in a food processor or blender. Cool completely before packaging. To speed up cooling, spread the puree in a baking dish set in a large pan of ice water and let stand, stirring occasionally, until completely cooled.

Dry Pack Pack in a freezer-safe container or bag, leaving the proper headspace.

Storage Freeze for 8 to 12 months.

Tomatoes, unpeeled Need a quick and easy way to keep up with your tomato harvest? Freezing whole tomatoes with the skins on is a time-saver. Don't worry about the skins; they slide right off after thawing. The downside? Storage is shorter, and whole tomatoes can also take up a lot of space in the freezer.

Prep Rinse and pat dry. Remove stem and core.

Dry Pack Pack in a freezer-safe bag, pressing out as much air as possible and leaving the proper headspace.

Storage Freeze for 6 months.

Tomatoes, peeled Roma is my favorite variety to freeze. Choose ripe, firm, brightly colored tomatoes. Thawed tomatoes lose their texture and are not desirable for fresh uses. But they are wonderful for making sauce and juice or used in cooked dishes.

Prep Rinse. Using a sharp paring knife, score the bottom of each tomato with an X. Blanch in boiling water for 30 to 60 seconds, or until the skins split. Transfer immediately to an ice bath for the same amount of time. Drain. Use the knife to peel away the loosened skins, reserving the skins to dehydrate into a powder (see page 113). Remove the stem and core. Leave whole, halve, quarter, dice, or crush.

Dry Pack Pack in freezer-safe containers or bags, pressing out as much air as possible and leaving the proper headspace. Pack crushed tomatoes in bags and, once frozen, store flat and stacked to maximize storage space.

Storage Freeze for 10 months.

Tomatoes, stewed Frozen cooked tomatoes are great to have on hand for sauces and stews.

Prep Rinse. Blanch and peel as for Tomatoes, peeled (page 33), then quarter. Add to a saucepan and bring to a simmer over medium heat. Cover and cook, stirring occasionally, until tender, 15 to 20 minutes. To quickly cool, place the semi-cooled saucepan in a larger pan of ice water and let stand, stirring occasionally, until the tomatoes are completely cooled.

Dry Pack Pack in a freezer-safe container or bag, leaving the proper headspace.

Storage Freeze for 10 months.

Turnips and parsnips These root vegetables will make your soups and stews extra hearty.

Prep Rinse well. Remove stem and root ends, no need to peel. Slice or dice into ½-inch pieces. Blanch in boiling water for 2 minutes. Transfer immediately to an ice bath for the same amount of time. Drain and pat dry.

Dry Pack Pack in a freezer-safe container or bag, leaving the proper headspace.

Storage Freeze for 10 months.

Troubleshooting Home Freezing

With careful prep, you won't have any of these problems. But just in case . . .

Issue	Cause	Solution
Oxidation/browning of foods, diminished quality	Exposure to oxygen due to poor storage	Use moistureproof, airtight containers, bags, and wraps specifically designed for freezing.
Freezer burn affecting quality (not safety) and causing discoloration and changes in texture and flavor, resulting in an off taste	Exposure to the cold air in the freezer due to poor storage	Wrap foods tightly in moisture- and vaporproof freezer paper or heavy-duty aluminum foil, and secure with freezer tape. For added protection, place wrapped foods inside freezer-safe bags, removing as much air as possible.
Ice crystals forming on foods	Freezing foods too slowly	Make sure the freezer is set at 0°F or lower. Twenty-four hours before adding food, turn the freezer temperature down to −10°F. Freeze in small batches. Over-filled freezers can also contribute to slowing down the freezing process.
Broken containers, lids ajar	Improper headspace for frozen foods to expand	Follow the headspace guidelines on page 19 to ensure there is enough space in the storage container for the foods to expand when freezing.

Ice Box Treats

The freezer isn't just great for preserving ingredients; it's also a fabulous tool for making frozen treats to have at the ready. I remember being outside on summer nights with the kids, after a long hot day, watching them enjoy an icy treat. They'd sit under the stars, talking and laughing, while whatever frozen treat they had was dripping down their chins, arms, and all over their clothes. I would cringe, but they loved it!

Garden Yogurt Pops

MAKES 8 ICE POPS

This summer favorite combines fruits and vegetables to create a delicious and healthy treat. You will need ice pop molds to make these.

1 cup sliced fresh, thawed frozen, or rehydrated freeze-dried carrots

1 cup fresh orange juice

1 cup sliced fresh, thawed frozen, or rehydrated freeze-dried strawberries

½ cup plain Greek yogurt

½ cup chopped and packed spinach leaves

1 tablespoon raw honey or Infused Honey (page 213)

1 · Puree the carrots, orange juice, strawberries, yogurt, spinach, and honey together in a blender.

2 · Place an ice pop mold on a rimmed baking sheet (for stability). Fill the molds with the puree and add the tops (and sticks, if needed).

3 · Freeze until solid, about 24 hours. Unmold and serve.

Strawberry Patch Ice Cream

We harvest quite a bit of strawberries and blackberries, along with other berries, from our garden every year. We also love going to one or two of the many u-pick berry farms near our home each season. Making homemade ice cream with berries from the patch is the perfect treat after a long day of picking.

MAKES ABOUT 1½ QUARTS

1 pound fresh or thawed frozen strawberries, hulled

2 cups heavy cream

1 (14-ounce) can sweetened condensed milk

1 · Chop enough strawberries to measure ½ cup to use later as an optional add-in. Puree the remaining berries in a blender; you should have about 1½ cups puree.

2 · Whip the cream in a chilled large bowl with a handheld electric mixer or stand mixer set at high speed until stiff. Beat in the puree and condensed milk, then fold in the chopped berries, if using.

3 · Pour the mixture into a 9-by-5-inch metal loaf pan and smooth the top. Cover tightly with plastic wrap pressed on the surface and freeze for at least 8 hours or overnight. (The ice cream can be frozen for up to 2 months.) When ready to serve, let stand at room temperature for a few minutes to soften slightly. Scoop and serve immediately.

VARIATION
Strawberry Chocolate Chunk Ice Cream: Stir ½ cup chopped semisweet chocolate into the ice cream before freezing.

Strawberry Rose Sorbet

Homemade sorbet is simple and versatile and requires only three ingredients: fruit, citrus juice, and flavored simple syrup. We enjoy the refreshing combination of strawberries and lime with a hint of roses. Want an adults-only version? Add a splash (or two) of vodka or clear rum before freezing.

MAKES ABOUT 6 SERVINGS

1 pound fresh or semi-thawed frozen strawberries, hulled

½ cup rose simple syrup (see page 224)

1 tablespoon fresh lime juice

Edible flowers or mint leaves, for garnish

1 · Puree the strawberries, syrup, and lime juice in a blender until smooth. Pour into an 11-by-7-inch loaf pan. Freeze for at least 6 hours.

2 · Let sit at room temperature for a minute or two before scooping. Scrape the mixture using an ice cream scoop to form a single serving and put into a cute little dish. Serve immediately.

Ice Box Treats

Berry Good Freezer Smoothie Cubes

Making freezer smoothie cubes is a great way to save you time during the week. For a pair of smoothies in a flash, process 6 of these frozen cubes with ¾ cup milk (dairy, oat, coconut, or nut) in a blender until smooth and serve chilled.

MAKES ABOUT 42 CUBES

½ cup orange juice

¼ cup floral or herb-infused honey (see flavoring menu, page 213) or raw honey

1½ cups nonfat or low-fat vanilla Greek yogurt

1 cup fresh or thawed frozen blueberries

3 cups coarsely chopped fresh or thawed frozen strawberries

1 cup fresh or frozen banana slices

1 · In this order, put the orange juice, honey, yogurt, blueberries, strawberries, and banana in a blender, then process until smooth. Place 2 or 3 ice cube trays on a rimmed baking sheet (for stability). Divide the puree among the ice cube cells. Freeze until solid, about 24 hours.

2 · Pop the frozen cubes out of the trays and transfer to a freezer-safe bag. Label and date. The cubes can be frozen for up to 6 months.

Fresh Mint Chocolate Chip Ice Cream

This simple recipe doesn't require an ice cream maker. Who has time to clean that thing? Instead, it gets whipped up in one large bowl using only a hand mixer. So easy! The cream can be infused with other herbs or edible flowers. Lavender, lilac, basil, and rose petals are all delicious flavors sure to impress your guests and please your family.

MAKES ABOUT 1½ QUARTS

2 cups heavy cream

1 cup packed fresh or thawed frozen mint leaves (such as spearmint, peppermint, or chocolate mint), torn, or ½ cup dried

1 (14-ounce) can sweetened condensed milk

1 to 5 drops plant-based green food coloring (optional)

¼ teaspoon mint extract, or to taste (optional)

1 cup mini chocolate chips

1 · Heat the heavy cream in a small saucepan over medium heat until small bubbles form around the edges. Remove from the heat. Add the mint (if using dried, gently crush the leaves as you add it to the cream). Set aside to infuse for 30 minutes. Strain through a fine-mesh strainer over another bowl, pressing hard on the leaves with a wooden spoon. Cover and refrigerate until very cold, at least 3 hours.

2 · Whip the cream in a chilled large bowl with a handheld electric or stand mixer set at high speed until stiff. Beat in the condensed milk and food coloring, if desired. (Without coloring, the ice cream will be beige, not green.) Taste, and if you want a stronger mint flavor, add the mint extract. Fold in the chocolate chips.

3 · Pour the mixture into a 9-by-5-inch metal loaf pan and smooth the top. Cover tightly with plastic wrap pressed on the surface and freeze for at least 8 hours or overnight. (The ice cream can be frozen for up to 2 months.) When ready to serve, let stand at room temperature for a few minutes to soften slightly. Scoop and serve immediately.

VARIATION

Lavender Ice Cream: Substitute ¼ cup fresh lavender buds or 2 tablespoons dried for the mint. Substitute ½ to 1 teaspoon butterfly pea powder or a few drops of blue food coloring for the green food coloring. Add 1 teaspoon vanilla extract. Omit the chocolate chips.

CHAPTER 2

No-Can Jams
& Quick Pickles

46
Quick Jam Session
Grandma's Raspberry Freezer Jam 47
Quick Rhubarb Jam 48
Blueberry Basil Lilac Spread 49
Black Pepper Plum Jam 50
Nectarine Jam 51

53
Quick, Pickle It!

When I first began preserving food at home, canning was not part of my routine. I had heard stories of it being difficult, maybe even a little scary. So instead, I mastered the art of quick pickles and no-can jams, which can be made in repurposed food jars, bail jars, and designer jelly jars. These no-can options have a shorter shelf life than canned foods (1 to 3 months in the refrigerator versus 1 to 2 years on a cabinet shelf), but they allow you to experiment with flavor combinations that canning recipes don't always offer. The best part: There is no need for large quantities of produce; if all you have is a handful of green beans, for example, you can pickle in the morning and bring them to a potluck in the afternoon, and they will be delicious. Freezer jam can be made in minutes, simply by crushing fruit and mixing it with no-cook or instant pectin, then stored in the freezer.

Fruit and Vegetable Pickle Prep

Recipes
Basic Quick-Pickled Fruit 59
Basic Quick-Pickled Vegetables 59
Quick-Pickled Lavender Carrots 60
Quick-Pickled Garlic Scapes 60

Quick Jam Session

Making jam is my jam! Jam is a thick mixture of fruit, sugar, and sometimes pectin. Apart from no-cook jams such as Grandma's Raspberry Freezer Jam (page 47), the fruit is cooked until spreadable. In chapter 3, I do a deeper dive into canning jams and jellies for long-term storage. **The recipes in this chapter, however, are designed for jam beginners, kitchen creators, and everyday cooks. This is the perfect place to wade into making jam.**

Containers: Unlike heat-processed canned jam (which requires canning jars with two-part lids), quick jam can be stored in bail jars or repurposed jam or sauce jars from the supermarket. Be sure to sterilize (see page 65) and check that the lids are tight fitting. For freezer jams, use freezer-safe jars or rigid, hard-sided plastic containers designed for freezer storage.

No-Cook Method: Fruit is simply crushed and combined with sugar and pectin. This is my go-to method for our seasonal strawberry and raspberry jams. For decades I've made it on the back patio, with my kids as helpers.

Cooked Method: Most jam and jelly recipes require cooking. A fruit (or fruit juice) mixture is heated to a hard rolling boil for a designated amount of time. The instructions for exact timing and processing will be provided in the recipes.

Cooked jams and jellies get extremely hot and must be watched constantly to avoid boiling over. Proper pot size is a must. Most recipes call for a heavy-bottomed 8- to 10-quart pot. It's also best to do when little ones are napping or at a safe distance, as the boiling mixture may splash outside the pot from time to time. Wearing an apron will help keep your clothes from getting stained and an oven mitt while stirring may also be useful.

No-can jams offer an opportunity to make custom flavored recipes with preserved ingredients from your pantry. For example, you can replace the plain sugar with infused sugar (see page 216). Add a drop or two of flavored extracts or mix fresh or dried herbs (page 90) into your jams. For recipes that call for water, you can use Botanical Water (page 165) instead.

Grandma's Raspberry Freezer Jam

This recipe brings me back to the jam that my grandma made from her garden raspberries. You never left her house without a container full of it! This small-batch recipe is perfect for small harvests or reasonable amounts of store-bought produce. It can also be made using strawberries, blackberries, marionberries, and boysenberries.

MAKES 2 TO 3 HALF-PINTS

3 to 3½ cups fresh raspberries

1⅔ cups sugar

2 tablespoons instant no-cook or freezer pectin, such as Ball RealFruit Freezer Pectin

1 tablespoon ground cinnamon

1 · In a large bowl, mash the raspberries with a potato masher or large fork.

2 · In another large bowl, combine the sugar and pectin. Measure 1⅔ cups mashed berries and add it to the bowl with the sugar-pectin mixture. Add the cinnamon and stir for 3 minutes. Set a timer: It is important to mix for the entire amount of time to evenly distribute and activate the pectin so the jam will thicken as it chills. Stirring also reduces any clumping that can effect the texture of the jam.

3 · Transfer the mixture to half-pint freezer-safe jars or rigid containers, leaving ½-inch headspace. Cover and let cool completely. Store in the refrigerator for up to 3 months or in the freezer for up to 1 year.

VARIATION

Strawberry Rose Jam: Substitute mashed strawberries for the raspberries and Rose Sugar (page 218) for the regular sugar. Omit the cinnamon.

Quick Rhubarb Jam

A trash-to-treasure recipe! This quick jam was born out of my desire to use every scrap of food. Sometimes there's magic in the discard. Use the leftover mash from making Rhubarb Simple Syrup (page 229) to make this three-ingredient jam. No need to add sugar since it's already sweetened, nor do we need pectin because it is naturally found in rhubarb. How cool is that?

MAKES 2 HALF-PINTS

1⅔ cups sweetened rhubarb mash (see Note) from Rhubarb Simple Syrup (page 229)

2 tablespoons fresh orange juice

Finely grated zest of 1 orange (optional)

1 · Sterilize 2 half-pint jars according to the instructions on page 65. Bring the mash, orange juice, and orange zest (if using) to a boil in a medium saucepan over medium heat. Turn the heat down to medium-low and simmer, stirring occasionally, until slightly reduced, about 10 minutes.

2 · Transfer to the jars, leaving ½-inch headspace. Secure the lids, then let cool completely. Store in the refrigerator for up to 2 months.

NOTE
If you are short on rhubarb mash, make up the difference with mashed strawberries.

Blueberry Basil Lilac Spread

This chunky spread, with fruity, herbal, and floral notes, is sure to please the senses. It can be used as a pie filling, spooned as a topping over cheesecake or ice cream, served with French toast or pancakes, spread over warm toast, or our favorite, tucked into pocket pies (see page 337)!

MAKES ABOUT 3 CUPS

4 cups fresh or thawed frozen blueberries, drained

½ cup plus 2 tablespoons water

2 tablespoons cornstarch

2 tablespoons bottled lemon juice

⅔ cup lilac-infused sugar (see page 216)

1 tablespoon chopped fresh basil or 1 teaspoon dried

1 · Combine the blueberries and ½ cup of the water in a medium saucepan. Cook, stirring occasionally, over medium-low heat until the berries begin to break down, 5 to 8 minutes.

2 · While the berries cook, combine the cornstarch, the remaining 2 tablespoons of water, and lemon juice in a small bowl and set aside.

3 · Add the sugar and basil to the berries and stir to combine. Stir in the cornstarch mixture. Cook, stirring occasionally, until the mixture thickens and becomes bubbly, 1 to 2 minutes.

4 · Transfer the mixture to a container or bowl. Cover the warm filling with plastic wrap pressed on the surface to avoid a skin forming on the top and cool completely at room temperature. Use immediately or store in a covered container in the refrigerator for up to 2 weeks.

Black Pepper Plum Jam

In this sweet and savory jam, every bite begins with sweet notes and finishes with a peppery spice. It's delicious on toast and biscuits or served with roasted chicken. Sweet Japanese black plums help balance the spice, but experiment with the plums you have available.

MAKES ABOUT 3 PINTS

3 pounds unpeeled plums, pitted and cut into ½-inch pieces (8 to 9 cups)

3½ cups sugar

Grated zest of 1 large orange

¼ cup fresh orange juice

1 tablespoon freshly cracked ground black pepper

1 · Before you get started, place a few metal spoons in the freezer for testing the gel of your jam. If you're planning to freeze your jam, sterilize 3 freezer-safe pint jars or rigid plastic containers. For refrigerated jam, sterilize designer jelly or reused food jars.

2 · In a heavy-bottomed 8- to 10-quart pot, stir together the fruit, sugar, zest, orange juice, and pepper. Set aside to infuse for 10 minutes. Place the pot over medium heat and cook, stirring, until the sugar is dissolved. Increase the heat to medium-high and bring the mixture to a boil. Cook the fruit, stirring frequently, until soft, about 10 minutes. Turn down the heat only slightly as needed to keep the mixture from overflowing, while still maintaining the constant boil.

3 · For a chunky jam, mash the fruit using a potato masher. For a pureed jam, remove the pot from the heat and use an immersion blender until smooth, then return the pot to the heat. Continue to boil, testing the gel periodically until it's set (see page 76), 5 to 10 minutes. Fill your jars, leaving ½-inch headspace. Secure the lids, then let cool completely. Label and date. Store in the refrigerator for up to 3 months or in the freezer for up to 1 year.

Nectarine Jam

Nectarines are my favorite stone fruit. We have two nectarine trees in our backyard. But I do love apricots, too. Cherries and plums are also delicious. Oh, and peaches! Okay, I love them all. Thankfully this recipe works for any stone fruit, so I can savor each of them all year long.

MAKES ABOUT 4 PINTS

4 pounds unpeeled nectarines, pitted and cut into ½-inch pieces (about 10 cups)

4½ cups sugar

Grated zest of 1 large lemon

¼ cup bottled lemon juice

1 · Before you get started, place a few metal spoons in the freezer for testing the gel of your jam. If you're planning to freeze your jam, sterilize 4 freezer-safe pint jars or rigid plastic containers. For refrigerated jam, sterilize designer jelly jars or reused food jars.

2 · In a heavy-bottomed 8- to 10-quart pot, stir together the fruit, sugar, zest, and lemon juice. Cook over medium heat, stirring, until the sugar is dissolved. Increase the heat to medium-high and bring the mixture to a boil. Cook the fruit, stirring frequently, until soft, about 10 minutes. Turn down the heat only slightly as needed to keep the mixture from overflowing, while still maintaining the boil.

3 · For a chunky jam, mash the fruit using a potato masher. For a pureed jam, remove the pot from the heat and use an immersion blender until smooth, then return the pot to the heat. Continue to boil, testing the gel periodically until it's set (see page 76), about 10 minutes.

4 · Fill the jars, leaving 1-inch headspace for freezing or ¼-inch headspace for the refrigerator. Secure the lids, then let cool completely. Label and date. Store in the refrigerator for up to 3 months or in the freezer for up to 1 year.

VARIATION

Peaches and Cream Jam: Substitute peaches for the nectarines and add 1 vanilla bean, split, to the mixture while cooking. Remove before filling the jars.

Quick, Pickle It!

Vinegar is the main ingredient in pickle brine. Vinegar works as a natural preservative by inhibiting the growth of certain types of bacteria. It brings out the flavor of vegetables and fruit (yes, fruit). But vinegar alone is too acidic for a pickling liquid. Here's what you need to get you on your way.

- **Vinegar:** Choose a good-quality vinegar with 5% or higher acidity (which you'll find on the label), avoiding those that contain additives such as sugar or artificial sweeteners. Most canning recipes call for apple cider vinegar or distilled white vinegar, both of which complement fruits and vegetables.

- **Water:** Believe it or not, the type of water you use matters. Hard water contains minerals that can adversely affect the quality of the pickles. For best results, use soft tap water or filtered water for making brines.

- **Salt:** Salt not only preserves but adds flavor and crispiness to whatever you are pickling. Use pickling or canning salt, which dissolves readily and is free of additives. Iodized salt makes a brine cloudy and causes pickles to discolor and go limp.

- **Sugar:** Unless the recipe specifies otherwise, use granulated cane or beet sugar. Infused sugars can offer additional flavor to your recipes.

- **Additional flavor:** Fresh herbs or spices add extra flavor to your pickling recipes. These flavor boosts are sometimes added to the brine in a spice bag or included in the jar with the food.

- **Pickle firming agent:** Calcium chloride is widely used in the pickling industry for a crunchy pickle. These optional, generic granules are also sold under various names and can be found in the canning section at the store. Follow the manufacturer's instructions for use and measurements.

Packing and Storage

There are two ways to pack jars for pickling, whether you're canning or not.

Fresh Pack Method Raw, uncooked produce is packed directly into a clean, heatproof jar and then covered with a hot or cooled vinegar solution. Foods packed this way will retain texture and crunch longer than the hot pack method, although the flavors may take longer to develop.

Hot Pack Method This method offers the quickest results. Produce is simmered in the pickling brine, packed, and covered with hot brine.

Regardless of method, leave $1/2$-inch headspace. Remove the air bubbles with a nonmetallic spatula or chopstick or a canning accessory known as an air bubble remover (see page 64). Then wipe the rims with a damp cloth, secure the lids, label, and date.

Quick pickles can be stored in new or repurposed glass jars. Just make sure the lids are nonreactive. Bail jars—glass jars with clamp lids—also work well. Before packing, wash the jars in hot soapy water and rinse well.

IMPORTANT NOTE

To avoid a metallic taste in your pickled foods, use a nonreactive pot and utensils, as metal can react with vinegar and leave an off flavor. Stainless steel, glass, nonstick, and enamel-covered cookware are all nonreactive. Avoid aluminum, cast iron, or copper cookware.

Quick Pickle Partners

You can pickle almost any fresh fruit or vegetable. The following charts will get you inspired with flavor possibilities, but feel free to mix and match. Then pick your brine (there are two on page 59). As you get more comfortable, experiment with different herbs and spices.

Keep track of your recipes in your journal pages at the back of the book.

A few other things to keep in mind:
- Cutting or slicing produce accelerates brine absorption.

Fruits	Fresh Herbs	Whole Spices
Blackberries	thyme, bay leaves (dried), mint	peppercorns, allspice berries, ginger, juniper berries
Blueberries	thyme, rosemary, bay leaves (dried)	cinnamon stick, peppercorns, allspice berries, cloves
Cherries	rosemary, thyme, red pepper flakes	cinnamon stick, cloves, coriander seeds, peppercorns
Grapes	bay leaves (dried), tarragon, mint	chiles, star anise, cinnamon stick, ginger, peppercorns
Mangoes	dill, garlic, bay leaves (dried), red pepper flakes	mustard seeds, cumin seeds, ginger, peppercorns
Melons	mint, cilantro, lavender	star anise, cinnamon stick, cloves, ginger
Peaches	thyme, mint	cinnamon stick, cloves, cardamom pods, star anise, allspice berries, ginger
Pineapples	basil, mint, cilantro	cloves, cinnamon stick, chiles, ginger, allspice berries, star anise
Strawberries	thyme, basil, mint, lemon zest	peppercorns, ginger, coriander seeds

NOTE

Garlic, when left in the pickling jar, can turn blue due to oxidation. This is totally normal and a harmless reaction. However, if giving your pickled creations as gifts, you may want to leave garlic out of the jars for appearance.

- Clean and pat dry herbs before adding to the jar or the brine.
- Use whole, not crushed spices as they tend to make the liquid murky.
- Store quick pickles in the refrigerator. They are best used within 1 to 3 months; after that, flavor and crispiness diminish. As with all preserved foods, be aware of signs of spoilage.

Vegetables	Fresh Herbs	Whole Spices
Asparagus	dill, bay leaves (dried), garlic, rosemary, thyme	mustard seed, coriander seeds, peppercorns
Beets	garlic, rosemary, bay leaves (dried), thyme	cinnamon stick, cloves, allspice berries, peppercorns, ginger
Carrots	lavender, thyme, dill, red pepper flakes, tarragon	cinnamon stick, cloves, ginger, coriander seeds, mustard seeds
Cauliflower	bay leaves (dried), garlic, sage, oregano, cilantro	mustard seed, coriander seeds, celery seed, allspice berries
Cucumbers	dill, red pepper flakes, bay leaves (dried), garlic, red pepper flakes	mustard seeds, chiles, dill seeds, coriander seeds, allspice berries
Green beans	dill, garlic, red pepper flakes, thyme	mustard seeds, peppercorns, dill seeds
Onions (sliced or pearl)	thyme, garlic, bay leaves (dried), oregano, rosemary	Cumin seeds, chiles, peppercorns, coriander seeds
Peppers	garlic, thyme, rosemary, red pepper flakes	mustard seeds, peppercorns, cardamom pods, cloves
Radishes	bay leaves (dried), thyme, dill, rosemary	ginger, mustard seeds, star anise, coriander seeds
Tomatoes (grape and cherry)	garlic, rosemary, dill, thyme, bay leaves (dried)	peppercorns, mustard seeds, fennel seeds, celery seeds
Zucchini	garlic, marjoram, red pepper flakes, thyme, dill	peppercorns, coriander seeds, fennel seeds, ginger

No-Can Jams & Quick Pickles

Fruit and Vegetable Pickle Prep

Since produce prep can vary, use these charts as a guide. Always begin with produce that is perfectly ripe, undamaged, and free of bruises or blemishes.

Fruit	Preparation
Blackberries	Keep whole.
Blueberries	Remove stems. Poke holes with a wooden skewer through the skins to speed up flavor infusion.
Cherries	Slice pitted cherries in half or leave whole. Poke holes with a wooden skewer through the skins of whole cherries to speed up flavor infusion.
Grapes (seedless)	Slice in half or leave whole. Poke holes with a wooden skewer through the skins of whole grapes to speed up flavor infusion.
Mangoes	Peel, pit, and cut into ½-inch chunks
Melons	Peel, remove seeds, and cut into ½-inch chucks, sticks, or small shapes using a cookie cutter.
Peaches	Pit, peel, and slice or cut into ½-inch pieces.
Pineapples	Peel, core, and cut into ½-inch chunks.
Strawberries	Hull and cut in half or slice.

Vegetable	Preparation
Carrots	Remove greens, peel, rinse, and cut into spears or rounds. Or get fancy and use a metal cookie cutter on large slices to cut out shapes. How cute would pickled carrot hearts be?! Perfect for a gift!
Cauliflower	Cut into small florets.
Cucumbers	If using slicing cucumbers, peel and remove any large seeds.
Green beans (dilly beans)	Snap or cut off the ends. Leave whole.
Onions	Peel and slice large varieties into thin rings. Leave peeled pearl onions whole.
Peppers	For spicy peppers: Working with food-safe gloves, remove the tops and slice into thin strips or rounds. Leaving the seeds will add extra heat. For bell peppers: Remove the tops and cut into thin strips. Or remove the top and bottom, slice the pepper open and lay flat on a work surface, and use a small metal cookie cutter to cut out small shapes. Especially cute for gifts!
Radishes	Trim and slice or cut in half.
Tomatoes	Slice in half or leave whole.
Zucchini	Slice into rounds or sticks.

Basic Quick-Pickled Fruit

Apples, blueberries, and cherries are all easy fruits to pickle. Add them to salads and cheese boards, or incorporate them into a sweet or savory sauce. The sweet and tangy brine can also be used in place of vinegar to make a vinaigrette.

MAKES ABOUT 1 QUART

1 pound fresh fruit, prepared as needed (about 2 cups)

1 cup apple cider vinegar or distilled white vinegar

1 cup water

½ cup sugar

1 tablespoon pickling or canning salt

Herbs and spices (optional; see page 55 for ideas)

1 · Pack the fruit into a sterilized wide-mouth quart jar.

2 · In a nonreactive saucepan, bring the vinegar, water, sugar, and salt to a boil over high heat, stirring until the sugar is dissolved.

3 · Ladle the hot brine over the fruit until completely covered, leaving ½-inch headspace. Remove any air bubbles, wipe the rim clean, and secure the lid. Completely cool. Label and date. Store in the refrigerator for up to 3 months.

Basic Quick-Pickled Vegetables

Use this base recipe for creating your own flavor combinations with one or several types of vegetables for a medley effect. See the Quick Pickle Partners chart on page 54 for herb and spice inspiration. See the Note below for sweet and savory adjustments.

MAKES ABOUT 1 QUART

1 pound fresh vegetables of any kind, prepared as needed

1 cup apple cider vinegar or distilled white vinegar

1 cup water

Sugar (see Note) or herb-infused sugar (see page 216)

Pickling or canning salt (see Note)

2 garlic cloves, peeled

1 to 2 herb sprigs or leaves (optional)

1 to 2 teaspoons whole spices (optional)

1 · Pack the vegetables into a sterilized wide-mouth quart jar.

2 · In a nonreactive saucepan, bring the vinegar, water, sugar, salt, garlic, and herbs and spices (if using) to a boil over high heat, stirring until the sugar is dissolved.

3 · Ladle the hot brine over the vegetables until completely covered, leaving ½-inch headspace. Remove any air bubbles, wipe the rim clean, and secure the lid. Cool completely. Label and date. Store in the refrigerator for up to 3 months.

NOTE

For sweet pickles: Use 3 tablespoons sugar and 2 teaspoons salt.

For savory pickles: Use 2 teaspoons sugar and 1 tablespoon salt.

Quick-Pickled Lavender Carrots

The combination of lavender and carrots results in a delightfully spiced pickled snack. Add them to salads or use as garnish for a Bloody Mary.

MAKES 2 PINTS

4 fresh lavender sprigs

2 fresh thyme sprigs

1 pound fresh carrots, peeled and cut into 3-inch-long sticks or ⅓-inch-thick rounds

1 cup apple cider vinegar

1 cup water

½ cup sugar

2 teaspoons pickling or canning salt

1 teaspoon coriander seeds

½ teaspoon whole black peppercorns

1 (3-inch) cinnamon stick

3 whole cloves

1 · Divide the lavender and thyme sprigs between 2 sterilized wide-mouth pint jars. Pack in the carrots, trimming the ends as needed, leaving a little more than ½-inch headspace.

2 · In a nonreactive saucepan, bring the vinegar, water, sugar, salt, coriander, peppercorns, cinnamon stick, and cloves to a boil over high heat, stirring until the sugar is dissolved. Turn the heat down to low and simmer for 10 minutes to blend the flavors.

3 · Ladle the hot brine over the carrots until completely covered, leaving ½-inch headspace. Remove any air bubbles, wipe the rims clean, and secure the lids. Cool completely. Label and date. Refrigerate for 1 to 3 days before opening, and use within 3 months.

Quick-Pickled Garlic Scapes

The scapes of the garlic plant (see page 106) are often overlooked or discarded. Not only are they edible, they're also less pungent than garlic bulbs and even more versatile. Garlic scape season is short. Quick pickling lets you capture the harvest to enjoy for months to come.

MAKES 1 PINT

18 to 20 whole or chopped garlic scapes

½ cup white wine vinegar

½ cup water

2 teaspoons sugar

1 teaspoon pickling or canning salt

3 to 4 whole black peppercorns

¼ teaspoon red pepper flakes (optional)

1 · Pack the garlic scapes tightly into a sterilized wide-mouth pint jar.

2 · In a nonreactive saucepan, bring the vinegar, water, sugar, salt, peppercorns, and pepper flakes (if using) to a boil over high heat, stirring until the sugar is dissolved. Turn the heat down to low and simmer for 10 minutes to blend the flavors.

3 · Ladle the hot brine over the scapes until completely covered, leaving ½-inch headspace. Remove air bubbles, wipe the rim clean, and secure the lid. Cool completely. Label and date. Infuse for 1 to 2 weeks in the refrigerator before opening, and use within 3 months.

CHAPTER 3
Boiling Water Canning

Canning Tools

Prep Steps

Boiling Water Canning: Step-by-Step

Once I became confident in my quick-pickling and jam-making skills, I decided to take the plunge and learn to make my favorite fruits and vegetables shelf stable. After doing my own research on boiling water canning, a well-known home preservation method my grandma called "water bath canning," I realized that the key to success was following the steps and recipes precisely for safe preservation. There are many steps, but the process itself is easy!

70
Troubleshooting Home Canning

72
Canning Whole Fruit

79
Recipes for Canning Jams and Jellies

Spiced Raspberry Jam 79

Apple Pie Applesauce 80

Concord Grape Juice 81

Wild Violet Jelly 82

Homestead Berry Syrup 84

Homestyle Pickles 85

Unlike quick pickles and jams that require refrigeration, boiling water canning makes perishable foods shelf stable for a long period of time. The high-heat process deactivates enzymes that cause spoilage and destroys any potential mold, harmful yeasts, bacteria, and microorganisms that can make you sick. After processing, the jars cool and the food contracts to create an airtight seal. Hearing the pop of a successful vacuum seal always makes me happy!

Boiling water canning is designed for high-acid foods with a pH of 4.6 or lower. Pickles, jams, jellies, and acidic fruits like apples, peaches, and cherries all apply here. Borderline low-acid fruits, such as tomatoes and rhubarb, when processed with additional acid (bottled lemon juice or citric acid), can also be canned this way.

For step-by-step instructions, see page 66.

UNSAFE CANNING PRACTICES

A number of unsafe canning practices are often promoted on social media as safe for food preservation. "Open-kettle canning" in an oven, microwave, or dishwasher, is not *safe. This method does not prevent all the possible spoilage that can occur, and it leaves you and your family at risk for foodborne illness. Another dangerous method that gets attention online is called "dry canning." Canning fresh food without liquid is also* not *recommended.*

Several electric multicookers have a built-in functionclaiming to work for canning. Use these appliances with caution, and follow the manufacturer's instructions precisely.

Whenever I have questions about any preserving method, my go-to resource is the National Center for Home Food Preservation (https://nchfp.uga.edu/).

Canning Tools

Boiling water canning requires a core group of tools. You can find most of them in the supermarket canning section or online, and they can often be purchased together in a kit.

- **Canner** A boiling-water canner, including a canning rack to hold the jars and lid, is the most important tool. The standard canner is made from aluminum or porcelain-covered steel and holds seven 1-quart jars. A ridged or flat bottom can be used on a gas burner, but if you're using an electric range, choose a flat-bottom canner. A see-through lid is great because you can check to see when the water is boiling.

- **Jars** Often called mason jars, these glass jars are recommended for home canning. They come in two shapes, standard and tapered, with two mouth (opening) sizes, regular and wide. They are sold in sizes ranging from 4 to 64 ounces, but the most common for canning are half-pint, pint, and quart. Mason jars can be reused for future canning projects.

- **Lids and bands** Canning jars are sold with self-sealing lids and bands designed for canning. The lid is a circle that fits right on top of the jar's mouth and has a rubber seal underneath, and the band is the round metal part that keeps the lids in place. Both should be washed with soap and hot water before using. Heat the lids in simmering (but not boiling) water, keeping them heated until ready to use. The bands do not need to be heated and can be reused if they are in perfect condition without any rust or dents. However, reusing lids can result in failed seals and is not recommended. Lids, however, can be reused to store dry goods. I like writing directly on top of lids with an indelible pen, using as labels. If I see writing on the lid, I know that it has been used before.

- **Jar funnel** A wide-mouth plastic funnel makes it easy to transfer hot food into jars.

- **Jar lifter** This essential tool allows you to transfer hot jars in and out of the canner.

- **Lid lifter** This pencil-size tool has a magnetic end that lifts the lid out of the heated water when you're ready to place it on the jar.

- **Headspace tool/air bubble remover** Playing two roles, this long plastic tool can both measure headspace—the space between the food inside a jar and the top edge of the jar—and remove any air bubbles inside the jar before processing. (This is also helpful for making the quick pickles in chapter 2.)

- **Kitchen towels** I use cotton towels as a protective liner between jars and my work surface before and after processing. Setting hot jars on a cloth will protect them from the shock of an abrupt temperature change, potentially causing jars to crack.

- **Food scale** I rely on a digital scale to weigh produce and help calculate how much I need for a recipe.

- **Nonreactive cookware** Because acids can react with metal and cause discoloration or, even more important, alter flavors, it's important to use a nonreactive saucepan or pot. Stainless steel, glass, nonstick, and enamel-covered cookware are all nonreactive. Avoid aluminum, cast iron, or copper cookware.

- **Canning salt** Also called picking salt, this fine-grained salt is best for canning because it has no preservatives. Other kinds of salt often have chemicals and anticaking agents that cloud the canning liquid.

Prep Steps

Washing Wash all jars, lids, bands, and canning equipment in hot water with a mild soap and rinse well by hand, or in the dishwasher.

To sterilize jars or not? It's all about processing time. All pickled foods, jellies, jams, and juices processed in *less than 10 minutes* should be packed into sterilized jars. Foods processed for *longer than 10 minutes*, including fruits, tomatoes, and some pickle recipes, do not require sterilized jars.

How to sterilize canning jars: Place empty jars, upright, on the rack inside the canner. Fill the canner and jars with hot but not boiling water, filling the canner to 1 inch above the jars. Bring the water to a rolling boil over high heat and boil for 10 minutes. (At elevations higher than 1,000 feet, boil for 1 additional minute for each additional 1,000-foot elevation.) Use the jar lifter to remove the hot jars, one at a time, pouring the water inside the jars back into the canner. Alternatively, your dishwasher may have a sterilizing cycle. Jars should be hot when you fill them because the warmth helps soften the rubber on the lid to make a tight seal.

Pretreating Fruits for Canning As with freezing, some fruits will retain their color and texture better when coated with a pretreatment solution before processing. See page 17 for pretreatment options.

Packing

There are two ways to pack jars for canning: hot pack and raw pack. The canning recipe you use will indicate its preferred pack.

> *Raw Pack Method* Uncooked food goes into hot jars and then is covered with a hot brine, syrup, or other liquid. This method is used for many types of pickles and whole fruits.

> *Hot Pack Method* Food is heated in a syrup, brine, juice, or water. The hot food is then transferred into hot jars. This is the preferred method for most fruits, salsas, relishes, and some pickles.

Syrups for Canning

The right canning syrup helps retain the color and flavor of your fruit. The chart on page 66 provides measurements for extra-light to extra-heavy syrups. **Each ratio makes enough for about 9 pints or 4 quarts.** Choose a syrup that complements the sweetness level of the fruit. If you need a larger or smaller volume of syrup, scale the recipe up or down. Other sweeteners, such as corn syrup or honey, may be used to replace up to half the sugar that's called for in each syrup.

To make the syrup, bring the water and sugar to a boil in a medium saucepan over high heat, stirring occasionally to dissolve the sugar. Follow the specific recipes on how to use.

Altitude Matters!

The canning recipes in this book are based on a maximum elevation of 1,000 feet above sea level,

Boiling Water Canning

unless otherwise noted. Higher altitudes change the atmospheric pressure, so it takes longer for water to reach the boiling temperature that kills harmful organisms in the jar. Use the chart on page 67 to make the necessary adjustments for your elevation. (To find your elevation, use an internet search engine or check WhatIsMyElevation.com.)

Boiling Water Canning: Step-by-Step

Follow these step-by-step instructions for boiling water canning and before you know it, you'll have a pantry full of tasty, colorful, shelf-stable foods that you can add to your everyday and special occasion cooking. Consider working with a partner to make preparing and packing move more quickly and smoothly. My husband and I always can together.

1. Gather your canner, clean canning equipment (see page 64), and clean jars with their bands and new lids.
2. Before prepping the food, fill the canner halfway with water. This is just an approximate amount of water needed for a full load of pint jars—you will add more hot water as needed to reach at least 1 inch above the jars. Cover the canner and bring the water to a simmer (180°F) over high heat.
3. While the water is heating up, heat the jars on the raised rack in the canner or keep in a hot dishwasher until ready to use.
4. Bring a small saucepan of water to a low simmer and add the lids. Keep the water hot but not boiling. Bring a kettle to a boil.
5. Prep your ingredients and make the recipes.
6. Fill the hot jars one at a time (so the jars stay hot) and measure the headspace (see page 19).
7. Remove air bubbles: After the jars have been filled and the headspace double-checked, slide the air bubble remover (or a nonmetallic chopstick or spatula) in between the jar and the food. Gently press on the food, while turning the

Syrups for Canning

Syrup Type	% of Sugar	Water	Sugar	Uses
Extra-light	10	6½ cups	¾ cup	Similar sweetness to natural sugar levels of most fruit; use for oranges, grapefruit, and berries.
Light	20	5¾ cups	1½ cups	Use when packing naturally sweet fruit such as sweet cherries, grapes, and pineapple.
Medium	30	5¼ cups	2¼ cups	A good choice for sweet, hardy fruit like apples, pears, and peaches.
Heavy	40	5 cups	3¼ cups	Use for tart fruit like plums and pears.
Extra-heavy	50	4¼ cups	4¼ cups	Extremely sweet; use only for very sour fruits like sour cherries.

jar, releasing any air trapped inside. Move around the jar, repeating these steps a few times until all the bubbles are released. Double check the headspace.

8. Wipe the rims clean with a damp cloth, making sure they're free of any bits of food that may prevent the lids from sealing.

9. Center a lid on each jar and secure the band fingertip-tight. You want it snug but not tight. Overtightening can prevent a successful seal.

10. Using a jar lifter, making sure it is securely positioned below the neck of the jar, transfer each upright jar to the rack. (Tilting the jars, even slightly, could loosen the lid and compromise the seal.)

11. Lower the filled rack into the simmering water. Adjust the water level with the kettle of boiling water to measure 1 to 2 inches above the tops of the jars. For processing times over 30 minutes, the water level needs be at least 2 inches above the tops of the jars.

12. Cover the canner. Increase the heat to high and bring the water to a rolling boil.

13. Once the water is rapidly boiling, set a timer. Make sure the water is at a full boil for the entire time and always covering your jars. If the water stops boiling, start over. If water level gets too low, add more to cover your jars and start over. (This is when a see-through lid really comes in handy!)

14. When the timer is done, turn off the heat and uncover the canner. Carefully lift the full canning rack, securing it to the sides of the canner so it is resting above the water. Let the jars sit for 5 minutes to cool before removing from the canner. This allows the jars to gradually adjust to room temperature.

15. With a jar lifter secured just below the band, transfer each upright jar to a cloth towel, spacing them at least 1 inch apart. (Tilting the jars, even slightly, can compromise the lid seal or cause the food to siphon out.) Cool at room temperature, undisturbed, for 12 to 24 hours. If the bands are loose, do not tighten; it could compromise the lid. If water has pooled on the lids, resist the urge to wipe it. It will evaporate.

Altitude Adjustments for Boiling Water Canning

Altitude in Feet	Increase Processing Time
1,000 to 3,000	5 minutes
3,001 to 6,000	10 minutes
6,001 to 8,000	15 minutes
8,001 to 10,000	20 minutes

Checking the Seal

Once the jars have cooled for 12 to 24 hours, check the seals. You may have heard the pops of the lids as they sealed. I love that sound! But there are other ways to make sure a lid is sealed. Remove the band and gently try to press down on the center of the lid, making sure it stays concave. Then try to lift the edges of the lid with your fingertips. If it stays in place, you did it!

If a lid comes off, or the center of the lid pops back when you press down, the seal is unsuccessful. You have two options:

- Refrigerate and use the food within a week or freeze in a freezer-safe container with the proper headspace for up to 1 year.

- Reprocess within 24 hours. Transfer the contents of the jar into a pot and reheat. Fill a new hot, clean jar with a new lid, and reprocess for the full time indicated in the recipe.

Storage and Use

With a clean, damp towel, wipe the lids clean without disturbing the seal. Be sure to remove any possible food residue, which can encourage mold.

Label and date the jars. Remove the bands; without them, you can easily see if a lid is leaking or looks domed.

Store in a relatively cool and dark place, preferably between 50° and 70°F. Avoid storing near a range, furnace, or hot pipes, or in direct sunlight. Do not stack jars more than two high to prevent disturbing the seals. Consider adding a layer of support (thin wooden boards or even cardboard) between rows of jars.

Home-canned foods are best when used within 1 to 2 years. After that, the flavor and color begin to deteriorate.

Now that you've got the pantry stocked, how do you open the darn things? There are a few ways to get that tightly sealed lid off when you're ready to use. My hubs uses his muscles to lift off the lid. That doesn't work for me. Instead, I use a jar opener (also called a church key) to pop it open. You can also use a spoon or butter knife to lift the edge of the lid, releasing the vacuum seal. Once opened, return the band to secure the lid, refrigerate, and use within 1 week.

Signs of Spoilage for Home-Canned Foods

It's important to inspect your canned foods from time to time. It is critical to remove any spoiled jars quickly from the pantry to maintain a safe environment. Here are a few things to look for:

Leaking jar
Dried food crusting along the top of jar
Swollen or bulging ("domed") lid
Unnatural color
Signs of mold
Gassiness or cloudiness
Broken jar
Foul or off-putting odor when opened
Rising, moving bubbles
Spurting or fizzing liquid when opened

If you suspect a jar has been spoiled but the jar is still sealed, place the entire jar in a heavy garbage bag. Secure the bag closed and place it in the trash. If the jar is leaking, broken, or unsealed, follow the detoxication guidelines from the National Center for Home Food Preservation.

Troubleshooting Home Canning

Issue	Possible Causes	Remedy
Seal failure	Incorrect processing time; improperly secured lid or band; wrong headspace; not adjusting for altitude; jar chips or cracks on rim; dirty rim	Refrigerate and use within 24 hours. For next time, follow the canning processing times and use the jar size and headspace specified in the recipe. Make sure the rims are clean, lids are centered, and bands are finger-tight. See the altitude adjustments on page 67. Examine the jars carefully for imperfections before selecting. Be sure to wipe the rim of the jar with a damp cloth before applying the lid, as food particles can compromise the seal.
Loss of liquid during processing	Overpacking the jar; raw pack was used; air bubbles not removed; lid failure; starchy food	Still safe to consume and store. Next time, pack the food more loosely, leaving space for the liquid to circulate around all the pieces. Use the hot pack method to fully hydrate food before canning. Remove air bubbles before processing. Make sure the lid is new and unblemished and wipe the rim clean before adding the lid.
Floating fruit	Raw pack was used; fruit was lighter than syrup; air trapped in food; jar improperly (loosely) packed	Still safe to consume and store. Use the hot pack method and select a lighter syrup. Pack the fruit until snug but not crushed. Use the correct headspace and remove air bubbles from the jars before adding the lids.
Escaping liquid after processing (siphoning)	Jars removed from the canner too soon	As long as the lids are sealed, food is safe to consume and store. For next time, turn off the heat, remove the lids, and lift the rack or jars over the water to rest for 5 minutes before removing the jars for complete cooling.

Issue	Possible Causes	Remedy
Warped or buckled lids after processing	Band too tight	Adjust the band only finger-tight before processing.
Warped or buckled lids during storage	Incorrect canning process that did not stop the growth of harmful microorganisms.	See page 68 on how to handle spoiled jars.
Darkened food around the top of the jar	Insufficient liquid; too much headspace, allowing food to oxidize; processing time too short	Still safe to consume and store as long as lids are sealed and signs of spoilage (page 68) are not present. For next time, be sure the syrup, water, juice, or brine completely covers the food in the jar, leaving the exact headspace required. Process according to the times provided.
Sediment at the bottom of the jar	Harmless yeast has formed; table salt was used; starchy vegetables	Safe to consume and store. Some sediment from green vegetables or onions is a harmless natural occurrence. Be sure to use pickling or canning salt for best results.
Cloudy liquid in jar	Minerals in hard water or table salt; starchy foods	If you suspect spoilage, discard (see page 68). Next time, use filtered or soft water instead of treated local water. Canning or pickling salt is best.
Undesirable color change of food	Overprocessed; contact with iron, zinc, or copper while cooking; unripe or overripe foods; exposure to light; possible spoilage; harmless natural color changes occur in foods like peaches, apples, pears	If you suspect spoilage, discard (see page 68). Be sure to follow the processing time in recipes and use sanitized nonmetallic utensils and do not let food touch uncoated metals during cooking. Use only ripe, high-quality, unblemished foods for canning. Keep jars stored in a cool, dark, dry location away from direct sunlight.

Canning Whole Fruit

A well-stocked pantry of home-canned fruit will empower you to make pies, fruit-filled baked goods, and more. Note that the processing times shown are for elevations up to 1,000 feet. Use the altitude chart on page 67 for adjustments.

Refer to page 66 for step-by-step instructions for prepping your jars for the canner and processing. Processing times for each fruit vary and are not interchangeable.

Apples Choose apples that are crisp, sweet, and juicy. Estimate 2½ to 3 pounds per quart jar.

> *Prep* Rinse. Peel and core. Cut into slices or chunks. Drop into a pretreatment solution (see page 17) during cutting. Drain again.
>
> *Hot Pack* Put the apples in a large saucepan. For every 5 pounds of fruit, add 2 cups medium canning syrup or water. Bring to a boil and cook, stirring occasionally, for 5 minutes. Using a slotted spoon, fill hot jars with the cooked fruit, then cover with the hot syrup, leaving ½-inch headspace. Process pints or quarts for 20 minutes.

Apricots Choose ripe, firm, unblemished apricots. Estimate 2 to 2½ pounds per quart jar.

> *Prep* Rinse. Using a sharp paring knife, score the bottom of each fruit with an X. Blanch in boiling water until the skins begin to split, 30 to 60 seconds. Transfer the apricots to an ice bath for an equal amount of time. Drain and pat dry. Remove the skins (keep for dehydrating into powder; see page 113). Halve, pit, and slice, dropping the pieces into a pretreatment solution (page 17) as you cut. Drain again.
>
> *Raw Pack* Fill hot jars with the raw fruit, cut side down, leaving ½-inch headspace. Cover with hot light or medium canning syrup, water, or apple juice, leaving ½-inch headspace. Process pints for 25 minutes and quarts for 30 minutes.
>
> *Hot Pack* In a large saucepan, combine the fruit with enough light or medium canning syrup, water, or apple juice to cover and bring to a boil. Immediately transfer the hot fruit into hot jars, cut side down, and top off with the hot syrup, leaving ½-inch headspace. Process pints for 20 minutes and quarts for 25 minutes.

Berries (blueberries, blackberries, currants, elderberries, huckleberries, loganberries, mulberries, and raspberries)—No-Sugar Method No-sugar berries are great for baking, infusions, syrups, ice creams, sorbets, and beverages. Estimate 1 to 2 pounds per quart jar.

> *Prep* Rinse. Remove stems as needed. Simmer berries in enough water to cover until heated through. Do not drain.
>
> *Hot Pack* Fill hot jars with the berries using a slotted spoon, leaving ½-inch headspace. Cover with boiling hot water, leaving ½-inch headspace. For elderberries, ladle in the fruit and hot liquid at the same time. Process pints and quarts for 15 minutes.

Berries (blueberries, blackberries, currants, elderberries, huckleberries, loganberries, mulberries, and raspberries)—Sweetened Canned soft berries won't hold their shape, but boy are they delicious! Use in pies, cobblers, crisps, ice cream, sauces, and syrups. Estimate 1 to 2 pounds per quart jar.

> *Prep* Rinse. Remove stems as needed.
>
> *Raw Pack* Use for blackberries, loganberries, mulberries, and raspberries. Fill hot jars with the raw berries, leaving ½-inch headspace and gently shaking the jar while filling to fill any gaps. Cover with hot extra-light or light canning syrup, leaving ½-inch headspace. Process pints for 15 minutes and quarts for 20 minutes.
>
> *Hot Pack* Use for blueberries, currants, elderberries, and huckleberries. Place berries in a large saucepan. For each quart of berries, gently stir in ½ cup sugar to coat. Cover loosely and let stand for 1 hour in a cool place. Heat over medium-low until the berries are heated through and the sugar has dissolved. Ladle the hot berries and juice into hot jars, leaving ½-inch headspace. Process pints and quarts for 15 minutes.

Cherries, sweet or sour Choose mature, brightly colored, cherries. Estimate 2 to 3 pounds per quart jar.

Prep Rinse. Remove stems and pits, if desired. Pretreat pitted cherries in an ascorbic acid solution (see page 17), then drain. If leaving the cherries whole, poke through the skin on opposite sides with a clean skewer or needle to prevent splitting.

Raw Pack Pour ½ cup hot canning syrup of choice, water, or apple or white grape juice into each hot jar. Fill with the raw cherries, gently shaking the jar to fill any gaps and leaving ½-inch headspace. Cover with additional hot liquid, maintaining ½-inch headspace. Process pints and quarts for 25 minutes.

Hot Pack For every quart of cherries, add ½ cup canning syrup of choice, water, or apple or white grape juice to a large saucepan. Add the cherries and bring to a boil. Fill hot jars with the hot fruit and liquid, leaving ½-inch headspace. Process pints for 15 minutes and quarts for 20 minutes.

Nectarines Use in fruit salad or sorbet or to make fruit leathers. Estimate 2 to 2½ pounds per quart jar.

Prep Rinse. Halve and pit. Leave in halves or cut into wedges.

Raw Pack Fill hot jars with the raw fruit, cut side down, leaving ½-inch headspace. Top off with hot light or medium canning syrup, water, or apple juice, leaving ½-inch headspace. Process pints for 25 minutes and quarts for 30 minutes.

Hot Pack In a large saucepan, stir together the fruit with enough light or medium canning syrup, water, or apple juice to cover. Bring to a boil. Immediately transfer the hot fruit into hot jars, cut side down, leaving ½-inch headspace. Top with the hot syrup, leaving ½-inch headspace. Process pints for 20 minutes and quarts for 25 minutes.

Peaches Select mature, ripe peaches with bright yellow flesh. Estimate 2 to 2½ pounds per quart jar.

Prep Rinse. Using a sharp paring knife, score the bottom of each fruit with an X. Blanch in boiling water until the skins begin to split, 30 to 60 seconds. Transfer the peaches to an ice bath for 30 to 60 seconds. Remove the skins (keep for dehydrating into powder; see page 113). Halve and pit. Leave in halves or cut into wedges, dropping the fruit into a pretreatment mixture (page 17) as you cut them. Drain.

Raw Pack Fill hot jars with the raw fruit, cut side down, leaving ½-inch headspace. Add hot light or medium canning syrup, water, or apple juice, leaving ½-inch headspace. Process pints for 25 minutes and quarts for 30 minutes.

Hot Pack In a large saucepan, stir together the fruit with enough light or medium canning syrup, water, or apple juice to cover. Bring to a boil. Immediately transfer the hot fruit into hot jars, cut side down, leaving ½-inch headspace. Top with the hot syrup, leaving ½-inch headspace. Process pints for 20 minutes and quarts for 25 minutes.

Pears Pears require the addition of bottled lemon juice to increase acidity. Estimate 2 to 2½ pounds per quart jar.

Prep Rinse. Peel, halve, and core. Leave in halves or slice into wedges or chunks, dropping the pieces into a pretreatment solution (page 17) as you cut. Drain again.

Hot Pack In a large saucepan, stir together the fruit and enough medium or heavy canning syrup (see page 66), water, or apple or white grape juice to cover. Bring to a boil, turn the heat down to medium-low, and simmer for 5 minutes. **IMPORTANT:** Before packing, add 1 tablespoon bottled lemon juice per pint or 2 tablespoons per quart. Ladle the hot fruit and liquid into hot jars, leaving ½-inch headspace. Process pints for 20 minutes and quarts for 25 minutes.

Pineapples Choose firm, ripe pineapples. Estimate 3 pounds per quart jar.

Prep Rinse. Cut off both ends and rind, trim sides, and remove eyes. Cut the peeled pineapple in half from top to bottom. Quarter lengthwise and remove core from each quarter. Cut into chunks.

Hot Pack In a large saucepan, stir together the fruit and enough extra-light or light canning syrup (see page 66), water, or (apple or white grape) juice to cover. Bring to a boil, turn the heat down to medium-low, and simmer for 10 minutes. Transfer the hot fruit and liquid into hot jars, leaving ½-inch headspace. Process pints for 15 minutes and quarts for 20 minutes.

Plums Choose mature, deep-colored fruit. Estimate 2 to 2½ pounds per quart jar.

Prep Rinse. Remove stems. For whole plums, use a fork or skewer to poke the skin on opposite sides to prevent splitting. Freestone varieties can be halved and pitted, if desired.

Raw Pack Fill hot jars with the raw fruit, leaving ½-inch headspace. Top off with hot extra-light to medium canning syrup (see page 66), leaving ½-inch headspace. Process pints for 20 minutes and quarts for 25 minutes.

Hot Pack In a large saucepan, bring medium or heavy canning syrup or water to a boil. Add the fruit and boil for 2 minutes. Remove from the heat, cover, and let stand for 20 minutes. Fill hot jars with the hot fruit and hot liquid, leaving ½-inch headspace. Process pints for 20 minutes and quarts for 25 minutes.

Rhubarb (stewed) Stewed rhubarb is great for pies, ice pops, and cobblers. Choose young, brightly colored stalks. Estimate 1 to 1½ pounds per quart jar.

Prep Remove leaves and trim ends. Rinse. Cut into 1-inch pieces.

Hot Pack For every quart jar, combine fruit and ½ cup sugar in a large saucepan. Let stand until juice appears, about 1 hour. Bring to a boil. Fill hot jars with the hot fruit and liquid, leaving ½-inch headspace. Process pints for 15 minutes and quarts for 20 minutes.

Tomatoes, Three Ways

There are many options for canning tomatoes. Whole, crushed, sauces, juice, oh my! **IMPORTANT**: Acidity in tomato varieties can vary. *Always add the specified amount of bottled lemon juice to home-canned tomatoes to increase the acidity for safe processing. See the chart on page 67 for altitude adjustments.*

For all variations: Estimate 2½ to 3 pounds per quart jar. Rinse. Using a sharp paring knife, score the bottom of each tomato with an X. Blanch in boiling water for 30 to 60 seconds, or until the skins split. Transfer immediately to an ice bath for the same amount of time. Drain. Use the knife to peel away the loosened skins, reserving the skins to dehydrate into a powder (see page 113).

Tomatoes, crushed Use canned crushed tomatoes in chilis, stews, soups, rice, and pasta dishes.

Prep Cut blanched and peeled tomatoes into quarters.

Hot Pack Working in batches, add just enough tomatoes to fill the bottom of a saucepan and crush with a wooden spoon. Bring to a boil, stirring constantly, gradually adding and crushing the remaining tomatoes. When everything is boiling, turn the heat down and simmer for 5 minutes. Before packing, add 1 tablespoon bottled lemon juice per pint jar or 2 tablespoons per quart. Ladle into hot jars, leaving ½-inch headspace. Add ½ teaspoon canning salt per pint jar or 1 teaspoon per quart jar. Process pints for 35 minutes and quarts for 45 minutes.

Tomatoes in juice These tomatoes can be roasted to become Roasted Marinara Sauce (page 297), which in turn can be used for Creamy Roasted Tomato Soup (page 262).

Prep Core blanched and peeled tomatoes. Leave small tomatoes whole; cut larger tomatoes into halves or quarters.

Raw Pack Before packing, add 1 tablespoon bottled lemon juice per pint jar or 2 tablespoons per quart. Fill hot jars with the raw tomatoes, pressing them down gently with a wooden spoon to release the juice as you fill, leaving ½-inch headspace. Add ½ teaspoon canning salt per pint jar or 1 teaspoon per quart. Process pints and quarts for 1 hour 25 minutes.

Tomatoes, water-packed Canned tomatoes make wonderful sauces and stews and salsas.

Prep Core blanched and peeled tomatoes. Leave small tomatoes whole; cut larger tomatoes into halves or quarters.

Raw Pack Before packing, add 1 tablespoon bottled lemon juice per pint jar or 2 tablespoons per quart. Fill hot jars with the raw tomatoes, leaving ½-inch headspace. Add ½ teaspoon canning salt per pint jar or 1 teaspoon per quart. Process pints for 40 minutes and quarts for 45 minutes.

Hot Pack Put the tomatoes in a large saucepan and add enough water to cover. Bring to a boil. Turn the heat down to medium-low and simmer for 5 minutes. Before packing, add 1 tablespoon bottled lemon juice per pint jar or 2 tablespoons per quart. Fill hot jars with the hot tomatoes and liquid, leaving ½-inch headspace. Add ½ teaspoon canning salt per pint jar or 1 teaspoon per quart. Process pints for 40 minutes and quarts for 45 minutes.

Canning Jams and Jellies

Jams are sweet, thick spreads made by combining whole fruit that's been crushed or chopped with an acid (such as lemon juice), a sweetener (usually sugar), and sometimes pectin, for thickening.

Jellies are made by combining fruit juice or Botanical Water (page 165) with lemon juice, sugar, and pectin to create a clear, firm spread that holds its shape when spooned out.

For best results, do not scale up, or even double, canned jam or jelly recipes unless otherwise specified or your spread may not set. Jellies hold up best when processed in a boiling water canner or refrigerated. Frozen jellies can be loose after thawing.

Sugar plays a vital role in soft fruit spreads. It helps retain the infused flavors, aids in color retention, and helps preserve the spread naturally by preventing the growth of microorganisms. It's tempting to want to lower the amount of sugar called for in a jelly or jam recipe, but don't do it. Granulated white cane or beet sugar is the best option. Avoid using sweeteners like molasses, brown sugar, or sorghum, as they can overpower the flavor of the spread; artificial sweeteners interfere with the gelling process, so avoid those, too.

Pectin is a thickener used to gel jams and jellies. Most canning recipes call for powdered or liquid commercial pectin. Each pectin acts differently, so be sure to follow the jam or jelly recipe using the precise amount of the specified pectin. There are some fruits, like apples, rhubarb, and plums, that contain enough natural pectin to gel without adding commercial pectin.

Testing for Proper Gel

Testing the set of jam and jellies is unnecessary when commercial pectin is used. But when using recipes that call for natural or no added pectin, testing the set can give you peace of mind. My preferred method is the spoon test.

Before you get started on your recipe, place a few metal spoons in the freezer. As the spread is getting closer to doneness, carefully dip a cold metal spoon into the boiling mixture. Lift the spoon and allow the mixture to fall back into the pot. Undercooked droplets will be light and syrupy. As the fruit cooks, the drops will become thicker and will start to fall off the spoon two at a time. When the two drops form together and "sheet" off the spoon, you know that your spread is done.

The actual firmness of your spread will not be known until it's completely cooled. Most soft spreads are successfully set within 24 hours. But some may take up to 2 weeks to set, especially jellies.

Stiff Jellies or Jams

We often hear about jams or jellies turning out too loose, but they can also become too stiff. (I know, it's always something!) But no worries, you can still put your spread to use. Use unset spread to glaze vegetables or meat. Stiff spreads can be heated and poured over waffles or pancakes, and a dollop would jazz up any vinaigrette.

Storage

Canned jams and jellies are best stored in a cool, dark, and dry place, between 50° and 70°F. For best quality and flavor, use within 1 year, but they can last much longer. Light-colored jellies or jams may darken slightly, but this is a normal occurrence. Once a jar has been unsealed, store the jar in the refrigerator and use within 1 month.

WHY BOTTLED LEMON JUICE?

Unlike fresh lemons, which vary in acidity, bottled lemon juice contains a standardized amount of acidity that also helps to prevent the growth of bacteria. So don't feel bad reaching for the bottle!

Spiced Raspberry Jam

Our pantry wouldn't be complete without this jam. We use the organic raspberries from our backyard for this, but of course it is also delicious with any fresh raspberries available to you. Not a spice girl? No prob, omit the nutmeg and keep it plain, Jane. Both are so good!

MAKES 8 HALF-PINTS

6½ cups sugar

½ teaspoon ground nutmeg or cinnamon (optional)

2 quarts fresh raspberries

1 (1.75-ounce) package powdered fruit pectin, such as Sure-Jell

1 · Gather your half-pint jars, lids, bands, and canning utensils. Prepare the boiling water canner (see page 66). Sterilize the jars.

2 · Combine the sugar and nutmeg (if using) in a medium bowl. Set aside. Put 1 cup of the raspberries in another large bowl and crush with a fork or potato masher. Continue crushing, 1 cup at a time, until you have 5 cups crushed raspberries.

3 · Transfer the raspberries to a heavy-bottomed nonreactive 8- to 10-quart pot. Stir in the pectin. Cook over high heat, stirring constantly, until the mixture comes to a full, rolling boil. Boil for 1 minute. Stir in the sugar mixture and return to a boil, stirring constantly. Boil hard for 1 minute. Remove from the heat. If necessary, use a large metal spoon to skim off any foam from the surface.

4 · Working with one hot jar at a time, ladle in the jam, leaving ¼-inch headspace. Wipe the rim, center the lid, and adjust the band. Using a jar lifter, place the jar in the canning rack raised above the simmering water.

5 · Lower the filled rack into the pot, being sure that the simmering water covers the jars by 1 inch. Add additional hot water as needed. Cover and bring the water to a rolling boil over high heat. Set a timer and process the jars for 5 minutes (see page 67 for high-altitude adjustments). Remember that timing does not start until the water comes to a full boil. Turn off the heat and uncover the pot. Raise the canning rack above the water and let the jars stand for 5 minutes.

6 · Using a jar lifter, transfer the jars, keeping upright (without tipping), to a kitchen towel and cool, undisturbed, for 12 to 24 hours. For best flavor use within 1 year. Once opened, refrigerate and use within 1 month.

Apple Pie Applesauce

Nothing says fall like spiced applesauce. When it's canned, it's the gift that keeps giving all year. I love to use it in muffins, cakes, quick breads, and oatmeal. For the sweetest applesauce, use Golden Delicious, Fuji, McIntosh, Pink Lady, Honeycrisp, or Gala apples. If sweet is not your thing, choose a tart variety, such as Granny Smith or Gravenstein.

MAKES ABOUT 6 PINTS OR 3 QUARTS

8 to 10 pounds fresh or thawed frozen apples, peeled, cored, and quartered

¼ cup fresh lemon juice

1½ teaspoons apple pie spice

1 (3-inch) cinnamon stick

2 cups water

1 cup packed light brown sugar

1 · Gather your pint or quart jars, lids, bands, and canning utensils. Prepare the boiling water canner (see page 66).

2 · Bring the apples, lemon juice, apple pie spice, cinnamon, and water to a boil in a heavy-bottomed nonreactive 8- to 10-quart pot over high heat, stirring often to minimize scorching. Turn the heat down to medium-low and simmer, stirring often, until the apples are tender, 20 to 30 minutes. Be flexible with the cooking time, which will vary according to the apple variety. Discard the cinnamon stick.

3 · Using an immersion blender or stand blender, process the applesauce to the desired consistency. For a chunky sauce, do not blend—simply mash with a fork or wooden spoon.

4 · Stir in the brown sugar. Increase the heat to medium-high and return the applesauce to a boil, stirring almost constantly, until the sugar is dissolved.

5 · Working with one hot jar at a time, ladle in the sauce, leaving ½-inch headspace. Wipe the rim, center the lid, and adjust the band. Using a jar lifter, place the jar in the canning rack raised above the simmering water.

6 · Lower the filled rack into the pot, being sure that the simmering water covers the jars by 1 inch. Add additional hot water as needed. Cover and bring the water to a rolling boil over high heat. Set a timer and process pints for 15 minutes and quarts for 20 minutes (see page 67 for high-altitude adjustments). Turn off the heat and uncover the pot. Raise the canning rack above the water and let the jars stand for 5 minutes.

7 · Using a jar lifter, transfer the jars, keeping upright (without tipping), to a kitchen towel and cool, undisturbed, for 12 to 24 hours. For best flavor, use within 1 year. Once opened, refrigerate and use within 1 to 2 weeks.

Concord Grape Juice

Homemade grape juice in September is a sweet reward for a gardener, and a prize I look forward to every year. Don't grow grapes? No problem! Take advantage of them at the grocery store in season when their taste and the price are the best. Can or freeze this juice to enjoy all year long.

MAKES 2 TO 3 QUARTS

20 cups stemmed Concord grapes (about 8 pounds)

3 cups water

1 cup sugar (less or more depending on the sweetness of the grapes and preferred taste)

1 · Combine the grapes and water in a heavy-bottomed nonreactive 8- to 10-quart pot. Cover and bring the mixture to a boil. Reduce the heat to medium-low and simmer, covered, occasionally mashing with a potato masher, until the grapes are softened, about 10 minutes. Fit a colander over another large pot that will fit in your refrigerator. Line the colander with a few layers of cheesecloth. Pour the grape mixture into the colander and stir and press with a large spoon to gently release the juices. Cover with the pot lid or plastic wrap and refrigerate to drain for 24 hours. Trust me, it's worth waiting for!

2 · Discard or compost the grape mash. (Or even better, feed it to your backyard flock—they'll love you even more!) Set a fine-mesh strainer over another large pot. Line the strainer with rinsed and wrung cheesecloth. Taking care not to disturb the sediment at the bottom of the pot, carefully pour the grape juice through the strainer. Stir in the sugar until it reaches the desired level of sweetness. Bring to a simmer over medium heat, stirring until the sugar is dissolved. Using a wide spoon, skim any foam as it collects.

3 · Store the juice according to one of the following methods:

Fresh Completely cool. Transfer to an airtight container and refrigerate for up to 2 weeks.

Freeze Completely cool. Pour into ice cube trays and freeze until solid, at least 4 hours. Transfer the frozen cubes to a freezer-safe bag and freeze. Best enjoyed within 12 months.

Can Gather quart jars, lids, bands, and canning utensils. Prepare a boiling water canner (see page 66). Sterilize the jars. Working with one hot jar at a time, ladle in the juice, leaving ¼-inch headspace. Wipe the rim, center the lid, and adjust the band. Using a jar lifter, place the jar in the canning rack raised above the simmering water. Lower the filled rack into the pot, being sure that the simmering water covers the jars by 1 inch. Add additional hot water as needed. Cover and bring the water to a rolling boil. Set a timer and process the jars for 5 minutes (see page 67 for high-altitude adjustments). Remember that timing doesn't start until the water comes to a full boil. Turn off the heat and uncover the pot. Raise the canning rack above the water and let the jars stand for 5 minutes. Using a jar lifter, transfer the jars, keeping upright (without tipping), to a kitchen towel and cool, undisturbed, for 12 to 24 hours. Once opened, refrigerate and use within 1 to 2 weeks.

Boiling Water Canning

Wild Violet Jelly

Jelly is my favorite way to capture the essence and flavor of flowers. Wild violet jelly is delightfully sweet and is the most stunning shade of hot pink! You'll find variations below using other flowers. Be sure to have all the ingredients measured and ready as working quickly is key in this recipe.

MAKES ABOUT 6 HALF-PINTS

2 cups packed fresh organically grown wild violet flowers

4½ cups boiling water

¼ cup bottled lemon juice

1 (1.75-ounce) package powdered pectin, such as Sure-Jell

4 cups sugar

1 · Make a strong botanical water, which will be used to make the jelly: Place the flowers in a heatproof bowl and add the boiling water. Cover with a kitchen towel and let stand until completely cooled, 2 to 3 hours. For the best flavor, cover with plastic wrap and refrigerate overnight.

2 · Drain the botanical water into another bowl, pressing hard on the flowers to extract as much flavor and color as possible. Discard the solids. Measure 4 cups, adding more water as needed.

3 · Gather your half-pint jars, lids, bands, and canning utensils. Prepare the boiling water canner (see page 66). Sterilize the jars.

4 · Stir the lemon juice into the purple tea. (It will turn pink, so gather the kids around to watch—they will think you are amazing!)

5 · Pour the mixture into a heavy-bottomed 8- to 10-quart pot and stir in the pectin. Bring to a rolling boil over medium-high heat. Boil for 1 full minute. Stir in the sugar all at once and return to a full boil, then cook for 1 minute, stirring constantly. Watch it carefully, so it doesn't boil over. (I blow on the foam in the pot, which discourages overflow.) Remove from the heat. Using a wide metal spoon, skim any foam.

6 · Working with one hot jar at a time, ladle in the jelly, leaving ¼-inch headspace. Wipe the rim, center the lid, and adjust the band. Using a jar lifter, place the jar in the canning rack raised above the simmering water.

7 · Lower the filled rack into the pot, being sure that the simmering water covers the jars by 1 inch. Add additional hot water as needed. Cover and bring the water to a rolling boil over high heat. Set a timer and process the jars for 5 minutes (see page 67 for high-altitude adjustments). Remember that timing does not start until the water comes to a full boil. Turn off the heat. Raise the canning rack above the water and let the jars stand for 5 minutes.

8 · Using a jar lifter, transfer the jars, keeping upright (without tipping), to a kitchen towel and cool, undisturbed, for 12 to 24 hours. The jelly is best used within 1 year. Once opened, refrigerate and use within 1 month.

VARIATIONS

Refrigerator Jelly: Ladle the hot jelly into heatproof jars or containers, leaving ¼-inch headspace. Let cool completely. Cover, label, and date the jars. The jelly can be refrigerated for up to 3 months or frozen for up to 1 year. Note that thawed jelly can be thin and soak through bread. Canning will yield better results.

Dandelion Jelly: Substitute dandelion flowers for the violets, removing all bitter green parts. Yellow dandelions make a sweet jelly with a golden hue.

Mint Jelly: Substitute mint leaves for the violets. If you like, add 4 to 5 drops green food coloring to the mint tea before stirring in the pectin.

Rose Jelly: Substitute brightly colored, fragrant rose petals for the violets to make a beautiful red to pink jelly. Cut off the white tips of the petals for the best flavor.

Homestead Berry Syrup

Use a fresh harvest or your frozen stash of berries to make this canned syrup, delicious on pancakes and cheesecake.

MAKES 4 TO 5 HALF-PINTS

12 cups fresh or frozen berries, such as blackberries, raspberries, or hulled strawberries

2 cups water

3½ cups sugar

1 · Using a potato masher, mash the berries in a large saucepan. Stir in the water. Bring to a boil over medium heat. Turn the heat down to medium-low and simmer until the berries are soft, 5 to 10 minutes.

2 · Place a fine-mesh strainer over a bowl and line with a double layer of cheesecloth. Pour the berries into the strainer and let drain, pressing on the fruit (except strawberries) to release the juice. Drain and cool. Discard the pulp. Measure 6 cups of juice, adding water if needed.

3 · Gather your half-pint jars, lids, bands, and canning utensils. Prepare the boiling water canner (see page 66). Sterilize the jars.

4 · Return the juice to the saucepan and bring to a boil over high heat. Stir in the sugar. Turn the heat down to medium and simmer, stirring occasionally, until the mixture is slightly thickened and syrupy, about 20 minutes.

5 · Working with one hot jar at a time, ladle in the hot syrup, leaving ¼-inch headspace. Wipe the rim, center the lid, and adjust the band. Using a jar lifter, place the jar in the canning rack raised above the simmering water.

6 · Lower the filled rack into the pot, being sure that the simmering water covers the jars by 1 inch. Add additional hot water as needed. Cover and bring the water to a rolling boil over high heat. Set a timer and process the jars for 10 minutes (see page 67 for high-altitude adjustments). Remember that timing does not start until the water comes to a full boil. Turn off the heat and uncover the pot. Raise the canning rack above the water and let the jars stand for 5 minutes.

7 · Using a jar lifter, transfer the jars, keeping upright (without tipping) to a kitchen towel and cool, undisturbed, for 12 to 24 hours. For best flavor use within 1 year. Refrigerate after opening and use within 2 weeks.

Homestyle Pickles

The perfect pickle for the pantry!

MAKES 8 PINTS!

2½ tablespoons pickling spice mix

1 quart distilled white vinegar

4 cups water

¾ cup sugar

½ cup pickling or canning salt

8 bay leaves

8 garlic cloves, peeled

8 small fresh or dried chiles (optional; use mild to hot chiles, depending on your taste—I use cayenne)

8 fresh dill heads or ¼ teaspoon dill seeds

4 teaspoons yellow mustard seeds

6 pounds pickling cucumbers, trimmed and cut into ¼- to ½-inch rounds

1 teaspoon pickle firming agent (optional)

1 · Gather jars, lids, bands, and canning utensils. Prepare the boiling water canner (see page 66).

2 · Cut two 6-inch squares of cheesecloth. Stack them together, place the pickling spice in the center, bring up the ends to form a bundle, and tie the bag closed with kitchen twine.

3 · Combine the vinegar, water, sugar, salt, and spice bag in a medium nonreactive saucepan and bring to a boil over high heat, stirring until the sugar and salt are dissolved. Turn the heat down to low and simmer for 15 minutes. Discard the spice bag.

4 · Working with one hot jar at a time, add 1 bay leaf, 1 garlic clove, 1 chile, 1 dill head (or a pinch of dill seeds), and ½ teaspoon mustard seeds. Pack in the cucumbers, leaving ½-inch headspace, and add pickle firming agent (see page 53), if using. Ladle in the hot brine, making sure that the cucumbers are covered, maintaining ½-inch headspace. Remove any air bubbles, wipe the rim, center the lid, and adjust the band. Using a jar lifter, place the jar in the canning rack raised above the simmering water.

5 · Lower the filled rack into the pot, being sure that the simmering water covers the jars by at least 1 inch. Add additional hot water as needed. Cover and bring the water to a rolling boil over high heat. Set a timer and process for 15 minutes (see page 67 for high-altitude adjustments). Remember that timing does not start until the water comes to a full boil.

6 · Turn off the heat. Raise the canning rack above the water and let the jars stand for 5 minutes. Transfer the jars, keeping them upright (without tipping), to a kitchen towel and cool, undisturbed, for 12 to 24 hours. For best flavor, use within 1 year. Once opened, refrigerate and use within 2 to 3 weeks.

Boiling Water Canning

CHAPTER 4
Dry It!

88
Drying Herbs

90
Culinary Herbs

95
Drying Edible Flowers

105
Drying Chiles

105
Curing Homegrown Alliums

105
Drying and Pasteurizing Shell Beans

As much as I love my dehydrator (see chapter 5), I still find drying herbs, flowers, and chiles and curing garden-grown garlic and onions an effective natural process. I dedicate an entire room to preserving this special bounty and fill it with loaded drying racks, hanging herbs, pressed flowers, and curing alliums. It's dreamy.

Recipes

Herbs de Provence Seasoning Blend 109

Greek Seasoning Blend 109

Italian Seasoning Blend 110

Flower-fetti 110

Chili Powder 111

Mild Taco Seasoning 111

Dried Chile Hot Sauce 112

Culinary Powders

Drying Herbs

We grow more than a dozen different perennial herbs as well as a handful of annuals that we start from seed each spring. I use both fresh and dried herbs to add flavor to all my cooking. Explore the detailed list of culinary herbs on page 90.

There are several different methods for drying herbs naturally, but the preparation is always the same.

Prep Steps

- Rinse the herbs quickly under cold water. Some may benefit from a quick dunk into a cold-water bath followed by vigorous shaking to remove any debris.

- Discard any bruised or imperfect leaves.

- Pat dry with a cloth or paper towel. I like to lay mine in a single layer on top of cloth or paper towels on the counter until they're completely dry, usually 2 to 3 hours.

Methods

Air drying

Indoor air drying is my number one method to dry most of my herbs and flowers and there are a few ways I do it. For each option, select a warm, dry, location with good airflow and away from a sunny window.

Hang Drying This method is ideal for hardy herbs like rosemary and sage. Gather rinsed and dried sprigs in groups of five or six. Note that overbundling can decrease air flow and result in mold. With twine, tie bundles by the stems—you will hang them by the stems, too—removing any leaves where the twine will be tied. Label the bundles. Hang in a location with good airflow. I use a string line hanging from the ceiling and attach my bundles to the line using clothespins. Avoid hanging flat against a wall, as this may cause the herbs to mold. Drying time varies, depending on the hardiness of the herbs, room temperature, and humidity. On average, it takes 1 to 2 weeks to completely dry most herbs. The leaves should break easily in your fingers when dried.

Drying in Paper Bags If dust is an issue in your space, consider hanging herbs inside paper bags to dry. Bundle as if you were hang drying, then secure a loose paper bag over the bundle with the bottom of the bag cut off or several holes poked into all sides of the bag. Good airflow is a must.

Screen Drying Herbs can also be dried directly on food-safe drying screens or wire cooling racks covered with cheesecloth. High-moisture leaves such as mint, basil, and lemon balm, dry more quickly when you separate the leaves from the stems. Arrange on screens, leaving space in between. Place the screens on utility shelving with open or wire construction to encourage airflow. Let dry for 1 to 2 weeks, or until the leaves can easily crush between your fingers.

Solar drying

Although direct sunlight will cause herbs to lose flavor and diminish in color, outdoor drying is still effective. A few hot days and a good spot in the shade will do just fine. The ideal outdoor temperature is 88° to 100°F with low humidity. Hang the herbs on something that can easily be transported. I tie my bundles onto the side of an old crib rail. Leaned up at an angle against something (shed, house, post), it provides good airflow for proper drying. Hangers, tomato cages, or screens are also good options. Bring the herbs indoors every night before dusk. Once the dew has dried in the morning, place them back out in the shade. This method takes 1 or more days, depending on temperature and humidity.

Store-bought or farmers' market fresh herbs can be dried at home, but if you're growing them yourself, harvest the herbs just before the flowers bloom for highest potency. Harvesting after the morning dew has dried is also ideal. But I've harvested in the dark with a flashlight so . . . do whatcha gotta do.

IMPORTANT NOTE
Dried herbs are three to four times more potent in flavor than fresh—and freeze-dried is even stronger. In recipes calling for fresh herbs, reduce the measurement by half for their dried counterparts.

Storage and Shelf Life

Store dried herbs in glass containers with tight-fitting lids away from direct sunlight, a heat source, or exposure to moisture. There's no need to hide jars in a dark cupboard. I've stored my seasonal dried herbs on my open kitchen shelf, out of direct sunlight, in airtight clear glass jars, year after year, without issue. Having them on display brings me joy and inspiration. Whole leaves stored this way have an average shelf life of 1 year before potency begins to diminish (but can last longer).

On average, ground herbs stay potent for 3 to 6 months. Adding an oxygen absorber, vacuum-sealing the jar, or using vacuum-sealed Mylar bags will extend the shelf life from months to years.

Pro tip! Always shake dried herbs out of the jar and into your hand, away from steam, when using. Place both hands together, rubbing back and forth, crushing the herbs to wake up the flavors before seasoning your food. If you shake the jar directly over food while it's cooking, the moisture from the stove will creep into the jar, resulting in moldy or discolored herbs.

Culinary Herbs

The following chart lists eighteen culinary herbs and how to use them. A few of the herbs also have edible flowers; you'll find more on edible flowers beginning on page 95. Herbs with an asterisk are suitable for tisanes. See page 171 for additional herbs and more on botanical teas.

Herb	Profile	Forms	Uses
*Anise, aniseed (*Pimpinella anisum*)	Tiny, delicate white flowers that produce flavorful seeds called aniseed. Sweet licorice flavor.	Seeds: fresh, dried Leaves: fresh, cooked Flowers: fresh	Use seeds in breads, sausages, and dressings or to flavor beverages and desserts. Use flowers in salads, as a garnish, or edible decor.
*Basil (*Ocimum basilicum*)	Distinctive clove-mint flavor. Cinnamon, lemon, and lime basil have notes of sweet, citrus, and spice. Purple leaf varieties make beautiful infusions and tea.	Leaves: fresh, dried Flowers: fresh, dried	Use in pesto, sauces, infusions, seasoning blends, and beverages. Use fresh flowers and leaves as garnish.
Bay, sweet bay, sweet laurel (*Laurus nobilis*)	Glossy green leaves with a strong spicy flavor that intensifies when dried. Fresh leaves have a slightly bitter taste.	Leaves: fresh, dried	Use in soups, sauces, oil infusions, and pickling. **NOTE**: Always remove whole bay leaves after cooking.
Chives (*Allium*)	A member of the allium family but classified as an herb. Straight stems with round purple or pink pom-pom blooms have a mild onion flavor. Harvest the flowers while young for best flavor.	Flowers: fresh Stems: fresh, freeze-dried	Use fresh stems and blooms for garnishes, salads, vinegar infusions (see page 185), compound butters, and savory baked goods. Add chopped dried stems to soups, sauces, and potato and egg dishes.
Cilantro/coriander (*Coriandrum sativum*)	Fragrant white, pink, and light purple flowers with light green leaves. Leaves and tender stems have a strong flavor. Seeds have notes of orange.	Seeds: dried Leaves: fresh, freeze-dried	Use seeds in pickling spice, marinades, curries, and relishes. Add leaves as a fresh garnish to tacos, black beans, and rice.

Herb	Profile	Forms	Uses
Dill (*Anethum graveolens*)	Fragrant, tiny flat seeds are mildly bitter. Dark green leaves are packed with flavor.	Seeds: dried Leaves: fresh, dried Flowers: fresh, dried	Use all parts, fresh or dried, in pickling brine, dips, breads, soups, and sauces. Add last minute when cooking so flavor isn't diminished.
*Fennel (*Foeniculum vulgare*)	Licorice-flavored feathery fronds. Aromatic flat seeds with yellow ridges are less sweet than aniseed, making them ideal for savory dishes.	Bulb: fresh Leaves/stems: fresh, dried Seeds: dried	Grill, braise, stew, or sauté bulbs. Use stems and leaves in sauces, soups, pesto. Add seeds to sausages, curries, breads, and crackers.
*Lavender, English or true (*Lavandula angustifolia*); fern leaf (*Lavandula multifida*)	Fragrant! Sweet, spicy flavor with hints of citrus packing big flavor so a little goes a long way. Adjust the amounts you use to fit your taste buds. As a tea, lavender is a natural sleep aid.	Stems: fresh, dried Leaves: fresh, dried Flowers: fresh, dried, pressed	Use in Botanical Water (page 165), ice cream (see page 43), baked goods (see page 308), granola (page 257), and infusions.
Lovage (*Levisticum officinale*)	Hollow stems and celery-like leaves in look and flavor. Small, brown, aromatic seeds. Add last minute to long-cooking dishes and use in moderation.	Stems: fresh Leaves: fresh, dried Seeds: dried	Use leaves in stuffing, salads, soups, and stews. Use seeds in sausages, marinades, and soups. Add last minute to long-cooking dishes and use in moderation.
*Marjoram, sweet (*Origanum majorana*)	Light floral, sweet flavor. Dark green leaves and tiny white flower clusters.	Leaves: fresh, dried Flowers: fresh	Use in infusions, vinegars, sauces, meats, and breads (see page 305). Marjoram has been used to make calming teas, rich in vitamin A and C, for centuries. Try it in combination with other herbs like basil and mint.

Herb	Profile	Forms	Uses
*Mint (*Mentha*), various	There are several varieties of mint with different flavors.	Leaves: fresh, dried Flowers: fresh	Use leaves in beverages, infusions, sugared (see page 222), soups, salads, fruit dishes, dips, and desserts. Use flowers for garnish, botanical tea (see page 170).
*Oregano (*Origanum vulgare*)	My favorite herb! Robust flavor. Flowers are also edible but slightly less flavorful than leaves.	Leaves: fresh, dried Flowers: fresh, dried	Use in infusions, compound butters, pizza, pasta, tomato sauce, and vinaigrettes. Makes a revitalizing tea that may soothe a sore throat, cough, and muscle aches.
Parsley: flat-leaf/Italian, curly (*Petroselinum crispum*)	Refreshing mild taste that can be added to almost any dish. Italian (flat-leaf) parsley is milder than curly-leaf types.	Leaves: fresh, dried Stems: fresh	Use in meatballs, pesto, stuffing, and compound butter. Add as a garnish on cooked dishes.
*Rosemary (*Rosmarinus officinalis*)	Aromatic herb. A delightful pine flavor with hints of citrus and mint. Makes a strong-scented revitalizing tisane that can be consumed every day.	Leaves: fresh, dried	Use in beverages, sauces, infusions, soups, stews, and vegetable dishes **ZERO WASTE:** *Use the fresh stems (leaves removed) soaked in water as a skewer for grilled meats or vegetables.*

Herb	Profile	Forms	Uses
*Sage, common (*Salvia officinalis*)	Musty, aromatic herb. When dried, the flavor intensifies.	Leaves: fresh, dried	Use in stuffing, sauces, infusions, butter, and sausages. Use leaves as a garnish, fresh or sugared (see page 222).
Savory, summer (*Satureja hortensis*); winter (*Satureja montana*)	Summer savory is aromatic with a minty-sweet thyme-like flavor. Winter savory has a strong, spicy, tangy flavor. Best used fresh.	Leaves: fresh, dried	Use in sauces, stuffings, soups, marinades, and salads.
*Tarragon (*Artemisia dracunculus*)	French tarragon has a subtle anise flavor. Russian tarragon is more pungent and slightly bitter. Dried leaves lose flavor quickly.	Leaves: fresh, dried	Use in infused vinegar, compound butter, béarnaise sauce, and rice.
*Thyme, English, French, and garden (*Thymus vulgaris*); lemon (*Thymus citriodorus*); wild (*Thymus serpyllum*)	As fragrant as it is flavorful. Tiny aromatic leaves on woody stems. Leaf color varies depending on variety. A complement to savory and sweet dishes.	Leaves: fresh, dried	Use in stews, soups, sauces, compound butter, infusions, stuffings, and fruit desserts

Drying Edible Flowers

Using edible flowers in culinary dishes might seem like a fad, but the practice dates back thousands of years. Use them to garnish a cocktail or dessert or for infusing flavor into jellies, teas, and sorbets—flowers are delightful ingredients. It is important to note that not all edible flowers taste good—some are best used as a decorative garnish.

Prep Steps

- Before bringing flowers indoors, place in a colander and give them a good shake to help remove any debris or insects.

- Remove any pistils and stamens as well as the bitter white part at the base of the petals called the heel. I sometimes use scissors to cut the petal away from the base, leaving the bitter white part behind.

- Rinse the flowers or petals quickly under gently running cold water. Some flowers, like bachelor's buttons, are tiny bug hotels and can benefit from a cold-water bath to force them out. More delicate flowers, like chamomile, pansies, or violas, can be wiped clean with a damp paper towel.

- Discard any bruised or imperfect petals. Pat flowers dry with a cloth or paper towel. I like to spread them out, facing down, on top of cloth or paper towels on my counter until they're completely dry—just an hour or so, depending on temperature and humidity. Now they're ready to use or preserve.

Fresh flowers, refrigerated in an airtight container, will keep for a few days.

Methods

As with herbs, there are several ways to dry edible flowers. These are my preferred methods.

Air Drying Indoors is my preferred method. Just like herbs, flowers like a warm and dry location with good airflow and away from direct sunlight.

Hang Drying Long-stemmed flowers, such as lavender and sunflowers, can be hung upside down to dry. Hang large head flowers at different lengths in the bunch to promote airflow. Overbundling will reduce air flow and may result in mold; this is especially true with lavender. With twine, tie bundles of eight to ten sprigs by the stems, removing any flower buds or leaves where the twine meets the stem. Dry any clipped blooms on a screen. Label if you need to identify flowers and hang bundles by the stems. As with herbs, I use a string line hanging from the ceiling and attach the bundles to the line with clothespins. Avoid hanging them flat against a wall as the flowers may mold. On average it takes 1 to 2 weeks to completely dry. Drying time will vary depending on the hardiness and size of the flower, room temperature, and humidity. Petals should be crisp to the touch.

Screen Drying Screen drying for edible flowers is the same process as herbs. See page 88 for more details.

How to Press Flowers

Drying flowers in a press gives you flat dried flowers for crafting and garnishing both baked and savory goods. Since I press mine for both crafting and culinary uses, I press them without the use of any preservatives.

Pressing works best for single flowers with delicate petals. Pressing larger blooms with several layers of petals can be tricky because they often develop mold in the process. It may take some trial and error to figure out the best method for your environment.

To press your flowers, you will need a flower press, either one you buy (usually a wooden press with bolts in each corner to tighten) or one you make. I use 12-inch square wood blocks stacked up, which allows me to press several layers of flowers at once. For smaller-scale flower pressing, use a large heavy book and a belt to tighten it closed.

Place your clean, air-dried flowers between sheets of nonglossy paper before placing them in your chosen press. Some folks add a piece of cardboard between the paper and flower press on the top and bottom of each layer. Drying flowers this way takes anywhere from 2 to 6 weeks, depending on the size of the flower, temperature, and humidity.

Storage and Shelf Life

Store dried flowers in glass containers with tight-fitting lids in a dry room, away from direct sunlight or a heat source. As with dried herbs, I've stored my dried flowers on an open shelf, out of direct sunlight, for many years without issue. They look so beautiful!

Whole dried flowers and dried petals have an optimum shelf life of 1 year before flavor, color, and fragrance diminish. Adding an oxygen absorber or vacuum sealing the jar will lengthen shelf life. Sealed Mylar bags with an oxygen absorber can preserve dried flowers for up to 5 years.

Store pressed dried flowers in resealable plastic bags and be sure to label and date. Keep in a moisture-proof box or binder, away from sunlight. Discard flowers if moisture, mold, or a foul odor is present.

Only organically grown edible flower varieties should be eaten. Those treated with fertilizers, insecticides, or pesticides, or purchased from big-box stores and garden nurseries (which are often treated) are not food safe.

When foraging, select only flowers grown far from roadways or sidewalks and use reliable plant identification, as some flowers look similar but can be harmful to humans. If you do not grow your own edible flowers, you can find them at specialty grocery stores and farmers' markets. Dried (and fresh) edible flowers are easy to find online.

IMPORTANT: People taking medications, those with asthma or plant allergies, and pregnant or nursing women, should all consult a doctor before consuming any flowers. Some edible flowers can interfere with medications and complicate health issues. It's always important to do your own research and seek advice from a physician before consuming.

Refer to the herb and botanical tea list (pages 172 to 175) for details on additional edible flowers. Flowers with an asterisk are suitable for tisanes. See page 170 for more on botanical teas.

* * *

Marigold flower heads can be strung into a strand of garland using a needle and thread. String them close together; they will shrink as they dry. Use them as seasonal decor. It's said that marigolds hung over doorways and windows will keep evil out. I think they just look pretty.

Edible Flowers

Edible Flower	Profile	Forms	Uses
Alyssum, sweet (*Lobularia maritima*)	Tiny compact flowers. Pungent flavor similar in taste as kale.	Leaves: fresh, pressed Flowers: fresh, pressed	Use as a garnish or in egg dishes. Mix the leaves and flowers into salads.
*Bachelor's button/ cornflowers (*Centaurea cyanus*)	Pom-pom shaped, multicolored blooms have very little fragrance but can have a sweet or spicy taste, depending on color and variety.	Flowers: fresh, dried, pressed	Use in desserts, baked goods, Flower-fetti (page 110), floral pasta, salads, and as a garnish or edible art.
*Borage/starflower (*Borago officinalis*)	Wide, fuzzy-textured, grayish-green leaves with star-shaped blue, pink, or white flowers. All have a refreshing cucumber-like taste. Remove center stamen.	Leaves: fresh, dried Flowers: fresh, dried	Use to flavor beverages. Use fresh leaves in stews, soups, and pesto. Sugar fresh flowers (see page 222) or freeze in ice cubes.
*Calendula/ pot marigold (*Calendula officinalis*)	Yellow, orange, pink, white, and cream-colored flowers. Tangy flavor. Makes a healing tea packed with antioxidant and anti-inflammatory properties.	Leaves: fresh, dried Flowers: fresh, dried, pressed	Make colorful infusions. Add fresh petals to salads, baked goods, or compound butter (see page 198). Use dried in herb blends.
Citrus blossoms (*Citrus aurantium, Citrus × limon, Citrus × latifolia*)	The flowers from the orange, lemon, lime, grapefruit, and kumquat plants have intense scent and flavor.	Flowers: fresh, dried	Use the flowers as a garnish, in infusions, or sugared (see page 222).
Dahlias (*Dahlia*)	All varieties are edible, with the flavor profile changing for each, ranging from spicy to fruity to carrot flavor.	Petals: fresh, dried	Use as a garnish or in ice cubes, infusions, garden butter, and Flower-fetti (page 110). Press whole flowers.

Dry It!

Edible Flower	Profile	Forms	Uses
Daisies (*Bellis perennis*)	Small white, blue, and purple blooms with a mildly bitter, spicy flavor. Use petals only. Use whole flowers as a garnish.	Flowers: Fresh, dried (pressed)	Use as a garnish or in salads, cookies, infused ice cubes, or sugared (see page 222).
*Dandelions (*Taraxacum*)	Young flowers have a sweet honey flavor, slightly bitter when fully mature. Remove the white part of the petals. Good source of vitamins A, C, and K. High in calcium and fiber.	Roots: dried Stems: fresh Leaves: fresh, dried Flowers: fresh, dried	Use as a garnish for savory or sweet dishes, jellies, infusions, or ice cubes. Roast roots for a coffee alternative or dry to make tinctures. Use leaves in salads or for pesto.
*Dianthus/carnation/pinks (*Dianthus caryophyllus*); sweet William (*Dianthus barbatus*)	Dianthus has a sweet nutmeg/clove-like taste. Enjoy petals of large carnations in fresh salads. Remove the white bitter part of the petals.	Flowers: fresh, dried, pressed	Use sugared for garnish (see page 222) or in infusions, ice cream, sorbets, and salads. Use dried to make Flower-fetti (page 110).
*Eastern redbud (*Cercis canadensis*)	Beautiful pink flowers have a mild slightly sweet flavor similar to snow peas.	Flowers: fresh	Use as a garnish or in salads, jellies, and infusions.
*Forget-me-nots (*Myosotis sylvatica*)	Tiny blue flowers with a delicate nutty taste.	Flowers: fresh, dried (pressed)	Use a garnish for sweet and savory dishes or in salads.
*Freesia (*Freesia*)	Strongly scented yellow flower with a sweet floral taste.	Flower: fresh, dried	Use in infusions, syrups, sorbets, and salads.
*Fuchsia (*Fuchsia*)	Uniquely shaped, purple-pink blooms have slightly acidic lemon pepper taste. Remove the stamen and green and brown parts before consuming.	Leaves: fresh, dried Flowers: fresh, dried Berries: fresh, dried	Use as a garnish or in beverages, ice cubes, infusions, and jellies. Use fresh leaves for pesto and salads.

Edible Flower	Profile	Forms	Uses
Gladiolus, sword lily (*Gladiolus*)	A rainbow of colors. Flowers have lettuce-like flavor. Remove anthers before eating. Pollen can be collected and used as a natural sweetener.	Flowers: fresh, dried, pressed	Use in salads, stuffed with cheese, or garden butter. Good for both sweet and savory dishes.
*Hollyhocks (*Alcea rosea*)	Hardly any flavor at all! Remove the center stamen before eating the flower.	Leaves: fresh Flowers: fresh, pressed	Stuff flowers with cheese filling. Eat leaves like spinach.
Impatiens (*Impatiens*)	Tiny colorful flowers with delicate flavor. The other parts of the plant are edible but bitter. Eat in moderation.	Flowers: fresh, pressed	Use as a garnish, sugared (see page 222), or in beverages, jelly, compound butter, food art, and infusions.
*Lilac (*Syringa vulgaris*)	Fragrant purple, lilac, pink, and white blooms. High floral tones with a slightly bitter aftertaste. These flowers can lose color and scent soon after being dried, so work with them fresh, slightly wilted, or just dried for best flavors.	Flowers: Fresh, dried, pressed	Use in jelly, infusions, Botanical Water (page 165), baked goods, and ice cream or as a garnish or sugared (see page 222). Purple blooms result in a colorful tea.
*Magnolia (*Magnolia*)	White, pink, purple, or yellow flowers. All magnolias are considered edible with slightly different flavor profiles. Some can be too intense in flavor. Select young blooms.	Flowers: fresh, pressed	Use as a garnish, sugared (see page 222), or pickled or in syrups, jelly, and salads.
*Marigolds (*Tagetes*)	French, signet, and gem varieties taste best. Fresh marigolds can sometimes be bitter or spicy with citrus notes. Remove the white parts of the flower. Consume in moderation.	Leaves: fresh, dried Petals: fresh, dried	Use in salads, infusions, baked goods, Flower-fetti (page 110), pasta, or rice. Can be a saffron substitute.

Edible Flower	Profile	Forms	Uses
Nasturtiums (*Tropaeolum majus*)	Seeds, greens, and blooms are all edible. Spicy flavor. Flowers grow in an array of colors. Harvest the green seeds after the bloom is spent for pickling.	Leaves: fresh, dried Flowers: fresh, dried, pressed Seeds: fresh	Use young leaves in pesto. Stuff blooms with soft cheese. Pickle the seeds to use like capers. Dry and grind flowers and leaves to use as a pepper substitute.
*Peony (*Paeonia*)	A popular edible flower in medieval times. Comes in a wide range of colors. Delightfully sweet and floral tasting. Petals impart color into your dishes.	Petals: fresh, dried, pressed Seeds: dried	Use fresh petals in tea, salads, desserts, ice creams, infusions, and beverages. Use seeds in mulled wine.
Primrose, common (*Primula vulgaris*)	Flowers have a delicate citrus flavor. Leaves are slightly bitter and should be used in small quantities.	Leaves: fresh Flowers: fresh, pressed	Use as a garnish, in salads and compound butters, or sugared (see page 222). Add leaves sparingly to salads.
*Roses (*Rosa*)	All roses are edible, but flavor varies depending on variety, color, and growing conditions. Remove white bitter part of the petals. Makes a colorful, flavorful tea rich in antioxidants.	Flowers: fresh, dried Hips: fresh, dried	Use in beverages, syrups, ice creams, jellies, and scones (page 310), sugar petals (see page 222).
*Scented geraniums (*Pelargonium*, such as *P. Clorinda*, *P. fragrans*, *P. graveolens*, *P. quercifolia*, and *P. tomentosum*)	A wide variety of colors. The flavor usually matches the scent ranging from fruity and floral, to minty or spicy. Leaves are more intense in flavor than flowers. **IMPORTANT**: The citronelle variety (*Pelargonium citronella*) should be avoided.	Leaves: fresh, dried Petals: fresh, dried, pressed	Use as a garnish or in salads, syrups, drinks, or ice cubes. Use dried in Flower-fetti (page 110) and oil infusions. Blend dried leaves and sugar for a sweet sugar infusion.
Snapdragons (*Antirrhinum*)	Flavor varies, from mild and bland to bitter and spicy. Best when used chopped up in small amounts or in combination with other flowers and herbs.	Flowers: fresh, dried, pressed	Use in salads, compound butter (see page 198), dried in Flower-fetti (page 110), or as a garnish.

Edible Flower	Profile	Forms	Uses
*Stocks (*Matthiola incana*)	Vibrant blooms in a variety of colors, with a sweet fragrance. Leaves and seed pods have a radish-like taste. Imparts color into foods.	Seedpods: fresh Leaves: fresh Flowers: fresh, dried, pressed	Use in infusions, jelly, garnish, Botanical Water (page 165), or food art.
*Sunflowers (*Helianthus annuus*)	Flowers can be eaten at the bud stage or fully mature. Most varieties have a tangy, slightly nutty taste. Roots and stalks can be cooked. Dried and roasted striped seeds are a delicious snack. Black seeds are perfect winter food for bird feeders.	Roots: cooked Stalks: cooked Petals: fresh, dried Seeds: dried	Petals can be used in salads, baked goods, infusions, and food art. Unopened buds can be steamed or blanched and tossed in herb butter.
Tulips (*Tulipa*)	Taste profile from slightly bitter to a lettuce or pea flavor. Only the flower petals should be consumed. Never eat the bulbs. **IMPORTANT**: If you have a skin reaction when touching tulips, do not eat.	Petals: fresh, pressed	Use as a garnish or in salads, ice infusions, compound butter. Stuff blossom with cheese spread; be sure to remove the pollen and stigmas before stuffing.
*Violas/pansies (*Viola cornuta*, *V. hybrida*, *V. tricolor*, *V. × williamsiana*, and *V. × wittrockiana*)	Subtle wintergreen-tasting flowers can be added to any dish without changing the flavor. Darker-colored blooms will impart color into infusions.	Leaves: fresh, dried Flowers: fresh, dried, pressed Whole plant (flower, stem, and leaves): pressed	Use as a garnish or in salads, infusions, floral butter, biscuits, Ham and Cheese Garden Quiche (page 254), and beverages.
Zinnia (*Zinnia*)	Strong bitter flavor. Resist using entire heads to decorate food or plan to remove before serving. Instead, use only the petals.	Petals: fresh, cooked, dried, pressed	Use as a garnish or in garden butter and pressed in ice infusions.

Drying Chiles

With a long shelf life and distinct flavors, dried chiles are a valuable ingredient for any kitchen.

Methods

Air-Drying This is my favorite way to dry my chile harvest. I like to string them up in clusters, so they double as decor while they dry. So pretty! Unlike herbs, chiles do well hanging in front of a warm, sunny window. Using heavy thread and a needle, string the thread through the base of the stems. For the first one, thread the needle through twice for extra security, then string on the remaining chiles, leaving enough thread at the top to make a loop for hanging. Chiles can also be air-dried whole on food-safe screens or racks that allow good airflow. Be sure to move the chiles around, turning them over a few times during the drying process to minimize risk of mold. Allow them to dry for several weeks. When successfully dried, chiles will darken, become wrinkled, and feel lightweight.

Solar Drying Live in a hot, dry climate? Oh, lucky you! Take advantage of those high temperatures by drying your chiles outdoors. Use the air-drying method, but make sure to bring your peppers indoors each night before dusk, returning them outdoors after the dew has dried in the morning. If insects are a concern, cover the chiles with a sheet of cheesecloth, which will still allow good airflow. Drying time will vary depending on temperature and humidity.

Storage and Shelf Life

Gently remove any dust your peppers may have collected with a soft dry cloth before storing. Dried chiles, placed in airtight containers and stored in a dark, cool location, away from direct sunlight, heat, or moisture exposure, will stay viable for 1 to 2 years before they start to diminish in flavor and quality. Vacuum-sealed bags or jars may lengthen shelf life. Ground chiles have a shorter shelf life than whole, averaging 3 to 6 months for the best flavor.

Refreshing

Wearing food-safe gloves or being careful not to touch your face while working, discard the stems and remove the seeds. Tear large chiles into smaller pieces or use scissors to snip them, being sure to clean the scissors before using and especially after, to remove any oils that might come back to haunt you later. Place the pieces in a small bowl and pour in enough hot water to cover them. Let them soak for about 1 hour, or until refreshed. Drain before using.

Curing Homegrown Alliums

Curing is the process of allowing produce to dry, removing just some of the moisture, so as to create better chances for long-term storage. In our garden we grow a lot of garlic and some onions. Curing garlic and onions is only necessary when you've grown your own; store-bought produce is already cured. Here are the methods we use to cure them.

DRYING AND PASTEURIZING SHELL BEANS

The simplest way to dry shell beans is right on the vine. Beans—whether soy, kidney, lima, great northern, scarlet runner, dragon tongue, navy, or lentils—all happily dry in the sunshine, right on the vine. Leave until the pods have browned and you can hear the beans rattle inside, then shell. If you find a few beans that are still not quite dry, put them in the dehydrator, in the oven on the lowest temp, or in the sun to prevent mold.

While heat from the sun is an effective way to dry beans outdoors, it doesn't kill harmful bacteria or destroy any insects or larva that might be inside the food. Fear not! There are two ways to safely pasteurize dry beans at home. Here is an overview of both:

Oven Method Place dried beans on a rimmed baking sheet in a single layer. Bake at 160°F for 30 minutes or at 175°F for 15 minutes. Cool before storing. Alternatively, a dehydrator may be used set at its highest temperature setting.

Freezer Method Place dried beans in a freezer-safe plastic bag. Set in the freezer (must be 0°F or below to be effective) for 48 hours. Transfer to a storage packaging of your choice.

Dry It!

- After harvesting, shake or brush off the excess dirt, but be sure to leave skin intact. It is essential to leave the stalks, roots, and leaves on the plant during curing; it prolongs the storage life of the bulbs. It also helps preserve nutrients and pungent flavors because the plant's stored energy is in the leaves and roots.

- Choose a warm, dry location with good airflow and out of direct sunlight. A shed, garage, covered porch, deck, or warm spot indoors are all good options. Lay the garlic heads and onions on food-safe screens or hang dry with kitchen twine, stems hanging down, allowing the moisture to wick away. Avoid curing onions in bundles because the bulbs touching can result in mold.

- Set the screens on open racks or blocks, or rest on top of two sawhorses to ensure good airflow. I use a stainless steel metal rack and place the onion or garlic, bulb side up, resting on the top rack with the greens weaving down through the lower racks. This option provides excellent airflow, is easy to move around, and uses something I already have on hand. If needed, add a fan to the space to ensure good air circulation.

Onions Select pungent, strong-flavored onions for best storage. Sweet onions tend to not last as long. Onions are best when cured in temperatures of 75° to 85°F for an average curing time of 3 to 4 weeks. Once cured, brush off any remaining dirt and trim the stalks, leaving about 1 inch, and cut off the roots.

Garlic Cure at a slightly cooler temperature, 70° to 80°F. Average drying time is 10 to 14 days, depending on the size of the bulbs. Keep the garlic bulbs, with greens attached, separated from each other while curing. Once cured, braid into bundles for space-saving storage.

Garlic Scapes Scapes are the flower stems that grow from hardneck garlic. They begin to appear a few weeks before it's time to harvest (typically the beginning of midsummer). If you remove the scapes, the bulbs will grow bigger in the final weeks. So not only are you helping the plant, but you are also eating a part that may otherwise have gone into the compost bin. Harvest the entire stem of the scape and discard the bloom. Scapes are flavorful but less pungent than the bulbs. They can be used fresh, cooked, or preserved. See the sections on freeze-drying (page 148) and dehydrating (page 126), and the recipes for Quick-Pickled Garlic Scapes (page 60), Turkey-Stuffed Lettuce Wraps (page 273), Creamy Garlic Scape Sauce (page 299), and Garlic Scape Vinaigrette (page 280).

Storage and Shelf Life

- Store cured onions or garlic in well-ventilated baskets or mesh bags. Or, if you leave the stems intact, onions can be braided and hung as mentioned for garlic. Place in a cool, dry, dark location such as a root cellar, basement, or unheated pantry. The ideal temperature for long-term storage is about 40°F.

- I don't recommend storing garlic in the kitchen. Kitchens get warm, and that may cause bulbs to spoil. The only exception is if you go through the bulbs quickly. For example, I store a few braids in a dark corner of my kitchen because I use them frequently. The garlic tends to last several weeks, but, once in a while, I will end up with a dried-up head. Avoid storing in the refrigerator as the cold, moist air will cause it to sprout and the flavor to change.

- Do not store onions near potatoes! Onions give off ethylene gas that will make the potatoes spoil prematurely. Also, the potatoes give off moisture that will create an environment for mold.

- Cured softneck garlic has an average shelf-life of 6 to 8 months; hardneck varieties, 4 to 6 months. On average, cured onions are best when used within 3 months.

Herbes de Provence Seasoning Blend

There are many ways to make this traditional French seasoning blend. I've found that the combination offers the right balance of flavor. We enjoy it in Vegetable Rice (page 290).

MAKES ABOUT ⅓ CUP

1 tablespoon dried basil

1 tablespoon crushed fennel seeds (crush in a mortar or under a heavy saucepan)

1 tablespoon dried lavender buds

1 tablespoon dried marjoram

1 tablespoon dried rosemary

1 tablespoon dried sage

1 tablespoon dried thyme

Lightly crush the basil, fennel seeds, lavender buds, marjoram, rosemary, sage, and thyme together with a large spoon in a small bowl or using a mortar and pestle. Transfer to a small jar or airtight container and store in a cool, dark place.

Greek Seasoning Blend

I use this seasoning so much I like to double or triple the recipe when I make it. The delicious combination of Mediterranean herbs and alliums can be used in a variety of dishes and cuisines. I use it to make Pretty in Pink Deviled Eggs (page 246), and dipping oils, to name a few.

MAKES ABOUT ⅓ CUP

2 tablespoons dried oregano

4 teaspoons dried thyme

2 teaspoons dried marjoram

2 teaspoons dried basil

2 teaspoons minced dried onion

1 teaspoon minced dried garlic

Lightly crush the oregano, thyme, marjoram, basil, onion, and garlic together with a large spoon in a small bowl or using a mortar and pestle. Transfer to a small jar or airtight container.

Dry It!

Italian Seasoning Blend

This is by far the most used seasoning in my kitchen. We love it in Herby Pizza Dough (page 300) and Potato Roses (page 286), to name just a few.

MAKES ABOUT ½ CUP

2 tablespoons dried basil

2 tablespoons dried oregano

2 tablespoons dried thyme

1 tablespoon dried rosemary

2 teaspoons garlic powder

¼ teaspoon red pepper flakes

Lightly crush the basil, oregano, thyme, rosemary, garlic powder, and pepper flakes together with a large spoon in a small bowl or using a mortar and pestle. Transfer to a small jar or airtight container.

Flower-fetti

Use your dried flower petals to make edible flower-fetti! Flower-fetti, like sprinkles, is used more for decorative bling than it is for the flavor. Any combination of dried edible petals will work, but here's a recipe to get you started. I love sprinkling this mixture on frosting, on top of salads, and into quick bread and muffin batters.

MAKES 1½ CUPS

½ cup dried calendula petals

½ cup dried bachelor's button petals

½ cup dianthus petals

Combine the calendula, bachelor's button, and dianthus petals in a medium bowl. Transfer to an airtight jar.

Preserving the Seasons

Chili Powder

Chili powder is different than a packet of chili seasoning. The latter sometimes contains a thickener and is mainly used to make chili. Chili powder is a mix of ground chiles and spices that can add heat to a variety of dishes. The measurements below can be adjusted to your liking. Create a one-of-a-kind blend by adding the dried chiles of your choice (keeping in mind heat levels). For the most authentic Tex-Mex flavor, use anchos (dried poblano), Anaheims, or hot banana peppers.

MAKES ABOUT ½ CUP

2 to 3 tablespoons dried and ground chiles or peppers (see headnote)

2 tablespoons sweet paprika

2 teaspoons ground cumin

1½ teaspoons ground oregano

1½ teaspoons garlic powder

1 teaspoon onion powder

½ teaspoon salt

Mix the ground chiles, paprika, cumin, oregano, garlic powder, onion powder, and salt in a small bowl. Transfer to a small jar or airtight container.

Mild Taco Seasoning

This mild seasoning blend makes an excellent rub, too. Try it on chicken, pork, or beef. Want to spice it up? Add 1 teaspoon chili powder to the mix.

MAKES ABOUT ¼ CUP

1 tablespoon kosher salt or Oregano Salt (page 207)

1 tablespoon ground cumin

1 tablespoon sweet paprika

2 teaspoons garlic powder

2 teaspoons onion powder

½ teaspoon dried oregano

½ teaspoon freshly ground black pepper

¼ teaspoon red pepper flakes

Mix the salt, cumin, paprika, garlic powder, onion powder, oregano, black pepper, and pepper flakes together in a small bowl. Transfer to a small jar or airtight container.

Dried Chile Hot Sauce

Making your own homemade hot sauce is easy. This recipe uses dried chile peppers, but fresh can be used, too (see the variation)! Be sure to wear food-safe gloves when working with chiles and remember not to touch your face while handling.

MAKES 1 PINT

2 ounces home-dried chiles, such as cayenne, Fresno, or jalapeño, or use store-bought dried chiles, such as New Mexico, ancho, or guajillo

2½ cups hot water

1½ cups distilled white vinegar, apple cider vinegar, or herb-infused vinegar (see page 186)

2 to 3 garlic cloves, minced

1 teaspoon salt

1 · Heat a large, heavy skillet over medium-high heat. Add the chiles and toast until the underside turns a darker shade, about 1 minute. Turn and toast the other side. Transfer to a medium bowl and add the hot water (the chiles should be completely covered; if not, add more hot water). Place a small plate on top to keep the chiles submerged. Let stand until softened and the water is tepid, about 20 minutes. Drain and reserve the soaking liquid.

2 · Wearing food-safe gloves, cut the tops off the chiles. For the spiciest sauce, include the seeds, but for milder results, cut the chiles open and remove the seeds.

3 · Transfer the chiles to a small saucepan. Add the vinegar, garlic, and salt. Bring to a boil, turn the heat down, and simmer for 10 minutes. Cool slightly.

4 · Pour the mixture into a blender and process on low speed to chop. Increase the speed to high and puree until you reach a sauce consistency. If needed, add some of the reserved soaking water. Let cool completely.

5 · Funnel the hot sauce into a sterilized bottle with a stopper. Date and label. The sauce can be refrigerated for up to 6 months. Shake well before using. Discard if mold, foul odor, or discoloration is present.

Roasting dried chiles in a dry nonstick or cast-iron skillet brings their flavors back to life. Using a wooden spoon, toss in a hot pan, pressing on the skins to sear and help release the oils. It takes just a minute or two until they're plumped and beginning to soften.

VARIATION

Fresh Pepper Hot Sauce: Substitute 8 ounces fresh chiles (cayenne, Fresno, or jalapeño), stemmed, seeded, and coarsely chopped. The fresh chiles do not need to be toasted or soaked. Start the recipe at step 2. Hot sauces made with fresh peppers have an average refrigerator shelf life of about 1 month, sometimes longer. Shake well before using. Discard if mold, a foul odor, or discoloration is present.

Culinary Powders

Powders are made by grinding dried (or dehydrated, or freeze-dried) vegetables, herbs, or flowers with an upright coffee grinder or high-powered blender.

You'll find many uses for your powder collection. Fruit and vegetable powders impart flavor and color in everyday cooking and baking projects. Seasoning powders level up dishes and are often a time-saver. Instead of cutting an onion, I may use my onion powder instead. Flower powders offer health benefits and some work as natural dyes.

Dried tomato skins do not thicken soups and sauces as well as dried tomato slices. Powder a mix of both for best results.

- **Fruit Powder** Add peach, strawberry, or blueberry powder to beverages, oatmeal, smoothies, and cereal to color your milk. Banana and apple powders can be used in muffin and pancake recipes. Avocado powder can be reconstituted into a delicious spread (see page 253). Fruit chips (page 134) are perfect for making powders.

- **Flower Powder** Marigolds, calendula, hibiscus, and butterfly pea flowers transform into beautiful natural colorings. Add them to syrups (see page 225), pasta (page 293), yogurt (see page 155), and more!

- **Seasonings** Grind dried herbs, onions, garlic, and chiles into fragrant and flavorful seasonings for all your savory recipes.

- **Vegetable Powder** The easiest way to sneak veggies into the kids' diet when they refuse to eat them is in powder form. Use mushroom, bean, or tomato power to thicken soups. Sweet pepper powder can be used to season sauces, butter, cheese spreads, and soups. Beet powder is prized for its natural coloring ability and is used to enliven Pretty in Pink Deviled Eggs (page 246). A mix of blanched greens like kale, spinach, and radish leaves create a nutrient-rich super powder that you can sneak into smoothies, soups, pasta, and pizza dough, or even sprinkle on the kids' macaroni and cheese.

Storage and Use

Freeze-dried powders are flavorful and vibrant, but they take on moisture from the air quickly, so it's best to use them immediately after grinding. Dehydrated powders, after a step called conditioning, are shelf stable for several months. Choose one of the following methods to condition your dehydrated powders:

Air Select a space with low to no humidity and good airflow. Place the powder in a shallow dish, cover loosely with cheesecloth, and let dry for several hours, stirring a few times for even drying and removing any clumps.

Dehydrator Place the powder in a coffee filter or muffin tin liner placed on the dehydrator tray. Dry at 90°F for 20 to 30 minutes. Unplug the dehydrator, leaving the powder in the machine until cool.

Transfer your powder to an airtight container, label, date, and store in a cool, dark, and dry place. For best results, add an oxygen absorber. The powder can be stored at room temperature, or refrigerated or frozen, if desired. Most powders stored at room temperature are best when used within 2 to 3 months. Stored in the refrigerator or freezer, they can last longer. Use in powder form or combine powder with an equal amount of water to create a paste.

HOMEMADE TOMATO PASTE

Tomato paste made from your homemade tomato powder is quick and easy. The ratio is always equal parts powder and water. So, if a recipe calls for 3 tablespoons paste, just mix 3 tablespoons each tomato powder and water in a small bowl, and you're on your way!

Dried tomato skins do not thicken soups and sauces as well as dried tomato slices. Powder a mix of both for best results.

CHAPTER 5
Dehydrate It!

116
How It Works

116
Prep Steps
Prepping Fruits 116
Prepping Vegetables 117

119
Rehydrating

119
Dehydrating Fruit

If you follow me on social media, you know that I have a sweet spot in my heart for dehydrating produce, herbs, and flowers and organizing them in my cupboard in a way that makes me twirl every time I open the doors. Raising our own basketball team made having healthy, affordable, and portable snacks at our fingertips important. What started with one dehydrator and a couple of trays is now three dehydrators and stacks of trays! I . . . can't . . . stop. Being able to load up the dehydrator and go about my day is the life hack that this mom needed. Dehydrating foods is a space saver, because the process causes food to shrink and shrivel, making it easier to store our garden harvests and take advantage of those seasonal sales that we just can't pass up.

Dehydrating Vegetables 123

Dehydrating Herbs and Flowers 128

Recipes 131
Basic Fruit Leather 131
Blueberry, Pear, and Basil Fruit Leathers 132
Berry Blast Oven Fruit Rolls 133
Fruit Chips 134
Chive Blossom Zucchini Chips 136
Vegetable and Bean Dried Soup Mix 136
Oven-Roasted Dried Beet Chips 137

How It Works

Dehydration is a form of drying in which *most* moisture is removed from the ingredient only comes from a home dehydrator, a small kitchen appliance, ranging in price from fifty to several hundred dollars, a home dehydrator gently heats and evenly circulates air, drying the food.

With a temperature range of 90° to 165°F, the heating element removes 80 to 95 percent of the moisture, while the fan carries away water vapor, finishing the job. As the water content of food evaporates, bacterial growth slows dramatically, creating shelf-stable food (see details for storage and shelf life on page 117). Machines are equipped with stainless steel or plastic trays to hold the food during drying. Accessories like fruit roll sheets or silicone mats that fit the trays can be purchased online or from the machine manufacturer.

Prep Steps

Always begin by selecting good-quality, ripe, unblemished produce. Rinse thoroughly and pat dry. See pages 119 to 128 for prep steps for specific fruits and vegetables.

PREPPING FRUITS

- Peel any fruit with skins (if desired) and remove any pits, seeds, or cores.

- Cut into ¼- to ½-inch-thick pieces, making sure the pieces are about the same size.

- Pretreat as needed (see page 17).

Pretreating Fruits for Dehydrating

Some fruit, like strawberries, can be placed directly on the drying racks without any extra effort. But some fruit will need special attention before dehydrating. For example, pretreating apples and pears in an acidic solution reduces oxidation, and ensures tastier and prettier results, while helping to retain nutritional value.

Along with the pretreatment options on page 17, there are a few more to consider when dehydrating:

Honey Dip Store-bought dried fruits are often treated with a honey dip treatment. Mix ½ cup granulated sugar with 1½ cups boiling water. Let stand until the syrup is lukewarm. Stir in ½ cup raw honey. Dip the cut-up fruit into the honey mixture; there is no need to soak. Drain well. Place on silicone or parchment paper–lined drying trays or racks.

Simple Syrup Soak A simple syrup is ideal for fruit like cranberries because simmering in the syrup splits the skins and imparts sweetness to an otherwise tart fruit. Bring equal parts water and sugar to a boil in a large saucepan over medium heat, stirring to dissolve the sugar. Remove from the heat. Soak the fruit in the hot mixture for 3 to 5 minutes. Drain well. Transfer to drying trays or racks.

Fruit Juice Soak Fruit juice, such as pineapple or orange, can be used to pretreat foods, although it is not as effective in preserving color and flavor as the other methods. Mild fruit juice (apple or grape) won't work. Soak fruit in the juice (no need to heat) for 3 to 5 minutes. Drain well. Transfer to drying trays or racks.

Fruits with thicker skins or wax coatings require additional steps before drying:

Checking Fruit "Checking" fruit refers to the process of breaking or splitting the skins of fruits like blueberries and cranberries. By checking the skins, moisture is allowed to escape more easily, ensuring the fruit dries evenly. The process is like blanching. Drop the fruit into boiling water over high heat, return to a boil, and cook for 30 seconds (90 seconds for cranberries). Drain and transfer immediately to an ice bath and let cool for an equal amount of time. Drain and pat dry.

Popping the Backs This is an effective method for larger skin-on stone fruits (peaches, nectarines, apricots, and plums), First, halve and pit the fruit. Then, place your thumb on the rounded side (where the skin is) and push inward, exposing more of the fruit. Think of an umbrella in a windstorm—you're effectively turning the fruit inside out. Place the fruit peel side down on the drying racks or trays and dry as directed.

PREPPING VEGETABLES

Blanching is an important step for dehydrating vegetables and should not be skipped. It brightens the color and softens the cell structure, allowing moisture to escape more readily. It also shortens drying and rehydration times. See more on blanching on page 18 and follow the individual dehydration recipes for exact blanching times.

Loading the Trays

Avoid overlapping foods on trays, as it will delay drying time. Different foods can be dehydrated at the same time, even on the same trays. Dry pungent items like onions or garlic separately.

Drying Times

Drying times vary, depending on the size, shape, and water density of the food, as well as external factors like air temperature and humidity. Even the location of your dehydrator can make a difference. It often takes a few attempts to get a feel for what will work best for your setup. Jot down what works and what doesn't and be sure to review the manufacturer's instruction guide for specific information. The following is a guideline for different food you might try dehydrating:

Flowers/herbs/spices/nuts 90° to 100°F
Fruit 125° to 140°F
Fruit leather 135° to 140°F
Vegetables 125° to 145°F
Meat and fish 165°F or highest temperature

Conditioning

This is an important step that ensures that the food is dried properly. It's also an opportunity for some of the well-dried pieces to absorb excess moisture from others. This may take up to a few days. Follow the easy instructions here.

- When dehydrating is done, unplug the machine or turn it off. Leave the food in the dehydrator to cool completely. Check for dryness.

- Fruits should be leathery and pliable. Tear a piece in half, then pinch to see if moisture appears. If not, the fruit is done. If the fruit still looks moist, return to the dehydrator and turn it back on to finish drying.

- See How We Roll (page 128) for how to tell when fruit rolls are done.

- Vegetables should be crisp or brittle.

- Loosely pack dried produce into a clear glass jar with a tight-fitting lid. Shake the jar once a day for 5 days. Look for signs of moisture or clumping food. If either is present, return the food to the dehydrator to reprocess. If mold or a foul odor is present, discard.

Packing and Storing

- Use any food-safe, moistureproof, airtight container to store. Canning jars with lids work well. Lightproof, vaporproof bags or vacuum sealed containers are excellent options. Adding an oxygen absorber will increase shelf life while also reducing the chance of insects or larva because they remove the oxygen in the packaging the insects need to thrive.

- Label and date packaging.

- Store in a cool, dark, and dry spot (ideal temperature is 50° to 70°F).

- Average shelf life for dried fruit is 6 to 12 months, slightly less for dried vegetables, but can last longer depending on storage conditions. Stored in vacuum sealed, light-, moisture-, and vaporproof bags with oxygen absorbers, some dehydrated food can last up to 15 years!

- While some people prefer to store dried produce in dark-colored containers to keep out the light, I like to store mine in glass canning jars, stored in a dark cupboard. This way I can easily see signs of spoilage or insects.

Rehydrating

Rehydrating, or "refreshing" dehydrated foods is not always necessary. If you plan to add dehydrated vegetables to liquid-based dishes like soup or rice, you can skip this step. In general, dehydrated fruits and vegetables rehydrate to about 80 percent. The process of soaking in just enough hot or cool water to cover usually takes anywhere from a few minutes to a few hours, depending on the food. Foods that soak for more than 2 hours should be kept in the refrigerator.

There are a few ways to rehydrate dried foods:

- **Vegetables** Soak in enough hot water to cover, usually double the amount of water to vegetables. Cover with a paper or cloth towel and let stand, stirring occasionally, until refreshed. For quicker rehydration, microwave-soak vegetables in 1-minute increments on high (100%) power until refreshed. You can also soak in cool water, but hydration will take longer. Blanched vegetables rehydrate more quickly than unblanched vegetables.

- **Fruits** Soak fruits in room-temperature or cool water that just covers the fruit, usually equal parts. Cover with a paper or cloth towel and let stand until refreshed. Avoid oversoaking, which can make food mushy and less flavorful. For quicker hydration, especially for fruit intended for baking, soak in hot water, cover, and let sit, stirring occasionally, until soft, 5 to 10 minutes. **NOTE:** You can also soak fruits and vegetables in unsweetened juice, milk, or low-sodium broth in place of water. Foods soaked in these liquids should be refrigerated during soaking to reduce the risk of spoilage.

- **Fruits for pie or dessert filling** Add just enough boiling water to cover. Cover bowl with a towel and let stand, stirring a few times, until the liquid is absorbed, about 1 hour.

- **Simmering** Place the fruit in a saucepan, add enough cold water to cover, and bring to a simmer; do not boil. Cover and cook over medium heat just until refreshed.

- **Directly in a recipe in process** Place food directly into hot, liquid-based recipes such as soups, stews, and sauces. Note that the texture may stay a bit shriveled when skipping the presoak.

Dehydrating Fruit

Dehydrated fruits have many uses. Enjoy it as a snack or in tea blends like Fruits and Flowers Tea Blend (page 177). Dried orange, apple, and pear slices make great seasonal decor. Refreshed fruit can be used in baked goods, sweet sauces, and syrups. Or add to yogurt, cereal, and oatmeal. See page 113 for details on powders.

Apples Select firm, unblemished apples. Enjoy them dried or rehydrated in my Apple Cinnamon Oatmeal (page 250).

Prep Rinse. Peel (reserving the peels to make powder; see below) and core. Cut the apples into ¼- to ½-inch slices. Pretreat (see page 17) or use a simple syrup soak (see page 116). Drain and pat dry.

Processing Load the trays, with the fruit not touching. Dry at 135°F until pliable without any pockets of moisture.

Drying Time 6 to 24 hours

NOTE
Do not add sugar to rehydrating fruit until it is tender. Sugar can make it tough.

ZERO WASTE ALERT!
Another win for the pantry! I like to coarsely grind and powder my dried apple peels and use in oatmeal, pancakes, muffins, cakes, and cookies. It's even good sprinkled over popcorn! It's best to use peels from unwaxed apples.

Apricots (see Nectarines)

Bananas Dehydrated bananas, once refreshed, are loaded with flavor. I like to smash them in the soaking liquid, creating a delicious mash that can be added to quick breads and muffins like Chocolate, Tahini, and Banana Muffins (page 313). Just like with freezing, the pretreatment step, which slows browning, is optional, especially if you plan to use the bananas in a batter.

Prep Peel. Cut into ¼- to ½-inch slices. Pretreat (see page 22), if desired. Drain and pat dry.

Processing Load the trays, with the fruit not touching. Dry at 135°F until pliable without any pockets of moisture.

Drying Time 6 to 12 hours

Berries, round (blueberries, cranberries, currants, gooseberries, and huckleberries) Select firm, ripe berries. Add dried berries to bagels, breads, trail mix, and granola. Refresh and use in muffins and pancakes.

Prep Remove stems and rinse. Check fruit (see page 116) or do a simple syrup soak (see page 116). Drain and pat dry.

Processing Load the trays, with the fruit not touching. Dry at 135°F until leathery.

Drying Time 12 to 24 hours

Cherries Select brightly colored ripe fruit. Dried cherries make a pretty powder and a colorful, flavorful syrup.

Prep Rinse. Remove stems and pits. Leave whole, halve, or chop. Check fruit (see page 116). Drain and pat dry.

Processing Load the trays, with the fruit not touching. Dry at 155°F for 3 hours. Turn the temperature down to 135°F and continue drying until sticky but leathery.

Drying Time 18 to 36 hours

Citrus peels (lemons, limes, oranges, grapefruit, and tangerines) Best to use only peels from organic, unwaxed citrus fruits. Use them as zest in your baked goods.

Prep Rinse well in warm water to remove any residue or possible pesticides. Peel fruit. Remove as much of the bitter white pith from the peel as possible.

Processing Load dehydrator trays, with the peels not touching. Dry at 125°F until brittle.

Drying Time 6 to 12 hours

Citrus slices (lemons, limes, oranges, grapefruit, and tangerines) Citrus can be dried with or without the peel and pith. If you leave the peel on, be sure to use organic, unwaxed fruit. I leave mine on and use in my Lavender Orange French Toast (page 251) and Rosemary Citrus Bundt Cake with Orange Glaze (page 334), to name a few.

Prep Rinse well. If desired, remove pith and peel. Cut into ¼- to ½-inch rings or slices.

Processing Load the trays, with the fruit not touching. Dry at 125°F until brittle.

Drying Time 6 to 12 hours

Elderberries Although this berry offers a wealth of health benefits, it can be tricky to work with. Harvest only the ripe black berries leaving behind the red and green. **Do not eat raw elderberries. Underripe berries, stems, and leaves of this plant are toxic. See page 231 for safe handling.** Dried ripe berries can be turned into powerful Elderberry Syrup (page 231) or good-for-you Homemade Elderberry Candies (page 331).

Prep Rinse well. Remove the stems and any unripe berries.

Processing Load the trays, with the fruit not touching. Dry at 125°F until dry.

Drying Time 5 to 10 hours

Grapes, seedless Homemade raisins! If leaving whole, do not skip the Checking Fruit step (page 116).

Prep Remove the stems. Rinse. Leave whole. Check the fruit. Drain and pat dry.

Processing Load the trays, with the fruit not touching. Dry at 135°F, until pliable but dry with no pockets of moisture.

Drying Time 12 to 24 hours

Nectarines/peaches/apricots Dried peaches make a delicious snack. Refreshed, they can be used in cobblers, oatmeal, muffins, and smoothies. Or grind into a power to flavor frostings and cakes.

Prep Rinse well. Halve and pit. Cut into quarters, ½-inch slices, or chunks. Pretreat (see page 17) or use a simple syrup soak (see page 116). Drain and pat dry.

Processing If you are drying with the skin on, cut in halves or quarters and pop the backs (see page 117). Load the trays, skin side down, with the fruit not touching. Dry at 135°F until pliable without any pockets of moisture.

Drying Time 24 to 36 hours

Pears Choose firm, unblemished, ripe fruit. Use dried in oatmeal, tea blends, and trail mixes. Refreshed, they can be used in baked goods.

Prep Rinse. Peel and core. Cut into halves, wedges, or ½-inch slices or rings. As you prepare them, drop into pretreatment solution (see page 17). Drain and pat dry.

Processing Load the trays, with the fruit not touching. Dry at 135°F until pliable (folds without breaking) but without any pockets of moisture.

Drying Time 6 to 24 hours

Pineapple Choose ripe pineapple. If the green leaves can be easily pulled from the fruit, it is ripe.

Prep Rinse. Peel and remove the sharp eyes. Slice lengthwise, core, and cut into ½-inch slices.

Processing Load the trays, with the fruit not touching. Dry at 135°F until leathery and not sticky.

Drying Time 24 to 36 hours

Plums Prunes are dried plums. But did you know that not all plums can become prunes? The two cultivars to look for are European (such as Italian purple) and Japanese (such as Mariposa).

Prep Rinse. Cut in half and pit. Cut into ½-inch slices. Pretreat (see page 17).

Processing If you are drying with the skins on, cut in halves or quarters and pop the backs (see page 117). Load the trays, skin side down, with the fruit not touching. Dry at 135°F until pliable with no moisture pockets.

Drying Time 24 to 36 hours

Strawberries Dried strawberries are a sweet snack. Use to flavor tea, drop into beverages to rehydrate as you sip, or toss into cereal. Refresh and use as a topping for pancakes or waffles, mix into yogurt or oatmeal, or make into syrup. Or grind into powder to add flavor and natural color to your creations.

Prep Rinse. Remove hulls. Cut in half or into ½-inch slices.

Processing Load the trays, with the fruit not touching. Dry at 135°F until almost crisp.

Drying Time 7 to 15 hours for sliced, 24 to 36 for whole fruit.

ZERO WASTE ALERT!
Use the tops to make Strawberry Thyme Simple Syrup (page 230).

Dehydrating Vegetables

Many vegetables require blanching before dehydrating (see page 18). Although most dried vegetables are refreshed before using in recipes, some make great grab-and-go snacks. See page 119 for details on rehydrating.

Asparagus Want a lesson in patience? Grow asparagus! These perennial plants take a long time to establish, but once you get them going, you'll have plenty to enjoy and maybe even enough to preserve. Buying seasonally, when it's inexpensive and at peak flavor, is also a great way to stock up.

Prep Rinse. Remove the woody ends. Dry whole or cut into ½-inch pieces. Blanch in boiling water for 1½ minutes for cut pieces or 2 to 4 minutes for spears, depending on size. Or steam blanch spears for 3 to 4 minutes. Transfer immediately to an ice bath and let cool for an equal amount of time. Drain and pat dry.

Processing Load the trays, with the asparagus not touching, at 135°F until brittle.

Drying Time 3 to 10 hours

Beans, green or wax Freezing beans for 30 minutes after blanching and before drying will help tenderize beans and retain better texture.

Prep Rinse. Remove the ends and cut into 1- to 2-inch pieces or cut in half lengthwise. Blanch in boiling water for 2 to 4 minutes, depending on size, or steam blanch for 4 to 5 minutes. Immediately transfer to an ice bath and let cool for an equal amount of time. Freeze the beans for 30 minutes before drying.

Processing Load the trays, with the beans not touching. Dry at 135°F until brittle.

Drying Time 8 to 14 hours

Beans, shelling (cranberry or pinto), fresh or canned Use in Vegetable and Bean Dried Soup Mix (page 136) and chili mixes. Or grind into a powder to thicken and flavor soups. Keep in mind that the beans will split open in the drying process. Not so pretty but still so tasty!

Prep Shell fresh beans, then rinse. Drain canned beans, then rinse. Drain and pat dry.

Processing Load the trays, with the beans not touching. Dry at 135°F until brittle. After 6 hours, begin checking on them, removing any beans that have dried completely and allowing the rest to keep drying.

Drying Time 6 to 12 hours for canned beans, 8 to 12 hours for fresh

Beets Deep red beets will yield a beautiful powder for cooking and decorating. Golden beets make beautiful and tasty chips!

Prep Rinse well. Leave unpeeled. To reduce bleeding, trim excess greens and roots, leaving ½ inch attached. Cook the beets in boiling water for 25 to 30 minutes for small beets, 45 to 50 minutes for large. Drain and cool until easy to handle, then remove the stem and root ends. Rub the skins off with a paper towel or use a vegetable peeler. Cut into slices or strips ¼-inch thick. For beet chips, cut into ⅛-inch slices.

Processing Load the drying trays lined with parchment paper to minimize staining, with the beets not touching. Dry at 125° to 140°F until brittle.

Drying Time 5 to 12 hours

Broccoli (see Cauliflower)

Cabbage Shredded cabbage can be used in soups or refreshed for stir-fries.

Prep Remove the outer leaves. Cut each head into quarters. Remove the core. Rinse. Cut into ⅛-inch strips. Blanch in boiling water for 2 minutes, or steam blanch for 3 minutes. Transfer immediately to an ice bath and let cool for an equal amount of time. Drain and pat dry.

Processing Load the trays, with the cabbage not touching. Dry at 135°F until brittle.

Drying Time 10 to 12 hours

Carrots or parsnips Carrots and parsnips are two of the most useful of all soup veggies, so they are good choices for your dehydrator. Don't toss the green tops, which can be dried along with leafy greens (see page 126) or used to make powder.

Prep Remove the stems and roots. Rinse. Peel. Leave small carrots whole, or cut into rounds or sticks, dice, or shred. Blanch in boiling water for 2 minutes for small cut pieces or 5 minutes for small whole carrots, or steam blanch small cut pieces for 3 minutes or small whole carrots for 6 to 8 minutes. Transfer immediately to an ice bath and let cool for an equal amount of time. Drain and pat dry.

Processing Load the trays, with the carrots not touching. Dry at 135°F until almost brittle.

Drying Time 6 to 12 hours

ZERO WASTE ALERT!
Keep the cleaned peels to make carrot powder

Carrot peels Carrot peels can be dried and turned into a powder to use in smoothies, homemade pasta, crackers, ice pops, baked goods, and more!

Prep Rinse. Pretreat (see page 17). Drain and pat dry.

Processing Scatter the peels onto trays in a single layer. Dry at 135°F until crispy.

Drying Time 4 to 10 hours

Cauliflower or broccoli Use in soups, stir-fries, pasta dishes, rice dishes, and casseroles.

Prep Rinse. Separate into florets. Cut larger florets into smaller pieces. Soak in salt solution, if desired (see page 29). Blanch in boiling water for 3 to 4 minutes, or steam blanch for 4 to 5 minutes. Transfer immediately to an ice bath and let cool for an equal amount of time. Drain and pat dry.

Processing Load the trays, with the florets not touching. Dry at 135°F until almost brittle.

Drying Time 6 to 12 hours

Celery Dry the leafy celery tops to make celery salt (see page 148).

Prep Rinse. If making powder, lightly run a vegetable peeler along the outer layer of the stalks to remove any fibrous strings. This step is not required, but it does help to create a finer powder. Cut the stalks into 1-inch pieces. Blanch in boiling water for 3 minutes, or steam blanch for 2 minutes. Transfer immediately to an ice bath and let cool for an equal amount of time. Drain and pat dry.

Processing Load the trays, with the celery not touching. Dry at 135°F until very brittle.

Drying Time 6 to 12 hours

Corn Dehydrated corn is a versatile pantry ingredient to use in soups and side dishes. Dent corn (also known as field corn) is a less sweet, high-starch variety. It's not the kind of corn that we eat fresh, but it's great dried and can be ground to make cornmeal, chips, or tortillas. It's also great for your backyard flock or visiting squirrels!

Prep Husk the corn and remove the silks. Rinse. Leave the ears whole for blanching. Blanch in boiling water for 1½ minutes or steam blanch for 2½ minutes. Transfer immediately to an ice bath and let cool for an equal amount of time. Cut the kernels from the cob.

Processing Load the trays, with the corn kernels not touching. Dry at 135°F until brittle.

Drying Time 6 to 10 hours

Flowers, edible (see page 128)

Garlic Minced or ground into a powder, dehydrated garlic sure comes in handy for quick cooking. Be sure to dry this on a warm day when you can have the windows open because the air is going to get pungent!

Prep Peel the cloves. Finely chop or just cut in half.

Processing Load the trays, with the garlic not touching. Dry at 135°F until brittle.

Drying Time 6 to 12 hours

Garlic scapes Drying this otherwise discarded part of the garlic plant will add wonderful flavor to your dishes. I grind my scapes into a culinary powder (see page 113) and use it in my Creamy Garlic Scape Sauce (page 299).

Prep Remove the flower buds and cut the scapes into 1-inch pieces.

Processing Load onto the trays, with the scapes not touching. Dry at 125°F until brittle.

Drying Time 6 to 12 hours

Herbs (see page 128)

Leafy greens (spinach, kale, collards, turnip greens, and chard) Many greens can be dried for soups, stews, and pasta dishes or turned into a powder (see page 113).

Prep Use blemish-free young leaves. Rinse. Remove the veins (they can be bitter) and cut the leaves into 2- to 3-inch pieces. Steam blanch until wilted, about 3 minutes. Transfer immediately to an ice bath to cool for an equal amount of time. Drain and pat dry.

Processing Line the trays with parchment paper or silicone mats. Spread the greens on the prepared trays, not touching. Dry at 135°F until crisp.

Drying Time 4 to 10 hours

Leeks Use in soups, stews, stir-fries, and sautéed dishes.

Prep Remove the root ends and discard the leafy tops. Rinse well to remove grit between the layers. Drain and pat dry. Cut into ¼-inch-thick slices.

Processing Load onto the trays, with the leeks not touching. Dry at 135° to 140°F until crisp.

Drying Time 3 to 9 hours

Mushrooms (edible varieties *only*) I love drying my bulk store-bought mushrooms. I use them in gravy, stuffing, and Vegetable, Beef, and Farro Soup (page 267). If you forage for your mushrooms, be certain you are working with edible varieties. Proper identification is a must!

Prep Wipe with paper towels to remove dirt. Remove the woody stems. Cut the caps into ¼-inch slices.

Processing Load onto the trays, with the mushrooms not touching. Dry at 125°F until dry and leathery.

Drying Time 4 to 10 hours

ZERO WASTE ALERT!
Save the woody stems to make Zero-Waste Vegetable Broth (page 163).

Onions, green (scallions) Use in seasoning mixes, dips, soft cheeses, dipping oils, marinades, and vinaigrettes. Add to dishes at the end of cooking.

Prep Rinse. Cut into pieces.

Processing Load onto the trays, with the onions not touching. Dry at 135° to 140°F until crispy and brittle.

Drying Time 3 to 9 hours

Onions, red, white, and yellow Dry these on a day you can have all the windows open because it can start to smell like a high school gym locker room after a while.

Prep Remove the outer papery skins, Cut off the ends. Cut into ¼-inch slices or dice.

Processing Load onto the trays, with the onions not touching. Dry at 135° to 140°F until brittle.

Drying Time 3 to 9 hours

Peas, shelling (green or English)

Prep Rinse. Shell the peas, reserving the pods (see below). Blanch in boiling water for 2 minutes, or steam blanch for 3 minutes. Transfer immediately to an ice bath and let cool for an equal amount of time. Drain and pat dry.

Processing Load onto the trays, with the peas not touching. Dry at 135°F until hard and wrinkled.

Drying Time 8 to 10 hours

ZERO WASTE ALERT!
Save the pea pods to use in Zero-Waste Vegetable Broth (page 163).

Peppers, hot (chiles) Be sure to wear food-safe gloves when handling, and remember not to touch your face. On the label when packaging, include name and heat level of chile for future cooking

Prep Rinse. You can leave them whole or remove the stems. Dice, slice, or cut in half, keeping or discarding seeds as desired (the seeds will add more heat).

Processing Load onto the trays, with the chiles not touching and separating the varieties so you can control the heat level of your dishes. Dry at 135°F until hard, wrinkled, and darkened.

Drying Time 8 to 12 hours

Peppers, sweet/bell Toss into soups, stews, marinades, or vinaigrettes. Or refresh and add to stir-fries, egg dishes, pizza, rice, and pasta dishes.

Prep Rinse. Remove the stems and seeds. Dice, slice, or cut in half. The bigger the pepper, the longer it will take to dry.

Processing Load onto the trays, with the peppers not touching. Dry at 135°F until brittle.

Drying Time 8 to 12 hours

Potatoes, red, white, or yellow I grew up eating scalloped potatoes from a box, and I still like them. But my homemade version (see page 291), made using dehydrated potato slices, is even better!

Prep Rinse, peel, and cut into $1/8$-inch slices. Toss the potatoes as you cut them into a pretreatment solution (page 17) to keep from turning brown. Drain. Bring ½ cup bottled lemon juice and 1 gallon water to a boil in a large nonreactive pot. Blanch the potatoes for 5 to 6 minutes or steam blanch for 6 to 8 minutes. Transfer immediately to an ice bath and let cool for an equal amount of time.

Processing Load onto the trays, with the potatoes not touching. Dry at 125° to 135°F until crispy.

Drying Time 6 to 12 hours

Potatoes, sweet (yams) Use in breads or muffins, or share with your furry friend as dog treats.

Prep Rinse. Peel and cut into ¼-inch slices or chunks. Steam blanch for 3 minutes. Transfer immediately to an ice bath and let cool for an equal amount of time. Drain and pat dry.

Processing Load onto the trays or racks, with the potatoes not touching. Dry at 135°F until crispy.

Drying Time 6 to 12 hours

Pumpkin (see Squash, winter)

Radish Dried and sliced thin radishes make a spicy little chip. Ground into a powder, they add a kick to spreads, sauces, dressings, and vinaigrettes.

Prep Rinse. Remove the stems and root ends. Rinse again. Using a mandoline, slice the radishes into $1/8$- to ¼-inch-thick rounds. Optional: Pretreat (see page 17) to keep from browning. Drain and pat dry.

Processing Load onto the trays, with the radishes not touching. Dry at 135°F until crispy.

Drying Time 3 to 8 hours

Squash, summer (crookneck, pattypan/scallop, straightneck, and zucchini) I look forward to combining my summer zucchini with my spring chive blossom vinegar every year to create healthy veggie chips (see page 156), unlike anything you can buy.

Prep Rinse. Remove the ends. Cut into ¼-inch slices or dice. Blanch in boiling water for 1 minute, or steam blanch for 2 to 3 minutes. Transfer immediately to an ice bath and let cool for an equal amount of time. Drain and pat dry.

Processing Load onto the trays, with the squash not touching. Dry at 135°F until crisp to brittle.

Drying Time 6 to 12 hours

Squash, winter (pumpkin) You might not think you need dried pumpkin in the pantry, but it can be added to "beef up" stews and soups. Or rehydrate and turn into puree for baking.

Prep Rinse. Cut open. Remove the seeds and inner stringy pulp. Cut into 1-inch strips. Peel. Cut the flesh strips into ⅛- to ¼-inch chunks. Blanch in boiling water for 1 minute, or steam blanch for 2 to 3 minutes. Transfer immediately to an ice bath and let cool for an equal amount of time. Drain and pat dry.

Processing Load onto the trays, with the pumpkin not touching. Dry at 135°F until brittle.

Drying Time 10 to 16 hours

Tomatoes Small varieties (such as cherry, grape, or Roma) work well for a delicious pop-in-your-mouth snack. We call the seasoned version "pizza chips," which are oh so good! Large tomatoes can also be used. Snip the dried tomatoes with scissors to mix into Herb and Dried Tomato Cheese Spread (page 243) or rehydrate to use in Tomato Basil Pasta Salad (page 296).

Prep Rinse. Halve smaller tomatoes. Slice or dice larger tomatoes.

Processing Load onto the trays, cut sides up, with the tomatoes not touching. For pizza chips, season the halves with Oregano Salt (page 207) and chopped fresh basil and thyme. Dry at 135° to 145°F until crisp.

Drying Time 10 to 18 hours

Dehydrating Herbs and Flowers

As detailed in chapter 4, natural drying is my go-to method for herbs and flowers, but not everyone has the time, or lives in a space or climate to dry indoors. If this describes you, the dehydrator is a good option; not only is it faster than air drying, but it's slow enough to preserve many of the valuable minerals and nutrients in herbs. It also maintains some degree of color and flavor, though not quite as much as natural drying.

Here's how you do it:

- Place the prepared herbs, whole flower heads, or petals (see page 95) on dehydrator racks in a single layer.

- Both are usually dried between 90 and 110°F. If you live in a very humid climate, you may need to increase the temperature up to 125°F.

- Many factors go into drying time, including temperature, humidity, hardiness of the herbs, and size of the flowers. Average drying time for both herbs and flowers is 1 to 4 hours, but some herbs or large flowers may need up to 18 hours to completely dry.

How We Roll: Fruit Leathers

Fruit rolls, or leathers, made with whole fruit (or a combination of fruits) and sweetener, are a popular snack in our pantry. Each of us has our own favorite flavors, but it's always exciting to try new fruit and flavor combinations.

The best method is the home dehydrator. It's quicker than other options while also maintaining most of the nutritional value and flavor, but you can also use

an oven set at its lowest temperature to make any fruit leather. Here are a few tips, a basic fruit leather recipe, and a few of our favorite combinations to get you started.

Tips for making fruit leathers:

- Sugar is great for sweetening, but corn syrup and honey extend shelf life.

- Applesauce gives a smooth texture and may extend shelf life. Add to fruit purees or dry alone to make an apple fruit leather.

- Flavored syrup, canned fruit, freeze-dried fruit, or even frozen fruit can all be used in place of fresh fruit.

- Feel free to get creative with herbs and spices.

The rolls can be stored in an airtight container in a cool, dark place at room temperature for up to 1 month. Or store in an airtight container (or a sealed bag with as much air removed as possible) in the refrigerator for up to 6 months or in the freezer for up to 1 year.

Basic Fruit Leather

MAKES 1 TRAY/SHEET

2 cups fresh or thawed frozen fruit (strawberries, peaches, plums, and mangoes are delicious options)

2 teaspoons bottled lemon or lime juice

1 to 2 tablespoons sweetener (honey, corn syrup, or granulated sugar)

Herbs and spices of choice (optional)

1 · If using fresh fruit, rinse. Peel, core, pit, and remove stems as needed. Coarsely chop. Puree the fruit, lemon juice, and sweetener in a blender.

2 · Line a dehydrator tray or rimmed baking sheet with parchment paper or a silicone mat. Spread the puree evenly, ⅛ to ¼ inch thick, onto the prepared tray. Dry until no indentations are left after touching with your fingertips and the leather easily pulls away from the tray.

Dehydrator Method Dry at 135° to 140°F for 3 to 8 hours. Check once an hour after 4 hours.

Oven Dry Method Preheat the oven to lowest temperature, 140° to 180°F. Check often to avoid burning. Dry time is 4 to 12 hours.

3 · While still warm, peel the leather off the silicone mat or parchment and transfer to a new sheet of parchment paper or plastic wrap. Let cool. Using scissors or a pizza wheel, cut into strips about 1 inch wide, including the parchment paper or plastic wrap underneath. Roll up the strips.

4 · Store in airtight jars in a dark, cool, dry location at room temperature for up to 1 month. Or store in an airtight container (or a sealed bag with as much air removed as possible) in the refrigerator for up to 6 months, or in the freezer for up to 1 year.

Blueberry, Pear, and Basil Fruit Leathers

This recipe uses canned pears and, thanks to the simple syrup, turns into an out-of-this-world shade of purple.

MAKES ABOUT 8 ROLLS

1 quart home-canned pears, drained, syrup reserved, or 1 (29-ounce) can pears in heavy syrup, drained, syrup reserved

½ cup Blueberry Basil Simple Syrup (page 225)

1 · Line a dehydrator tray or fruit roll tray with parchment paper.

2 · Puree the pears and syrup in a blender. If it seems too thick to spread thinly, blend in some of the drained pear syrup. Pour the puree onto the tray and spread evenly about ¼ inch thick, without any spaces or holes, and leaving a ½-inch border around the edges.

3 · Dehydrate at 135°F for 6 to 12 hours, checking every 30 minutes after 4 hours, until the leather is no longer sticky and pulls away easily from the tray.

4 · While still warm, peel off the tray and transfer to a new sheet of parchment paper or plastic wrap. Let cool completely. Using a sharp knife or a pizza wheel, cut the leather (including the parchment or plastic) into 6 strips. Roll up each strip.

Berry Blast Oven Fruit Rolls

Don't have a dehydrator? No problem. An oven will do the trick for making fruit leathers.

MAKES 6 TO 8 ROLLS

2 cups fresh or thawed frozen strawberries

1 cup fresh or thawed frozen blackberries

2 tablespoons agave nectar, raw honey, or floral infused honey (see page 213)

2 teaspoons fresh lemon juice

1 · Preheat the oven to the lowest setting—it needs to be between 150° and 180°F for the fruit leathers to dry properly. Line a large rimmed baking sheet with parchment paper or a silicone baking mat.

2 · Puree the strawberries, blackberries, agave, and lemon juice in a blender. If the puree seems like it has a lot of seeds, strain through a fine-mesh strainer. Pour the puree onto lined the baking sheet and spread evenly into about a ¼-inch-thick layer without any spaces or holes, leaving a ½-inch border around the edges.

3 · Place in the oven and dry for 6 to 12 hours, checking every 30 minutes after 4 hours, until the leather is no longer sticky to the touch. While still warm, peel off the paper and transfer to a fresh sheet of parchment paper or plastic wrap and let cool completely. Using a sharp knife or a pizza wheel, cut the leather (including the parchment or plastic) into strips. Roll up the leather.

VARIATION

Peach and Mango Oven Fruit Rolls: Make these beauties because we all need colorful jarred treats in the pantry! Substitute 1 cup each peeled, pitted, and chopped mango and peaches for the berries.

Fruit Chips

Replace your candy craving with these naturally sweet homemade chips made in your dehydrator. Dried fruit chips serve a double purpose: Not only are they a wonderful snack, they can also be pulverized to make versatile powders (see page 113). Store as chips and grind into powders as needed.

MAKES 1 DEHYDRATOR TRAY

2 cups fresh or thawed frozen fruit chunks

¼ cup water or fruit juice

Raw honey, as needed (optional)

1 · Puree the fruit and water in a blender. It should be easily spreadable but still hold its shape—blend in additional water, 1 tablespoon at a time, if needed. Taste the puree, and if it seems too tart, blend in some honey, if using, also 1 tablespoon at a time.

2 · Pour onto a fruit roll dehydrator tray. Dry at 135°F, for 8 to 14 hours, checking after 4 hours, until crisp.

3 · Let cool completely before breaking the fruit into chips. Store the chips in an airtight container in a cool, dark place at room temperature for up to 1 month.

VARIATIONS

Fruit Punch Chips: Combine leftover fruit or fruit salad to create a medley. Plus, you'll clean out the fridge at the same time. Winning! Use 2 cups any combination mixed fruit.

Spiced-Up Fruit Chips: For a "fruit, spice, and everything nice" version, add 1 teaspoon ground cinnamon when pureeing.

Floral Fruit Chips: Replace the water with your favorite Botanical Water (page 165). Strawberry-rose-blueberry-lilac chips are tasty!

Chive Blossom Zucchini Chips

Soaking in vinegar before dehydrating is a quick way to infuse flavor into your chips. This recipe uses the pungent and beautiful chive blossom vinegar, but get creative using different vinegar infusions to find your favorite flavor combination.

MAKES ABOUT 1 CUP

2 medium zucchinis (about 12 ounces total), scrubbed but unpeeled

1 cup Chive Blossom Vinegar (page 187)

½ teaspoon herb salt (see page 205)

1 · Using a mandoline or plastic V-slicer (or a large knife), cut the zucchini into ¼-inch rounds. Transfer to a medium bowl, add the vinegar, and soak, stirring occasionally, for 30 to 45 minutes. Strain, reserving the vinegar for another use (such as the Chive Blossom Vinaigrette on page 280).

2 · Place on dehydrator trays, with some space in between. Dry at 125°F for 5 to 9 hours, checking every hour after 5 hours, until crisp.

Vegetable and Bean Dried Soup Mix

Make-ahead soup mix! This dried soup mix made with a home dehydrator comes in handy for those days you just don't feel like going to the trouble to shop or roll up your sleeves and go through all the steps of making soup. It's also a great camping meal. The beans break open when dried. Not so pretty but still so tasty!

MAKES 3 CUPS

2 cups (½-inch) diced carrots

1 large yellow onion, cut into ½-inch dice

2 medium zucchini, cut into ½-inch dice

1 cup (½-inch) diced celery

½ cup shelled fresh peas

1 (15.5-ounce) can Great Northern beans or pinto beans, drained

1 (15.5-ounce) can kidney beans, drained

1 · Put the carrots, onion, zucchini, celery, and peas on dehydrator trays. (No need to blanch first.) Put the white beans and kidney beans on trays, separate from the vegetables, as they will dry in less time.

2 · Dry at 135°F for 10 to 12 hours, or until dried. Start checking the beans every hour after 4 hours of drying. Remove the beans before the vegetables, if necessary. Let all the ingredients cool and dry completely. Combine and transfer to an airtight container. Store in a cool, dry place.

Oven-Roasted Dried Beet Chips

Nothing beats that roasted flavor, but the crispness from the oven won't last long. But there is a solution! Dehydrating after roasting will extend the shelf life and hold the crisp.

MAKES 2 TO 3 CUPS

Nonstick cooking spray

2 to 3 small red or golden beets, scrubbed

Extra-virgin olive oil, for drizzling

Herb salt (see page 205) and freshly ground black pepper (optional)

1 · Preheat the oven to 375°F with a rack in the center of the oven. Line two rimmed baking sheets with parchment paper and grease with cooking spray.

2 · Roughly peel the beets, leaving some skin on—they don't have to be perfectly peeled. Using a mandoline or plastic V-slicer, slice the beets into ⅛-inch-thick rounds. Thin and consistent slices are the key to even roasting and crispiness.

3 · Divide on the prepared baking sheets in a single layer, leaving space in between. Spray, brush, or lightly drizzle with olive oil. Season with herb salt and pepper, if desired.

Bake until the beets are crisp and slightly brown, 15 to 20 minutes, watching closely after 10 minutes so they don't burn. Transfer to a wire cooling rack. If some are still soft, return to the oven for a few minutes more. Let cool, although they are good warm, too! Serve the chips the same day as baking.

4 · For longer shelf life and a crispier chip, arrange the roasted chips on dehydrator racks and dry at 135°F for 1 to 5 hours, checking hourly, until crispy enough to break between two fingers. Cool completely on the racks before storing in an airtight, moistureproof container.

CHAPTER 6
Freeze-Dry It!

140
How It Works

140
Drying Times

141
Storing Freeze-Dried Foods

142
Rehydrating

142
Freeze-Drying Fruits

146
Freeze-Drying Vegetables

With a home freeze-dryer, you can preserve raw, frozen, or cooked food, keeping them as fresh as the day as they were made. I wish I'd had a freeze-dryer back when we were having our babies. I would have freeze-dried so many meals to save during the postpartum months. Having a few meals at the ready would have also come in handy when I had six sick kids (say that five times fast) and worked a full-time job. These days I always have a few meals stashed away so I am prepared for power outages, natural disasters, and zombies (ha!).

Getting Even More From Your Produce

Baby Food 152

Dog Food 152

Recipes

Freeze-Dried Yogurt Drops 155

Freeze-Dried Vegetable Chips 156

Freeze-dried foods, better known by my generation as "astronaut" or "space" food, is the latest and greatest way to preserve. Eggs, dairy, meat, herbs, snacks, homemade pet food, and baby food are all fair game, and it's a no-brainer for camping and road trips.

Anything you freeze-dry, including fruits and vegetables, retains nearly all of its nutrients and color. Flavors can intensify, too. And the shelf life is wild—freeze-dried food can last for 25 to 30 years!

Beyond the many practical benefits, freeze-drying allows me to be creative in the kitchen.

But there is a catch. Actually, there are a few.

The freeze-dryer machine is an investment. Prices start at a couple thousand dollars. It also requires a designated space (it's larger than a microwave but smaller than a washing machine and is too heavy to move around) and the pump for the machine, which may require oil replacement from time to time depending on the model, is a bit loud. We keep ours in our laundry room. It's a big enough space for the machine to safely operate and the noise doesn't bother us. In addition, the freeze-drying process also takes time; some foods may take up to 48 hours to process. That being said, for us the pros far outweigh the cons!

How It Works

The automated machine goes through a few steps, starting with a deep freeze. Fresh, prefrozen, or cooked foods are placed on special trays that are frozen at –30°F or colder. Once the machine senses that the freezing part is complete, it creates a powerful vacuum around the food, lowering the pressure in the chamber.

While keeping the air in the chamber cool, the machine then slightly warms the trays, which causes the ice in the frozen foods to sublimate. (That's a technical word describing the transition from a solid to a gas.) This process removes about 98 percent of the moisture in the food, stopping the growth of bacteria. When the food is completely dried, you must immediately package it, as freeze-dried food quickly absorbs moisture from the air. Always follow the manufacturer's instructions for freeze-drying food and maintaining your machine.

The machine includes stainless steel trays (the number of trays depends on the size of machine) that the food is placed on for processing, including whole cooked meals. Specialty designed silicone molds can hold pureed foods or liquids. Silicone mats designed for the freeze-dryer or parchment paper can be used to line the trays for sticky foods or those foods that may stain. There are a few tricks to loading the trays:

- Fill each tray before processing. An empty tray can throw off the machine sensor, resulting in unevenly dried food.

- When working with liquid and purees, avoid spills by pouring directly onto trays, or molds placed on trays, already in the machine.

- Different foods can be processed at the same time, even on the same trays. But avoid mixing foods like onions, garlic, and peppers with other foods due to pungent odors and flavors that will transfer to other foods.

- Prefreezing in your home freezer can speed up the freeze-drying time.

- Semisolid foods (such as yogurt, applesauce, pudding, and ice cream) poured into silicone molds can make fun shapes.

- Placement on the trays is variable. Some items can be close together, and some can be spaced slightly part, or even heaped. See each recipe for spacing recommendations. In any case, do not stack higher than the tray's rim.

Drying Times

Each drying method takes time, but freeze-drying is the longest and most unpredictable. Several factors affect process time, including the density, size, shape, and moisture content of the food, load size, room temperature, and location of the machine. Keep track of the processing times that work for your setup so you can plan accordingly in the future. It's worth noting that you cannot overdo it when freeze-drying food; food processed longer than required will not be ruined.

Use these estimated freeze-drying times as a guide to get started.

Fruits/vegetables/meat 24 to 36 hours
Herbs and flowers 12 to 24 hours
Dairy 20 to 36 hours
Prepared meals 24 to 48 hours

To keep your machine running efficiently and reduce drying times, use the following check list:

- Temperature: A controlled temperature environment is best. High humidity and hot days can lengthen drying times.

- Placement and airflow: Machines placed in poorly ventilated areas or small rooms or near other appliances may have longer dry times. Good ventilation will help the machine run efficiently. Consider adding a fan if the room is warm.

- Food shape and size: Diced and thinly sliced foods will process more quickly than larger pieces. Keeping pieces the same size will ensure even drying.

- Moisture content: The moisture content in produce varies. Foods that are higher in water content will take longer to process.

- Machine maintenance: Keep your machine clean and maintain oil (if applicable).

Storing Freeze-Dried Foods

Be sure food is completely dry before packaging. Unlike dehydrated food that is conditioned before packaging, freeze-dried food quickly takes on moisture from the air and must be packaged immediately after processing. Even a small amount of moisture can begin to rehydrate the food.

Exposure to light or heat can affect color and quality. Store freeze-dried food in a cool, dry, and dark place, such as a cupboard, pantry, or closet, especially if packed in clear jars.

You can add oxygen absorbers (available online) to the packaging; these are packets that come in various sizes and can extend shelf life. But know that every time you open a container, the absorber needs to be replaced.

Containers to consider:

- **Canning jars** Canning jars are an inexpensive, moistureproof, airtight storage option. With their familiar two-part lids, they can be reopened as needed without the use of additional equipment.

- **Resealable glass jars** These are perfect for foods that you will access frequently. Reasonably priced glass jars (sometimes called bail jars) with tight clamps or locking fasteners fall into this category. Repurposed glass jars from store-bought foods with resealable, tight-fitting lids can also be used.

- **Vacuum-sealed glass jars** A moderately priced storage option, vacuum-sealed jars are good for longer-term storage. Vacuum sealing removes the oxygen in the jar, creating an ideal environment for your freeze-dried foods. Oxygen absorbers are unnecessary, but special jars, lids, and a vacuum sealer are required.

- **Vacuum-sealed bags** Vacuum sealers come with a variety of bag size or rolls of wrap. This reasonably priced option allows for long-term storage and protects freeze-dried food from all elements except light.

- **Mylar storage bags** This storage option can be an investment, but it will give you the longest possible storage. Mylar bags are moisture-, light-, and vaporproof. You can find them online in a variety of sizes, often including oxygen absorbers. Bags can be purchased as resealable, or heat sealed. The latter requires the purchase of a heat sealer, often sold by the same company or manufacturers. These bags are ideal for large, precooked meals. Another benefit: Boiling water can be added directly to the bag to rehydrate the food to enjoy wherever you are. It's perfect for college students, road trips, camping, or hiking.

Rehydrating

Spritzing and soaking are the two main ways to rehydrate freeze-dried food. Rehydrating times vary depending on the food and its size. See the tips on page 119 for details.

- Spritzing calls for a spray bottle. This method is ideal for herbs and leafy greens, which are delicate. Fill the bottle with lukewarm water and spray all over whatever you want rehydrated. Place the food on a plate or in a colander and repeat as needed, tossing, until refreshed.

- Soaking is what you might think: Cover freeze-dried items with water and let them sit. Cool (not cold) water is best, but warm or hot water will speed up rehydration—it can also adversely affect the texture and flavor of some fruit, so use this option selectively. Alternative soaking liquids, like broth or juice, can replace the water for added flavor. If you use alternative soaking liquids, rehydrate in the refrigerator.

Fruits and vegetables Use a ratio of 1 cup food to 1 cup water. You want the food covered, but not drowning, or it may become mushy. Cover fresh fruits and vegetables tightly with plastic wrap or a plate. Let stand, stirring occasionally, until refreshed. This can take from 5 minutes to a few hours. Berries rehydrate quickly, for example, but grapes and green beans may take an hour or more.

To speed things up, place vegetables in a microwave-safe bowl with enough water to cover and cook on high (100%) power, in 1-minute intervals, stirring, until refreshed. Or place in a saucepan of water and simmer until heated through.

For cooked vegetables, cover with hot water in a bowl. Cover tightly with plastic wrap or plate until refreshed, 10 to 15 minutes. Drain.

To add freeze-dried items directly to soup, sauces, and stews, add an additional ¼ cup of water for every 1 cup food. This will help reestablish the liquid ratio after the finished dish absorbs some of it in rehydration.

Soft foods (oatmeal, potatoes) Combine ½ cup freeze-dried food with 1 cup hot milk in a small bowl. Cover and let soak for 4 to 5 minutes. Stir before serving. For mashed potatoes, mash and season.

Purees and smoothies Put in a serving glass and gradually stir in cool water or juice until the desired consistency is reached.

Powders To make pastes for flavoring, seasoning, and coloring, stir equal parts powder and cool to warm water in a small bowl (see page 113).

Freeze-Drying Fruits

Freeze-dried fruit has become my new candy. The flavors are intensified, and the crunch is so satisfying.

- Process according to your machine manufacturer's instructions.

- Use the estimated drying times on page 141 as a guide.

- Some fruits may benefit from a dip into a pretreatment solution (see page 17).

- See page 119 for details on rehydrating and page 113 for details on grinding powders.

- For details on rehydrating, see page 119.

Apples Enjoy freeze-dried apples as a snack or use in Apple Cinnamon Oatmeal (page 250).

> *Prep* Rinse. Leave skins on for a freeze-dried snack, but peel for future baking. Cut into slices or wedges. Pretreat (see page 17). Arrange on the trays, overlapping up to the rim and leaving no space in between each slice. Process.
>
> *Optional* Sprinkle on a mix of sugar and cinnamon for a sweet snack. Or sprinkle the slices with a fruit powder (try raspberry) to add extra fruity flavor.

Rehydrate Cover with cool water in a bowl. Cover the bowl and soak until refreshed, stirring occasionally. Drain as needed.

Applesauce Enjoy as a crunchy snack, grind into a powder, or rehydrate to use in baby food, oatmeal, baked goods, and smoothies. Kick up the flavor by sprinkling ground cinnamon or a botanical powder on top before processing.

Prep Line the trays with parchment paper or silicone mats. Spread the applesauce evenly, filling the tray halfway to the edges. Do not overfill. Or pour into freeze-dryer-safe molds to make shapes. Process.

Rehydrate Combine 1 part applesauce to 2 parts cool water or apple juice in a bowl. Stir. Add additional water, as needed, to reach the desired consistency.

Apricots Freeze-dry sliced fruit or apricot puree. Rehydrate to use in baked goods, sauces, oatmeal, baby food, ice cream, and fruit leathers. Enjoy as a snack or grind into a powder.

Prep Rinse. Halve and pit. Slice into ½-inch wedges or leave halved. Arrange closely together on the trays, cut side up. Process.

Rehydrate Cover with cool water in a bowl. Cover the bowl and soak, stirring occasionally, for 5 to 10 minutes. Drain as needed.

Avocados Freeze-dried avocado is just the thing to have on hand when you crave guacamole. I like to use it to make Avocado Garden Toast (page 253). Be sure to use ripe avocados, as underripe avocados will have a bitter taste when rehydrated.

Prep Halve, pit, and peel. Dice, slice, or mash. For diced and sliced pieces, toss with a little lemon juice to help retain color, then arrange on the trays, leaving little space in between. For mashed avocado, add a teaspoon or two of lemon juice to the puree, then spread evenly onto trays lined with parchment paper or silicone mats. Process.

Rehydrate Grind into a powder. Pour into a bowl and gradually stir in cool water until you reach the desired consistency.

Bananas Enjoy as a snack, grind into a powder, or rehydrate to use for muffins, breads, pancakes, smoothies, and baby food. The soaking liquid for bananas becomes so flavorful! Be sure to use it, too.

Prep Slice about ¼ inch thick or blend into a puree. Pretreat slices, if desired (see page 17). Arrange the slices on trays closely together. For puree, spread evenly. Process.

Rehydrate Combine the bananas and cool water in a bowl. Cover the bowl and soak until refreshed, stirring occasionally. Mash with a fork or in a food processor.

Berries, tender (such as blackberries, boysenberries, raspberries) Tender berries generally have longer processing times than strawberries. Prefreeze for at least 6 hours to speed up processing time. Enjoy as is, or rehydrate for smoothies, fruit and simple syrups, baked goods, ice cream, fruit leathers, and sauces. Berries also make excellent powders.

Prep Rinse. Leave whole. Arrange the berries closely together on parchment paper–lined trays. Process.

Optional Sprinkle with sugar or spices, such as ground cinnamon or ginger.

Rehydrate Cover with cool water in a bowl. Cover the bowl and soak until refreshed, stirring occasionally. Drain as needed.

Blueberries Enjoy as is, or rehydrate to use in syrups, baked goods, ice cream, fruit leathers, and sauces. Blueberries are excellent ground into a powder to use for added flavor or food colorant.

Prep Rinse. Remove stems. Pierce the skin with a toothpick to help maintain the shape or check the berries in boiling water (see page 116). Arrange closely together on parchment paper–lined trays. Process.

Optional Sprinkle with sugar or spices, such as ground cinnamon or ginger.

Rehydrate Cover with cool water in a bowl. Cover the bowl and soak until refreshed. Drain as needed.

Cantaloupes and honeydew melons Enjoy as is, or rehydrate for syrups, fruit salad, sauces, smoothies, beverages, and fruit leathers, or grind into a powder.

Prep Peel. Cut into ½-inch slices. Arrange closely together on the trays, leaving no space in between. Process.

Rehydrate Cover with cool water in a bowl. Cover the bowl and soak until refreshed. Drain as needed.

Cherries Enjoy as is, or rehydrate for use in syrups, baked goods, fruit salads, ice cream, fruit leathers, sauces, and smoothies.

Prep Rinse. Pit and halve. Arrange closely together, cut side up, on the trays. Process.

Rehydrate Cover with cool water in a bowl. Cover the bowl and soak until refreshed. Stir occasionally. Drain as needed.

Citrus (such as oranges, lemons, and limes) Use in tea or to make juice. Grind into a powder for baked goods, sauces, marinades, and dressings.

Prep Rinse. Cut into slices or wedges. Remove the seeds. Stack, overlapping the slices on the trays and keeping them below the rim. Process.

Rehydrate Cover with cool water in a bowl. Cover the bowl and soak until refreshed. Drain as needed.

Grapes Enjoy a handful of this intensely sweet-and-sour crunchy treat. Or rehydrate for use in syrups, baked goods, ice cream, fruit leathers, and salads. Because of the high sugar content in grapes, freeze-drying and rehydrating times can be long. They're done when they're hard and crunchy.

Prep Rinse. Remove the stems. Blanch in boiling water for 1 minute. Transfer immediately to an ice bath and let cool for an equal amount of time. Drain and pat dry. Cut in half. To speed up the freeze-drying process, prefreeze overnight before freeze-drying. Arrange closely together on trays, cut side up. Process.

Rehydrate Cover with cool water in a bowl. Cover the bowl and soak until refreshed, stirring occasionally. Drain as needed.

Mangoes Freeze-dried mango is a delicious snack. But it can also be ground into a powder or rehydrated to use in smoothies, yogurt, oatmeal, baked goods, fruit leathers, fruit salads, syrups, ice cream, sorbet, and baby food.

Prep Peel. Slice or cut into small chunks. Mango takes a long time to process. Speed it up by prefreezing for 6 hours to overnight. Arrange closely together on the trays. Process.

Rehydrate Cover with cool water in a bowl. Cover the bowl and soak until refreshed. Drain as needed.

Peaches, nectarines Enjoy as a snack, grind into a powder, or rehydrate to eat or use in smoothies, yogurt, oatmeal, baked goods, baby food, fruit leathers, fruit salads, syrups, and jams.

Prep Peel and pit. Cut into slices, wedges, or chunks. Arrange closely together, cut side up, on trays. Process.

Optional Sprinkle with sugar or spices.

Rehydrate Cover with cool water in a bowl. Cover the bowl and soak until refreshed. Drain as needed.

Pears Eat as a snack, grind into a powder, or rehydrate to eat or use in tea, crisps, cobblers, smoothies, oatmeal, baked goods, baby food, fruit leathers, and fruit salads.

Prep Rinse. Peel if preserving for future baking. Cut into slices or wedges. Pretreat (see page 17). Pile on trays, no higher than the rim. Process.

Optional Sprinkle a mix of 2 tablespoons sugar and 1 teaspoon ground cinnamon per 1 pound fruit. Or sprinkle with fruit powder (blueberry is especially delicious) to add extra fruity flavor.

Rehydrate Cover with cool water in a bowl. Cover the bowl and soak until refreshed, stirring occasionally. Drain as needed.

Pineapple I love this as a snack! You can also grind into a powder or rehydrate to use in smoothies, beverages, fruit salads, marinades, oatmeal, and popsicles. But take note, pineapple can take more than 48 hours to process.

Prep Use fresh or frozen pineapple. If using fresh, remove skin and core. Cut into 1-inch chunks or rings. Prefreeze overnight to speed up processing time. Arrange closely together on trays. Process, making sure the largest pieces are not chewy.

Rehydrate Cover with cool water in a bowl. Cover the bowl and soak until refreshed. Drain as needed.

Plums Eat as a snack, rehydrate, or grind into a powder. If plums are tart, sprinkle with a little sugar before processing.

Prep Halve and pit. Cut into wedges or chunks. Arrange the plums closely together, cut side up, on parchment paper–lined trays. Process.

Rehydrate Cover with cool water in a bowl. Cover the bowl and soak until refreshed.

Strawberries These don't last long at our house. They make a delicious, freeze-dried snack and a beautiful powder.

Prep Hull and slice. Stack, overlapping slices on the trays and keeping below the rim. Process.

Rehydrate Cover with cool water in a bowl. Cover and soak until refreshed.

Freeze-Drying Vegetables

Get ready to have the most beautiful pantry on the block! Use the estimated drying times on page 141 as a guide. They may be shorter or longer depending on your machine and room temperature, as well as the shape, size, and water content of the food. Prefreezing for at least 6 hours to overnight will speed up processing time.

- Process according to your machines manufacturer's instructions.

- Although not required, most fresh vegetables benefit from blanching before freeze-drying. If you choose to freeze-dry cooked vegetables, there is no need to blanch. Adjust the blanching time to allow 1 minute longer if you are 5,000 feet or more above sea level.

- In general, it is best to arrange vegetables close together in a single layer and no higher than the tray rims.

- See page 119 for details on rehydrating and page 113 for details on grinding powders.

Asparagus Eat as a snack or rehydrate to use in soup and casseroles. For extra flavor, grill the asparagus for a few minutes before processing.

Prep Remove the woody ends. Lightly grill for 3 to 4 minutes or blanch in boiling water for 2 to 4 minutes, depending on size. Immediately transfer to an ice bath and let cool for an equal amount of time. Remove from the water and pat dry. Arrange the asparagus on the trays in a single layer, leaving no space between them. Process.

Rehydrate Cover with cool water (for raw asparagus) or hot water (for blanched asparagus). Cover the bowl and soak until refreshed. Drain as needed.

Beets Rehydrate to use in salads or pickles. Grind into a beautiful powder to use in smoothies, yogurt, juice, soft cheese, or homemade pasta, and use as a natural food dye.

Prep Rinse well. Steam blanch whole beets, covered, for 30 minutes. Cool completely. (No ice bath required.) Peel and slice into desired thickness. Arrange on parchment paper–lined trays in a single layer with no space in between. Process.

Rehydrate Cover with cool water in a bowl. Cover the bowl and soak until refreshed. Drain as needed.

Broccoli (see Cauliflower)

Brussels sprouts Rehydrate to enjoy sautéed, roasted, or in a warm salad.

Prep Trim the outer leaves. Rinse. Leave raw or blanch in boiling water for 3 to 5 minutes. Cool completely. (No ice bath required.) Arrange on the trays in a single layer, leaving no space in between. Process.

Rehydrate Cover with cool water (for raw sprouts) or hot water (for blanched) in a bowl. Cover the bowl and soak until refreshed. Drain as needed.

Cabbage Spritz back to life to use in soups, slaws, stir-fries, tacos, and sandwiches.

Prep Remove any blemished outer leaves. Rinse cabbage thoroughly under cold water. Remove core and shred into strips or cut into pieces. Fill the trays, stacking or layering the cabbage no higher than the rim. Process.

Rehydrate Spritz with lukewarm water from a spray bottle until refreshed. Rehydrate directly into soups or other liquid-based recipes.

Carrots Add freeze-dried or rehydrated carrots to soups, stews, pot pies, baked goods, or ice pops, or eat as a snack. Grind into a powder to flavor and color breads, cakes, muffins, and smoothies.

Prep Peel, remove tops and ends, and rinse well. Cut into slices or leave small carrots whole. Leave raw, blanch, or cook until tender. Blanch in boiling water for 2 minutes for cut carrots or 5 minutes for small whole carrots. Or steam blanch sliced carrots for 3 minutes or small whole carrots for 6 to 8 minutes. Transfer immediately (unless cooked) to an ice bath and let cool for an equal amount of time. Drain and pat dry. Pile on the trays, no higher than the rims. Process.

Rehydrate Cover with cold water (for raw carrots) or hot water (for cooked carrots) in a bowl. Cover the bowl and soak until refreshed. Drain as needed. Rehydrate directly into soups.

Cauliflower Rehydrate to roast, grill, sauté, or stir-fry. Use in soups, chowders, and casseroles.

Prep Rinse. Separate into florets. Steam blanch for 3 to 4 minutes, or cook. Transfer immediately to an ice bath and let cool for an equal amount of time. Drain and pat dry. Pile onto the trays, no higher than the rims. Process.

Rehydrate Cover with just enough cool water (for blanched florets) or hot water (for cooked) to cover. Cover the bowl and soak until refreshed. Drain as needed.

Celery Use how you would fresh celery. Rehydrate to use in chicken salad, potato salad, sauce base, stock, soups, and stir-fries. Grind into a powder as a seasoning. Freeze-dry the celery tops to use in celery salt (recipe follows).

Prep Dice or slice. Pile onto the trays, no higher than the rims. Process.

Rehydrate Cover with cold water in a bowl. Cover the bowl and soak until refreshed. Drain as needed. For fresh dishes, spritz freeze-dried celery with lukewarm water from a bottle, tossing to coat evenly, until refreshed. Rehydrate directly into soups and stews.

HOMEMADE CELERY SALT

To make celery salt, blend 1 cup freeze-dried or dehydrated celery and celery tops (see Leafy Greens, page 149) with ½ cup kosher or coarse sea salt and 1 tablespoon celery seed, until powdery. Use it to season seafood and poultry dishes.

Eggplants Rehydrate and add to pasta sauces, casseroles, cooked vegetables, skillets, and sheet pan dinners.

Prep Rinse. Slice or dice. Arrange closely together on the trays. Process.

Rehydrate Cover with cool water in a bowl. Cover the bowl and soak until refreshed. Drain as needed.

Garlic Freeze-dried garlic is a wonderful addition to the pantry. Grind into a powder, mix with salt or other seasonings, or leave plain. Use garlic powder in any dish that calls for garlic. Please note that processing freeze-dried garlic can leave behind an unpleasant odor that can transfer to other foods. After processing a batch of garlic, freeze-dry other savory foods next where the garlic won't be offensive. Or process bread slices on the trays to soak up the odors.

> *Prep* Peel. Slice or chop. Arrange closely on trays lined with parchment paper or silicone mats. Process.
>
> *Rehydrate* Garlic is best when used freeze-dried, so do not bother to refresh.

Green beans Use in soups, sheet pan dinners, skillet dinners, and stir-fries.

> *Prep* Remove the ends. Rinse. You can freeze-dry raw, blanched, or completely cooked beans. Blanch in boiling water for 2 to 4 minutes, or steam blanch for 4 to 5 minutes. Transfer immediately to an ice bath and let cool for an equal amount of time. Drain and pat dry. Pile onto trays no higher than the rims. Process.
>
> *Rehydrate* Cover with cool water (for raw or blanched beans) or hot water (for cooked) in a bowl. Cover the bowl and soak until refreshed. Raw, unblanched beans can take a long time to refresh. Drain as needed.

Herbs Freeze-drying is, hands-down, the best way to preserve herbs. It not only preserves the color and nutrients, but the flavors are also intensified in the freeze-drying process, making them better than ever before. Use slightly less than the recipe calls for when using freeze-dried herbs. Enjoy crushed freeze-dried herbs in all your favorite recipes and dishes.

> *Prep* Rinse. Pat dry. Remove the stems for herbs like mint, lemon balm, and basil. Keep the stems on for herbs with small leaves such as rosemary and thyme. Fill the trays, stacking or layering, no higher than the rim. For delicate herbs and leaves, cover with a paper towel to keep from blowing around during processing.
>
> *Rehydrate* Use herbs in the freeze-dried state. To refresh, use a spray bottle and lightly spritz the herbs with lukewarm water, tossing until refreshed.

Leafy greens (chard, collards, kale, and spinach) Grind into a powder to use as a seasoning or as an addition to smoothies and dips. Or add freeze-dried greens to soups and stews.

> *Prep* Rinse. Remove the stems and any hard ribs. Process raw or blanched. Steam blanch for 3 minutes. Transfer immediately to an ice bath and let cool for an equal amount of time. Drain and thoroughly pat dry. Layer on trays, no higher than the rims. Process.
>
> *Rehydrate* Using a spray bottle, lightly spritz the greens with lukewarm water until refreshed.

Mushrooms Only use store-bought mushrooms that you know are edible. Add to soups, stews, and sauces, or grind into a powder to add mushroom flavor to any dish.

> *Prep* Slice or dice raw mushrooms. Stack or layer the mushrooms in the trays, no higher than the rims. Process.
>
> *Rehydrate* Cover with cool water in a bowl. Cover the bowl and soak until refreshed. The soaking liquid is full of flavor, so use it in your recipe if you can.

Onions Use dried as a seasoning. Grind into a powder to add flavor to your dishes. Use refreshed in omelets, tacos, and hamburgers, or on top of chili. Caramelized or cooked onions can also be used. For best results, place in the freezer for a few hours before freeze-drying. Do this on a day you can open the windows, as the smell is pungent.

> *Prep* Remove the outer skin and dice. Pile on the trays no higher than the rims. Process.
>
> *Rehydrate* Add directly to dishes—no need to rehydrate when cooking. Or, using a spray bottle, lightly spritz with lukewarm water until refreshed.

Peas Toss into soups and stews. Rehydrate to use in pot pies, salads, pasta, and rice dishes. Grind into a powder to flavor sauces, soups, homemade pasta, or add water to the powder to make baby food.

Prep Shell the peas, reserving the pods to make Zero-Waste Vegetable Broth (page 163). Rinse. For fresh peas, blanch in boiling water for 30 seconds or cook for longer. Transfer immediately to an ice bath and let cool for an equal amount of time. Drain and pat dry. Frozen or canned peas do not need to be blanched. Pile peas in the trays no higher than the rims. Process.

Rehydrate Cover with cool water (for raw peas) or hot water (for cooked) in a bowl. Cover the bowl and soak until refreshed. Drain as needed.

Peppers, hot (chiles) Grind into red pepper flakes or into a powder to make chili powder. Add to chilies, marinades, and sauces. Rehydrate for use in savory dishes.

Prep Wearing food-safe gloves, slice in half lengthwise and remove the seeds. Leave in halves or cut into strips or small pieces. Process spicier peppers by themselves. It is best if chiles are not combined with other trays of foods when freeze-drying. Fill the trays, stacking or layering the chiles no higher than the rims. Process.

Rehydrate Cover with cool water in a bowl. Cover the bowl and soak until refreshed. Drain as needed.

Peppers, sweet/bell Rehydrate for use in rice, pasta, sauces, dips, or spreads. Grind into a powder to use as a seasoning.

Prep Stem, halve, and seed. Slice or dice. Arrange on the trays, no higher than the rims. Process.

Rehydrate Cover with cool water in a bowl. Cover the bowl and soak until refreshed. Drain as needed.

Potatoes, red, white, and yellow Rehydrate directly into casseroles, soups, and stews. Grind into a powder to make mashed potatoes. Potatoes must be blanched or cooked so that they don't turn black.

Prep Peel and rinse, then slice or dice. Coat raw potatoes in a pretreatment solution (see page 17). Drain. Blanch in boiling water for 5 to 6 minutes. Transfer immediately to an ice bath and let cool for an equal amount of time. Drain and pat dry. Arrange the potatoes closely together in a single layer on the trays. Cooked or mashed potatoes can be spread evenly on trays lined with parchment paper or silicone mats. Process.

Rehydrate Cover with cool water in a bowl. Cover the bowl and soak until refreshed. Drain as needed. For mashed potatoes, gradually stir hot water into freeze-dried mashed potatoes in a bowl until the desired consistency is reached.

Potatoes, sweet (yams) Grind into a powder to flavor baked goods or eat as chips. These also make great snacks for your pup!

Prep Slice or dice, trying to keep pieces the same size. For chips, use a mandoline to thinly slice. Steam blanch for 3 minutes. Transfer immediately to an ice bath and let cool for an equal amount of time. Drain and pat dry. Arrange closely together on the trays. Cooked or mashed sweet potatoes can be spread evenly on trays lined with parchment paper or silicone mats. Process.

Rehydrate Cover with cool water in a bowl. Cover the bowl and soak until refreshed, 10 to 20 minutes. Drain as needed. For mashed potatoes, gradually stir hot water into freeze-dried mashed potatoes in a bowl until the desired consistency is reached.

Radishes Eat as a spicy veggie chip or use as a crunchy topping for salads.

Prep Rinse. Slice thinly. Season if desired. Spread on the trays, overlapping slightly. Process.

Rehydrate Dried radishes are best when enjoyed freeze-dried. If rehydrating, cover with cool water in a bowl. Cover the bowl and soak until refreshed. Drain as needed. Or spritz with lukewarm water, wait a few minutes, then toss. Repeat the steps if needed.

Squash, summer (crookneck, pattypan/scallop, straightneck, and zucchini) Rehydrate shredded zucchini for quick breads, muffins, bars, cakes (see page 332), and more. Diced squash works in soups,

pot pies, and stir-fries. Sliced squash can be used in casseroles and vegetable lasagna.

Prep Peel (unless shredding). Slice, dice, or shred, keeping the pieces about the same size. Do not blanch shredded zucchini, but do pat dry. Blanch cut pieces in boiling water for 1½ minutes, or steam blanch for 2 to 3 minutes. Transfer immediately to an ice bath and let cool for an equal amount of time. Drain and pat dry. Pile the squash on the trays, no higher than the rims. Process.

Rehydrate For sliced or diced squash, cover with cool water in a bowl. Cover the bowl and soak until refreshed. Drain as needed. For shredded zucchini, place in a colander and lightly spritz, tossing and spraying until refreshed.

Tomatoes Freeze-dry in pieces or as a fresh tomato puree. Grind into a powder to flavor baked goods, rice, Tomato Basil Crackers (page 245), and homemade pasta (see page 293). Rehydrate to thicken and season soups, stews, and sauces.

Prep Rinse. Core, then slice, dice, or halve. Arrange closely together (cut side up for halves) on the trays. For puree, blanch and peel (see page 33). Puree in a blender. Spread the puree evenly on parchment paper-lined trays. Process.

Freeze-Dry It!

Rehydrate Cover with cool water in a bowl. Cover the bowl and soak until refreshed. Drain as needed. For tomato puree, gradually stir hot water into freeze-dried tomato puree in a bowl until the desired consistency is reached.

FLOWERS

I've learned a few interesting things experimenting with freeze-dried flowers. One, they are vibrant in color and, in some cases, like small whole roses, they puff up into beautiful works of art. In addition to uncompromised color, the fragrance, nutrients, and minerals all remain intact, with the flavor of the petals becoming intensified. They also don't shrink into tiny flowers like when dehydrated or air-dried. The downside? Most become extremely fragile, making them almost impossible to craft with. In the kitchen, though, they can be used in many ways.

Getting Even More from Your Produce

Baby Food

It seems we're learning more and more about harmful chemicals or preservatives inside some of the foods we've bought and trusted. Our need for convenience comes at a sacrifice to our health and diet. The more we know, the better we do. This includes baby and pet foods. Why include unwanted ingredients in these important meals when you can make healthy whole foods right at home, for a fraction of the price of convenience?

Always use fresh, unblemished fruits or vegetables that have been well rinsed. I recommend filtered water, too. Create a puree in the blender by combining cooked fruits or vegetables with water. Spread the puree mixture evenly on a freeze-dryer tray. Repeat the steps, making a different puree for each tray so you get the most out of one processing period. Or even better, use specially designed silicone molds to make perfect portions.

- **Applesauce** Blend 3 peeled, cored, and chopped apples, baked or steamed until tender, with 2½ cups water.

- **Bananas** Blend 3 ripe bananas with 1 cup water.

- **Broccoli** Blend 3 cups cooked broccoli with 1½ cups water.

- **Carrots** Blend 3 cups cooked sliced carrots with 1½ cups water.

- **Green beans** Blend 2 cups cooked green beans with 2 cups water.

- **Peas** Blend 2 cups cooked peas with 2 cups water.

- **Winter squash** Blend 2 cups peeled and chopped winter squash, roasted or steamed until tender, with 1 cup water.

Process each puree according to your freeze-dryer manufacturer's instructions. Once dried, break into chunks and store in jars or bags. Or grind into a powder. When you're ready to use, place chunks or powder into a bowl. Gradually stir in hot or cold water until the desired consistency is reached. Test the temperature before feeding your baby. Good job, mama! You're working hard and it will make a difference.

Dog Food

Whether it's a human baby or a fur baby, we want them to eat the very best. The freeze-dryer is an excellent, cost-effective way to prepare better pet food at home. And since your fur friend isn't a food critic, there is no need to measure! He's gonna love it! It's always recommended to check with your dog's vet before changing or adding foods to their

Preserving the Seasons

diet. Store dog treats in resealable Mylar bags in a dark, cool location. No need to rehydrate, as your pup will love the crunch.

- **Squash or sweet potato bites** Peel and cut sweet potatoes into 1-inch chunks or slices. Steam or roast until tender. Cool. Pile cooled squash on trays lined with parchment paper or silicone mats, staying below the rim of the tray, and process.

- **Veggie balls** Combine 2 cups cooked white rice, ½ cup cooked peas, ½ cup cooked finely diced carrots, and 1 beaten egg. Form into 1-inch balls. Place on the trays, leaving little to no space in between, and process.

Do Not Freeze-Dry It!

While there are hundreds of foods that can be freeze-dried, there are a handful that cannot. In the freeze-drying process, water gets removed from food, but the amount of oil stays the same. That means that foods high in oil content will not freeze well on their own, like peanut or other nut butters, butter, and chocolate. If these foods are used as an ingredient combined with others to create a food or dish being freeze-dried, it should process without any issues. Other foods that don't freeze well on their own include jellies, jams, honey, and syrups.

Troubleshooting Freeze-Dried Foods

From time to time, things happen when freeze-drying. Refer to the manufacturer's instructions for machine troubleshooting.

Issue	Possible Cause	Solution
Clumpy powder	Food was exposed to moisture during grinding or storing.	Grind only the amount you'll be using at one time.
Moisture in jar	Food was not completely dried.	Be sure that all the pieces of food are completely dry before packaging. Process in the freeze-dryer longer.
Stained trays	Food that bleeds color, like berries or beets, was placed directly on trays.	Line trays with parchment paper or a silicone mat designed for your freeze-dryer model.

Freeze-Dried Yogurt Drops

With their melt-in-your-mouth texture, yogurt bites are great for kids, because one drop fits perfectly in little hands. They make a good addition to the toddler travel snack bag (aka your purse). Oh, I remember those days when my purse was full of Cheerios and goldfish crackers. Moms with young kids are like walking vending machines. Any yogurt will work for this—with or without fruit, Greek, low-fat, nonfat, all the fat . . . whatever you like!

MAKES ABOUT 40 DROPS

2 cups flavored yogurt

Fruit, vegetable, or flower powder for additional flavor and color (optional)

1 · Line the trays with parchment paper. If using powders, mix into the yogurt 1 teaspoon at a time until the desired color is reached. Fill a pastry bag without a pastry tip with the yogurt (or use a 1-gallon resealable storage bag with one corner snipped off). Using a scant tablespoon for each, pipe about 40 mounds of yogurt onto the trays. (They will not expand much, so you can pipe them close together.)

2 · Process the drops according to the manufacturer's directions. Store in an airtight container in a cool, dark place, such as a cupboard. (For more storage information, see page 141.)

VARIATION

Raspberry Vanilla Drops: Use vanilla yogurt. Mix in 1 tablespoon raspberry powder page (113), and process as above.

Freeze-Dried Vegetable Chips

Freeze-dried veggie chips bring the crunch! You can make them sweet or savory. Use this basic recipe as a guide to get you started. See page 137 for Oven-Roasted Dried Beet Chips, page 136 for Chive Blossom Zucchini Chips, and page 128 for pizza chips.

YIELD VARIES

Vegetables: beets, carrots, kale, parsnips, radishes, squash, sweet potatoes, turnips, zucchini

Seasonings: ground cinnamon, red pepper flakes, cracked black pepper, garlic salt, ground ginger, herb salt (see page 205), chopped fresh herbs, Infused Sugar (see page 216), lemon pepper, onion powder, Mild Taco Seasoning (page 111), Chili Powder (page 111)

Extra-virgin olive oil, in a spray bottle, for spritzing

1 · Using a mandoline or sharp knife, cut the vegetables into ⅛-inch-thick rounds. Lightly spritz the vegetables with the oil, then sprinkle and toss with the desired seasoning until lightly coated. Arrange close together in a single layer on trays lined with parchment paper or silicone mats.

2 · Process according to the manufacturer's instructions. Immediately transfer the chips to an airtight glass canning jar or Mylar bag. Add an oxygen absorber for an extended shelf life.

Savoring the Seasons with Infusions

PART TWO

I keep my pantry interesting and flavorful by creating infusions. Infusions impart the flavors of one ingredient to another. Some, like vinegar, salt, and sugar, act as a form of preservation, extending the shelf life of seasonal ingredients. In this section, you'll learn to take the simplest of ingredients—water (and ice), butter, salt, sugar, and honey—to the next level.

160 • CHAPTER 7
Water Infusions

182 • CHAPTER 8
Savory Infusions

210 • CHAPTER 9
Sweet Infusions

CHAPTER 7
Water Infusions

162
Recipes
Garden Coolers 162
Zero-Waste Vegetable Broth 163
Botanical Water 165
Cucumber Body Mist 165

166
Fancy Pants Ice
Fancy Pants Ice Menu 166
Holiday Ice Cubes 169
Colorful Fruit Ice Cubes 169

It doesn't get any easier or more budget friendly than this. Water infusions, which make colorful and flavorful ice cubes, refreshing beverages, savory broths, and healing teas, are simple ways to get big flavor from few ingredients. Gather ingredients from your garden or clean out the produce drawer in the fridge—even scraps, like fruit and vegetable peels, can change a tall glass of water into something delicious and beautiful.

170
Botanical Teas (Tisanes)

177
Tea Flower Blend Recipes
Fruits and Flowers Tea Blend 177
Mediterranean Vibes Tea Blend 177
Floral Teas 178
Hibiscus Berry Tea 179
Rose Tea Latte 180
Herbal Whipped Cream 180

Garden Coolers

Staying hydrated is key for every gardener—and every person. Doing it with the help of the garden, well—that is just showing off! Try one of the following natural flavor combinations that pack a healthy punch or create your own. Be sure to keep track of your recipe creations on the journal pages at the end of the book.

MAKES 4 TO 6 SERVINGS

Strawberry, Cucumber, and Mint

½ cup sliced fresh or frozen strawberries

1 cucumber, scrubbed but unpeeled, thinly sliced

10 fresh mint leaves, torn

5 cups spring or filtered water

Blackberry, Orange, and Rosemary

1 cup fresh or frozen blackberries

1 orange, thinly sliced, or 6 to 8 slices dehydrated orange (see page 120)

6 fresh rosemary sprigs

5 cups spring or filtered water

Blueberry, Lemon, and Basil

1 cup fresh or frozen blueberries

1 lemon, thinly sliced, or 4 to 6 slices dehydrated lemon (see page 120)

5 large basil leaves, torn

5 cups spring or filtered water

1 · For each combination, mix the infusing ingredients in a large pitcher. Add the water.

2 · Cover and refrigerate for at least 1 hour and up to 24 hours. The longer it steeps, the stronger the flavor.

3 · Strain through a fine-mesh strainer and serve immediately or refrigerate for up to 5 days.

4 · To serve, pour over regular ice cubes or Fancy Pants Ice (page 166) and garnish as you like, using fresh herbs, edible flowers, or citrus slices.

Zero-Waste Vegetable Broth

Homemade vegetable broth is a satisfying zero-waste creation that uses veggie and herb scraps. Sip warm in a mug, use as a soup base, or make sauces. Best part, it's simple. This basic recipe will get you started, but use whatever you have on hand and adjust accordingly. If you prefer a low-sodium or salt-free broth, feel free to adjust or omit the salt in the recipe as needed.

MAKES ABOUT 3 QUARTS

1 tablespoon extra-virgin olive oil

6 to 8 cups vegetable and herb scraps

8 garlic cloves, smashed under a knife and left unpeeled

2 tablespoons dried parsley

2 teaspoons dried thyme

1 teaspoon dried rosemary

6 whole peppercorns

3 large bay leaves

2½ teaspoons salt (optional)

6 quarts water

1 · Heat the oil in a large pot over medium-high heat. Add the vegetable and herb scraps. Toss in the garlic, parsley, thyme, rosemary, peppercorns, bay leaves, and salt (if using). Cook until the vegetables soften, 2 to 3 minutes.

2 · Add the water and bring to a boil. Turn the heat down to low, cover, and simmer for 1 hour. Uncover and stir. Continue cooking uncovered until fully flavored, 1 to 3 hours. Remove from the heat and allow the broth to steep at room temperature until completely cooled.

3 · Set a fine-mesh strainer or colander over a large pot or bowl and line it with several layers of cheesecloth. Strain the broth. Store in an airtight container in the refrigerator for up to 1 week or in the freezer (leaving 1-inch headspace in the container) for up to 6 months.

Reserve and refrigerate your vegetable scraps throughout the week in a 1-gallon resealable bag until you have collected 6 to 8 cups of scraps. I'm able to collect enough to make a full bag for new broth every week. If it takes longer than a week to accumulate scraps, keep your scraps bag in the freezer. Freeze refrigerated scraps on a rimmed baking sheet until solid, 2 to 4 hours, before adding to the same bag. Once the bag is full, you have a batch ready to go. Thaw before using.

Broth-loving scraps: carrot peels and tops, corn cobs, pea pods, celery leaves and trimmings, white or yellow onion peels and trimmings, mushroom stems, leek greens and trimmings, chard, woody chive stems, parsnip peels and trimmings, herb stems (thyme, oregano, and parsley), and leftover roasted veggies

Ingredients to avoid: potato trimmings and peels (too starchy) and cruciferous vegetables, like cabbage, broccoli, or cauliflower (too strongly flavored). Also note that adding purple pea pods, red onions, or red beets will tint the stock purple. I think it is cool but, in some dishes, it may not look that appealing.

Water Infusions

Botanical Water

Use this recipe template to make infused water with your favorite edible flowers and herbs. The flavored, medicinal, and sometimes colored water can be used in so many magical ways. Some of my favorite flowers to infuse include rose petals, butterfly pea flowers, lavender buds, pansies, dandelion blossoms, and mint. Using berries as a natural colorant is a wonderful option for lavender and lilac. Refer to the list of Herbs and Flowers for Botanical Teas (Tisanes) on page 171 and the Edible Flowers chart on page 99 for inspiration. Always double-check that your flower choices are nontoxic and are grown without the use of insecticides or pesticides.

MAKES 4 CUPS

2 cups packed fresh edible flowers or herbs (or ½ to 1 cup dried)

¼ cup blueberries, blackberries, or raspberries, smashed (optional, for color)

4½ cups boiling water

1 · Place the petals and berries (if desired) in a large heatproof bowl. Cover with the boiling water, then cover the bowl with cheesecloth, a kitchen towel, or plastic wrap. Steep until completely cooled.

2 · Strain through a fine-mesh strainer into a 1-quart canning jar. Label and date, twist on a lid, and refrigerate for up to 2 weeks. Or, to freeze, pour into ice cube trays and freeze until solid, about 6 hours. Remove the cubes from the molds and store in a resealable freezer bag (removing as much air as possible) or in an airtight container. The cubes are best used within 3 months.

VARIATION
Cold Infusion: Use 4 cups cool water in place of the boiling water. Cover and steep at room temperature or refrigerate for at least 20 minutes but no more than 24 hours. Taste periodically, adding more steeping time as needed. Strain.

A LITTLE ME TIME
Cucumber Body Mist
MAKES 1 CUP

1 large or 2 small cucumbers, peeled and cut into 1-inch chunks

1½ cups water

Use a couple of small, misshapen, yellowing cucumbers you might otherwise compost for this light toner. And to think all those years we thought those ugly little guys were a garden fail!

Bring the cucumber and water to a simmer in a small saucepan over medium heat. Turn the heat down to low and simmer until the cucumbers are soft, 5 to 6 minutes. Do not boil.

Remove from heat and cool for 10 minutes. Process in a blender until smooth, about 20 seconds. Strain through a fine-mesh strainer set over a bowl. Cool completely. Transfer to a glass canning jar or a spray bottle. (The toner can be refrigerated for up to 1 week.) Use poolside to keep your skin hydrated, or to soothe a sunburn. It's also refreshing after a shower or just when the kids are driving you nuts.

Fancy Pants Ice

Infused ice cubes were one of the first "fancy pants" things I started making when the kids were all little. The days were long and hard. There was just something about a flower suspended in my ice that gave me pause in my day to find gratitude and a moment of peace.

- For best visual and flavor results, use filtered or distilled water, which make a clearer ice cube than plain tap water. Alternatively, bring tap water to a full boil in a large pot over high heat, remove from the heat, and let it cool completely before freezing.

- Ice can be made in traditional ice trays or in silicone molds, which come in all shapes and sizes.

- Choose your ingredients—see the Fancy Pants Ice Menu chart below. Avoid using tiny flowers or leaves and very small pieces of fruit that may be choking hazards. The solid ingredients (herb leaf, flower, fruit, or vegetable) should be big enough to be easily removed from the glass with your fingertip. When making infused ice for young children, opt for Colorful Fruit Ice Cubes (page 169) instead.

- Place the rinsed ingredients in the ice cube tray cells or individual silicone molds. If you are freezing more than one tray or mold at a time, place the trays on a baking sheet to keep them stable. Fill each cell halfway with filtered, distilled, or boiled and cooled tap water. Freeze for several hours, until the ice around the ingredient is solid. Top with additional water and freeze overnight. This two-step freezing will keep your ingredients suspended in the ice. Larger ice cubes do take longer to freeze.

- Keep the ice cubes in the trays or molds and use within 2 to 3 weeks of initial freezing. For longer storage, remove the cubes from their trays and transfer to a freezer-safe container or a resealable freezer bag (pressing out at much air as possible). They will last for several months.

Fancy Pants Ice Menu

Give plain ice cubes a makeover with one or more of these ingredients. Combinations like blackberries and basil leaves or lavender and citrus slices are sure to delight.

Edible Flowers	Herbs	Fruits and Vegetables
Bachelor's buttons	Basil leaves	Blackberries or raspberries
Borage	Lavender buds	Blueberries
Dandelions	Lemon verbena leaves	Citrus slices or small wedges
Forget-me-nots	Mint leaves	Cucumber slices or small wedges
Pansies/violas	Parsley leaves	Cranberries
Snapdragons	Rosemary sprigs	Grapes (seedless), halved
Stocks	Thyme sprigs	Strawberries, halved

Holiday Ice Cubes

These ice cubes, bright in color and flavor, are delightful in holiday mocktails, cocktails, and punches.

MAKES AS MANY AS YOU NEED

Fresh cranberries, as needed

1 large orange, thinly sliced into rounds (including the rind), then each round cut into quarters

4 to 5 large rosemary sprigs, broken into small pieces (small enough to fit into an ice tray cell)

Distilled, filtered, or boiled and cooled tap water

1 · In the cell of each ice cube tray, place 2 cranberries, 1 orange quarter, and a small rosemary sprig. Fill each mold halfway with water. Freeze until the ingredients are in place, then add more water to completely fill the molds. Return to the freezer and freeze until solid, about 6 hours.

2 · Remove the ice cubes from the molds and store in a resealable freezer bag (pressing out as much air as possible) or an airtight container.

VARIATIONS

Floral Ice: Substitute the petals of edible flowers (pansies, violas, lavender, dandelions, bachelor's buttons, or roses) for the cranberries, oranges, and rosemary. The petals should be big enough to be easily removed from the glass with your fingertip to avoid a choking hazard.

Lemonade Ice: Substitute fresh mint leaves for the cranberries, oranges, and rosemary and use your favorite lemonade in place of the water.

Colorful Fruit Ice Cubes

Add these naturally colored ice cubes to any beverage you want to cool down: sparkling water, seltzer, cocktails, mocktails, iced tea, lemonade. Freeze in pretty shapes. They'll even change the hue of your beverages!

MAKES ABOUT 2 DOZEN

1 cup fresh or frozen blueberries, raspberries, or blackberries

3 cups water

1 · Lightly crush the berries in a small saucepan to release the juices. Add the water and bring to a boil over high heat. Remove from the heat, crush the berries again, and let cool completely. Strain the fruit through a fine mesh strainer into a container with a spout. Pour into ice trays or silicone molds.

2 · Freeze until solid, about 6 hours. Remove the ice cubes from the molds and store in a resealable freezer bag (pressing out as much air as possible) or an airtight container.

Water Infusions

Botanical Teas (Tisanes)

Botanical teas, or tisanes (from the Middle English word for "medicinal brew"), are water infusions made from herbs, seeds, bark, roots, flowers, or fruits. Tisanes have been used as natural home remedies for millennia. Botanical teas are also naturally caffeine-free. I enjoy them warm, iced, frozen in ice pops, and even in baking recipes as a water substitute.

A benefit to having a collection of dried herbs and flowers in your pantry is that you can make a tisane for whatever you're feeling or needing in the moment. Lavender and chamomile are my go-to herbs when I need to feel calm and relaxed. Sage and oregano are high on my list when I'm not feeling well, and rosemary stimulates circulation, which comes in handy before a day of gardening.

IMPORTANT: People on medications, those with asthma or plant allergies, children under age 12, and pregnant or nursing women, should all consult a doctor before using tisanes. Some herbs can interfere with medications and complicate health issues. It's always important to do your own research and seek advice from a physician before consuming.

If you grow your own herbs for tea, organic is the way to go. Any chemicals on your plants will end up in you. If you forage for your tea herbs, choose a spot far from busy roads or sidewalks. Many plants look similar, so proper plant identification is a must when foraging. It probably goes without saying, but give fresh herbs a good rinse before making your tea. To dry your own tea herbs, see the chapters Dry It! (page 86), Dehydrate It! (page 114), and Freeze-Dry It! (page 138).

Methods

There are a few methods for infusing plant material with water. Keep in mind that steeping times are estimates. Steep less for lighter infusions or longer for stronger ones, as you wish. Experiment with proportions, herb combinations, and steeping times to discover what you like best. Crush, grind, or chop ingredients to get more flavorful extractions. You may choose to keep the solids in the tea or strain them out—another matter of taste.

Brew Brewing is a way to extract the beneficial medicinal properties and flavors of tisanes. Although not as powerful as an infusion, brewing is the quickest way to a cup of tea. Simply pour boiling water over loose dried herb leaves or petals (or filled tea bags, balls, or infusers), then cover and steep for 5 to 10 minutes. Flowers have a more delicate flavor, so steep for 5 to 10 minutes longer. Strain and enjoy immediately or refrigerate. Quick brews taste best when used within a few days.

I like a strong, flavorful tea, so I usually make mine with 1 tablespoon dried ingredients per 1 cup water, with exceptions of course—I use less for pungent herbs like lavender. If I'm making a pot of tea, I'll use ¼ cup per 1 quart water. Double the measurements for fresh herbs and flowers. Sweeten with honey, infused sugar (see page 216), a splash of simple syrup (see simple syrup soak, page 116), or other ingredients as you wish—or not at all. See the list of Herbs and Flowers for Botanical Teas (Tisanes) on pages 172 to 175 for preparation by herb.

Infusion A long steeping period in hot or cold water concentrates flavors even more than brewing. Steeping can be done in a covered pot, tea kettle, French coffee press, or canning jar. I make big batches to use in beverages, baking, and even beauty care. Infusions can be reheated or served as iced tea. Although best used within 24 to 48 hours, infusions keep in the refrigerator for up to 2 weeks. Discard if a foul odor or mold is present, or if the liquid becomes cloudy.

Hot infusion is the best method for dried ingredients, and for allowing fresh flower petals to impart colors deeply. Pour boiling hot water over the dried or fresh ingredients in a bowl, cover, and steep until completely cool, 1 to 2 hours. Some mineral-dense herbs (such as nettles) benefit from a longer steep, 4 to 6 hours. Steeping overnight (but no more than 24 hours) in the refrigerator will offer the deepest infusion. Strain.

Cold infusion is a good method for fresh leaves, flowers, and other delicate plant material. There is also a group of herbs called demulcents, including hibiscus, calendula, comfrey, and linden, that do better with cold water to infuse. Pour cold water over the ingredients in a bowl, cover, and steep at room temperature or refrigerate. Average steeping time for cold infusions is 20 minutes to 2 hours, but the longer you steep, the deeper the flavor. Taste periodically, adding more steeping time as needed. Strain.

See the cold infusion variation for Botanical Water (page 165) for large-batch infusion preparations.

Decoction This method is used for dense plant material, such as fresh or dried roots, bark, stems, and mushrooms. First, simmer the ingredients in water until the liquid is reduced by half, 20 minutes to 1 hour, depending on the size and density of the material. Chopping the ingredients into smaller pieces will help the extraction. Strain before serving or storing. Decoctions are best used within 48 hours but will keep in the refrigerator for up to 2 weeks depending on the plant material. Discard if a foul odor or mold is present, or if the liquid becomes cloudy.

Perfuming Use this method to infuse the flavors of fresh flowers into black, white, or green tea leaves. Intensely fragrant flowers work best for this method, so harvest the blooms in the early morning or evening when their aroma is strongest. Roses, lavender, jasmine, and lilacs are all good options.

Place 2 or 3 tea bags in a dry wide-mouth glass jar. Top with a single layer of fresh, clean, and patted dry organic edible flowers or petals. Be sure the flowers or petals are no longer wet from rinsing before layering with tea or they will mold. Cover the flower layer with 3 more tea bags. Top the tea with a smaller jar (or a flat object) to weight and press down the layered tea and flowers. This intensifies the flavor infusion.

Cover with a tight-fitting lid and allow the scents and flavors to marry in a dark, cool place for at least 24 hours, and preferably up to 1 or 2 weeks for stronger flavor. Open the jar once a day to test the scent. When the desired fragrance is reached, remove the smaller jar or weight and discard the flowers. The perfumed tea bags are best stored in an airtight container in a cool, dark place, far away from any moisture. For best flavor use within 6 to 12 months.

To use, for each serving, combine 1 tea bag and 1 cup boiling water in a mug. (Or, for sharing, use a couple tea bags and a teapot.) Cover and steep for 5 minutes.

JAZZ UP YOUR TEA!

- Add half-and-half or heavy cream, or plant-based milk, such as coconut, oat, or almond.
- Add a fresh or dried slice of citrus.
- Sweeten with Infused Honey (page 213), Infused Sugar (see page 216), or Infused Sugar Shapes (page 221).

Spill the Tea!

Herbs and Flowers for Botanical Teas (Tisanes)

I take pride in the process of growing, harvesting, drying, and enjoying my own tea herbs. A tea garden not on your bucket list? No problem: Many herbs for tisanes can be found in stores and online.

The formulas that follow are for a single 8-ounce serving, but you can use 6 to 10 ounces of boiling water based on your preferred strength. I like a robust tea, and the measurements reflect that. Experiment to find the perfect ratio for your taste buds. Crush or grind ingredients to get stronger, more flavorful extractions. Steeping times are a general guide. The longer they steep, the more flavorful the infusion will be. Tea that cools while steeping can be reheated before enjoying. To steep for hot infusions, water should be boiling.

IMPORTANT: The benefit information provided with each herb is for educational purposes only and should not be considered as an endorsement or recommendation of any medical treatment. Some herbs can interfere with medications and complicate health issues. People on medications, those with asthma or plant allergies, children under age 12, or pregnant or nursing women, should all consult a doctor before using tisanes.

Also see the charts of Culinary Herbs (page 90) and Edible Flowers (page 99) for additional tisane options not listed below.

Anise hyssop (*Agastache foeniculum*)

Profile Sweet, licorice-scented leaves and flowers used to decorate baked goods, infuse honey, liquor, or syrup. Makes a soothing tea with a minty, slightly bitter, flavor. Best when used fresh.

Benefits May reduce fever, coughing, and headache pain. Natural sleep aid.

Preparation 1 tablespoon fresh leaves and flowers or 2 to 3 teaspoons dried. Cover, steep for 15 minutes, and strain.

Bee balm/bergamot/Oswego tea (*Monarda*)

Profile Red blooms make the prettiest tea!

Benefits Good source of vitamins A and C. Calming. Supports digestive and respiratory health.

Preparation Try a cold infusion (page 170) or brew with 5 to 6 fresh or dried leaves or 5 to 6 flower petals. Cover, steep for 15 minutes, and strain.

Blueberry (*Vaccinium spp.*)

Profile A light and refreshing tea with a rich flavor made using the tender young leaves.

Benefits Revitalizing and packed with antioxidants.

Preparation 1 tablespoon crushed, dried blueberry leaves with 1 dried citrus slice. If desired, add 2 to 3 berries to flavor and color your tea. Cover, steep for 10 to 15 minutes, and strain.

Butterfly pea flower (*Clitoria ternatea*)

Profile A vibrant blue tea with a fresh, floral, earthy flavor, also known as blue pea tea. A good herb for tea blends. Enjoy hot or cold. Blue pea tea mixed with lemonade is delish! For a hot tea, try pairing with lemongrass and honey. Add a slice of a lemon and watch the blue color turn to pink. Magical tea! Dried flowers make a vibrant powder that can be used in a variety of culinary applications.

Benefits Rich in antioxidants, such as anthocyanins, which give the flowers the bright blue hue.

Preparation 1 teaspoon dried flowers for a dark blue, or ½ teaspoon for a lighter blue. Adjust these amounts to achieve less or more color. Cover and steep for at least 10 minutes. The longer it infuses, the darker the color. Strain.

Chamomile, German (*Matricaria chamomilla*) and **Chamomile, Roman** (*Chamaemelum nobile*)

Profile Tiny white or yellow daisy-like flower. Fragrant with a sweet earthy, apple flavor. Try a cold infusion (page 170) to reap all the medicinal benefits this little cutie has to offer. Also delightful in a honey infusion (see page 213).

Benefits Aids with sleep, calming, good for digestion. High in antioxidants.

Preparation ¼ cup fresh flowers or 1 tablespoon dried. Cover, steep for 10 to 15 minutes, and strain.

Coneflower (*Echinacea*)

Profile Strong floral, earthy taste that is best when combined with other bold-tasting herbs like mint. **NOTE**: Due to the medicinal properties in echinacea, drinking the tea can cause your tongue to tingle. This is perfectly normal.

Benefits Immunity booster and pain reliever. Soothes a sore throat and cough. Antioxidant and anti-inflammatory properties. Improves skin health.

Preparation ¼ cup chopped fresh leaves, flowers, or roots, or a combination of all three, or 1 to 2 tablespoons dried. Cover, steep for 30 minutes, and strain. Reheat. Sweeten with honey to improve flavor.

Elderberries (*Sambucus nigra*)

Profile Naturally sweet, small black berries that must be cooked before eating. These tiny berries pack a health punch and are used to make syrup (see page 231) and jelly candies (see page 331).

IMPORTANT: The stems, leaves, and unripe (red or green) berries are all toxic and should be removed before consuming.

Benefits A natural immune booster. High levels of vitamins A and C. Rich in antioxidants and flavonoids.

Preparation Bring 2 cups water, 2 tablespoons dried elderberries, ¼ teaspoon ground cinnamon, and ¼ teaspoon ground turmeric to a boil over high heat. Turn the heat down to medium-low and simmer for 15 minutes to reduce the liquid by half. Remove from the heat. Cover and steep for 10 to 15 minutes. Strain and sweeten with honey. For tea from Elderberry Syrup (page 231), add 1 to 2 tablespoons syrup to boiling water. No need to sweeten; the syrup has you covered!

Elderflower (*Sambucus nigra*)

Profile These delicate, tiny white clusters of flowers make a lovely cup of tea, hot or cold. Notes of honey and citrus and hints of floral. They're also wonderful in simple syrup (see simple syrup soak, page 116) and honey infusions (see page 213). Fresh flowers have a light flavor but can be hard on your stomach. Dried blooms are full of flavor and can be stored to use year round!

IMPORTANT: The stems, leaves, and unripe (red or green) berries are all toxic and should be avoided.

Benefits Natural immune booster. May reduce cough and sooth a sore throat. Calming. High levels of vitamins A and C. Rich in antioxidants and flavonoids.

Preparation ¼ cup fresh elderflowers or 1 tablespoon dried elderflowers. Cover, steep for 15 minutes, and strain.

Goldenrod (*Solidago canadensis*)

Profile Goldenrod has a mildly sweet, anise-like flavor with an earthy aftertaste. The blooms make a light golden tea, but the flavorful leaves can also be used. Pairs nicely with mint and ginger.

Benefits May reduce pain, swelling, muscle cramps, and joint pains. High in antioxidants and flavonoids.

Preparation 2 to 3 tablespoons leaves and new blossoms or 1 tablespoon dried. Cover, steep for 10 to 15 minutes, and strain.

Hawthorn (*Crataegus*)

Profile Fresh berries result in a red, sweet, tangy, and tart tea with a floral vibe. Dried berries have a slight pink hue and a pleasant subtle berry flavor. I don't even sweeten mine!

Benefits Rich in antioxidants. Supports heart health. May reduce anxiety and boost relaxation.

Preparation 1 tablespoon fresh, crushed berries, or 2 teaspoons smashed dried berries. Bring the water and smashed berries to a boil, turn the heat down, and simmer for 15 minutes. Remove from the heat, cover, and infuse for 10 minutes. Strain.

Hibiscus (*Hibiscus sabdariffa*)

Profile Edible varieties include roselle and cranberry hibiscus. Color ranges from ruby red to purple or pink with a cranberry-like flavor. The edible parts of the plant are the flowers, leaves, and fruit calyxes. Makes a pretty pink to red tea, delicious hot or cold.

IMPORTANT: Use in moderation, as it may cause headaches.

Benefits May support heart, liver, and kidney health and aid in weight loss.

Preparation Cold infusion (page 170) or brew with 1 tablespoon dried petals. Steep for 15 to 20 minutes. Strain and reheat if needed.

Holy basil/tulsi (*Ocimum tenuiflorum*)

Profile The leaves of this sacred, ancient herb have a sweet fragrance with flavor notes of mint and cloves. A delicious tea packed with zen.

Benefits Highly regarded adaptogenic herb that can reduce anxiety, boost mental health, and replenish energy.

Preparation Cold infusion (page 170) or brew 10 fresh leaves, or 1 tablespoon dried. Cover, steep for 15 to 20 minutes, and strain.

Jasmine (*Jasminum sambac, Jasminum officinale*)

Profile White blooms with a strong, sweet scent. A delightful tea.

Benefits Immune system booster. Detoxifier, high in antioxidants, and calming.

IMPORTANT: Not all jasmine are edible. True jasmine produces white, waxy flowers and leaves that are oval and shiny. False jasmine, also known as jessamine or yellow jasmine, woodbine, trumpet flower, and Carolina jasmine, are not related to jasmine and are all toxic.

Preparation 1 tablespoon fresh flowers, or 2 to 3 teaspoons dried. Cover, steep for 5 to 10 minutes, and strain. Or use the perfuming method (see page 171).

Juniper berries (*Juniperus*)

Profile The citrus-pine flavor and scent can be both sweet and spicy.

Benefits High in antioxidants. Anti-inflammatory.

Preparation 1 tablespoon fresh, crushed berries, or 2 teaspoons smashed dried berries. Bring water and smashed berries to a boil, turn the heat down, and simmer for 15 minutes. Remove from the heat, cover, and steep for 15 minutes. Strain. Reheat if needed.

Lemon balm (*Melissa officinalis*)

Profile Earthy, lemon-flavored leaves pair nicely with other tea herbs needing a hint of citrus. For the most medicinal benefit, try a cold infusion (see page 170).

Benefits Calming. Natural sleep aid. Supports brain, heart, digestive, and respiratory health.

Preparation Cold infusion (see page 170) or brew 5 to 6 torn fresh leaves, or 1 tablespoon dried. Cover, steep for 10 to 15 minutes, and strain.

Lemon verbena (*Aloysia citriodora* or *Lippia citriodora*)

Profile Slightly sweet, earthy-flavored leaves with a hint of lemon. Very aromatic plant makes a surprising mild tea. Also delightful in infusions, both savory and sweet (see chapters 8 and 9).

Benefits Rich in antioxidants and anti-inflammatory compounds. Natural sleep aid.

Preparation 3 to 4 torn fresh leaves, or 2 teaspoons dried. Cover, steep for 10 to 15 minutes, and strain.

Lemongrass (*Cymbopogon*)

Profile This earthy, lemon-flavored grassy herb makes a citrus-flavored herbal tea.

Benefits Rich in antioxidants. Antimicrobial and anti-inflammatory properties.

Preparation Bring 2 cups water to a boil over high heat. Stir in 1½ cups chopped fresh lemongrass. Cover, turn the heat down to medium, and boil for 10 to 15 minutes. The longer it cooks, the deeper the flavor. Strain.

Mint (*Menta*), various

Profile Distinctive sweet mint flavor that varies depending on variety. Often combined with bitter herbs to enhance the flavor of the tea.

Benefits Revitalizing and refreshing. Peppermint helps ease a head cold. Fights bacteria. Aids in oral and sinus health.

Preparation Cold infusion (see page 170) or brew 4 to 5 torn fresh leaves, or 2 to 3 teaspoons dried. Cover, steep for 10 to 15 minutes, and strain.

Raspberry (*Rubus idaeus*)

Profile Tastes like homemade Earl Grey tea! Harvest tender young leaves.

Benefits Rich in antioxidants. May reduce symptoms of PMS.

IMPORTANT: May induce labor for pregnant women.

Preparation 5 to 6 torn fresh leaves (or 2 to 3 teaspoons dried) and 1 dried orange slice. If desired, add 2 to 3 berries to color and flavor to your tea. Cover, steep for 10 to 15 minutes, and strain.

Red clover (*Trifolium pratense*)

Profile You likely have these "weeds" growing in your yard. Fresh blooms have a sweet and subtle, grassy flavor with hints of vanilla. Dried flowers have a sweet floral taste. Leaves can also be used for tea, fresh or dried. Fresh blooms make a pretty, pink tea.

Benefits Antioxidant. Rich in flavonoids, vitamins, and minerals. Detoxifying.

Preparation 2 to 3 teaspoons fresh or dried flowers. Cover, steep for 10 to 15 minutes, and strain.

Strawberry (*Fragaria × ananassa*)

Profile Young, tender strawberry leaves have a delightful subtle taste with a sweet aroma.

Benefits Loaded with antioxidants. Antibacterial, antifungal, astringent, and antimicrobial properties. Mild diuretic effect.

Preparation 1 tablespoon crushed dried leaves. If desired, add 2 to 3 berries to color and flavor your tea. Cover, steep for 10 minutes, and strain.

Wild violets (*Viola odorata*)

Profile Pretty tea! A bluish-purple tea that can turn pink by adding a little lemon juice. Delicately floral and fruity, earthy flavor. The flowers and young leaves are edible and used for tea. Use these sweet blooms for infusions like sugar, syrup, and honey (see chapter 9).

Benefits Rich in antioxidants. Source of vitamins A and C. Anti-inflammatory properties. Respiratory aid, helping to reduce coughs. Immune system boost. Supports heart and skin health.

Preparation Cold infusion (see page 170) or brew 1 tablespoon fresh leaves and flowers, or 3 teaspoons dried. Cover, steep for 10 to 15 minutes, and strain.

Fruits and Flowers Tea Blend

This blend uses dehydrated fruits and dried edible flowers to make a sweet and floral tea that's perfect for a tea party. Sweeten to taste as needed.

MAKES ABOUT 4½ CUPS TEA BLEND

½ cup dried strawberries

5 to 6 dried orange slices, peel and pith removed

8 to 10 dried apples slices

1 cup dried lemon balm or lemon verbena

½ cup dried rose petals

½ cup dried chamomile flowers

½ cup dried lavender buds

1 cup hot water per serving

1 · Using kitchen shears, snip the dried strawberries, orange slices, and apple slices into small pieces. Put the fruits in a medium bowl and add the lemon balm, rose petals, chamomile, and lavender and combine. Transfer to an airtight jar.

2 · To brew one serving, spoon 1 tablespoon of the tea blend in a tea infuser, tea bag, or tea ball. Put in a mug, pour in the hot water, cover, and steep for 10 minutes. Remove the infuser and serve hot.

Mediterranean Vibes Tea Blend

Let this blend made with warm herbs take you on a trip to the Mediterranean between doing loads of laundry. (Almost like being there!) Sweeten with an Infused Honey (page 213) or your preferred sweetener.

MAKES 1 SERVING

2 teaspoons dried mint

½ teaspoon dried oregano

¼ teaspoon dried rosemary

1 cup hot water

1 dried lemon slice (optional)

Put the mint, oregano, and rosemary in a tea infuser, reusable tea bag, or tea ball. Place in a mug and add the hot water. Steep for 5 minutes. Remove the infuser and add the lemon slice, if using. Serve hot.

Water Infusions

Floral Teas

Use your favorite botanical water to create your own floral teas. Serve hot or iced (see Variations below).

MAKES 1 SERVING

1 cup Botanical Water (page 165)

Flavorings:

- 2 dried lemon, lime, or orange slices, snipped with kitchen shears
- 2 to 3 dried apple rings, pear slices, or strawberries, snipped with kitchen shears
- 1 to 2 teaspoons dried tea herbs, such as lavender, mint, oregano, raspberry leaves, or wild violet
- Spices, such as cinnamon stick or star anise, broken up, or ½ vanilla bean, split lengthwise

1 tea bag of your favorite black or green tea

1 to 2 teaspoons sweetener, such as Infused Sugar (see page 216) or Infused Honey (page 213), sugar honey, or sugar alternative

Bring the Botanical Water to a boil in a small saucepan over high heat. Add your desired flavorings and the tea bag, and cover. Steep for 10 minutes. Strain, stir in the sweetener, and serve. Reheat, if desired.

VARIATIONS

Rose-Vanilla Tea: Use rose flower water, ½ vanilla bean, and 1 black tea bag.

Apple Spice Tea: Use chamomile flower water, 2 dried apple rings, 1 star anise, and 2 cloves, and 1 green tea bag.

Floral Iced Tea: Cool the brewed tea. Transfer to a covered container and refrigerate until chilled, at least 1 to 2 hours, or longer. Pour into an ice-filled glass and sweeten as desired.

Hibiscus Berry Tea

This beautiful red pitcher of sweet tea can be enjoyed both hot and on ice. If you're like me and don't grow your own red hibiscus flowers, you can purchase them dried from many grocery stores and online.

MAKES 8 SERVINGS

2 quarts water

2 cups fresh or frozen raspberries

1 orange, cut into ½-inch rounds

1 cup dried hibiscus flowers

6 to 8 fresh mint leaves, torn

3 tablespoons fresh lime juice

¼ to ½ cup honey, agave nectar, or maple syrup (optional)

For iced tea: Ice cubes (preferably Colorful Fruit Ice Cubes, page 169), fresh mint sprigs, and lime slices

1 · Combine the water, raspberries, and orange slices in a large saucepan and bring to a boil over high heat. Stir in the hibiscus flowers and mint. Remove from the heat and steep for 1 to 2 hours or more—the longer the stronger the flavor.

2 · Strain through a fine-mesh strainer into a pitcher, pressing hard on the solids. Discard the solids. Add the lime juice and sweetener (if using), adjusting the amount to reach the desired sweetness. Transfer to an airtight container and serve right away or refrigerate for up to 1 week.

3 · To serve, fill a glass with ice cubes and pour in the cooled brewed tea. Garnish with a mint sprig and a lime slice. For hot tea, reheat the desired amount of brewed tea in a small saucepan or microwave oven.

Rose Tea Latte

Use the rose petal version of Floral Teas (page 178) to create this warm and comforting tea. Kick it up a notch by adding herb or floral infused honey to sweeten. This recipe can also be made using other flower waters or teas, or black tea instead of green, if that's your preference. Make it your own special blend.

MAKES 1 SERVING

1 cup water

1 green tea bag, such as jasmine green tea (use store-bought or perfume your own—see page 171)

2 teaspoons Floral- or Herb-Infused Honey (see page 213)

2 tablespoons Botanical Water (page 165) made with rose petals

½ cup milk

Dried rose petals, for garnish (optional)

1 · Bring the water to a boil in a small saucepan over high heat. Remove from the heat and add the tea bag. Let the tea steep for 5 minutes. Remove the tea bag and stir in the honey and Botanical Water.

2 · Meanwhile, warm the milk in another small saucepan over medium heat, or heat in the microwave. Pour into the tea and stir to combine. Transfer the latte to a large mug and top with a few dried rose petals (if using).

Herbal Whipped Cream

MAKES ABOUT 1 CUP

1 cup heavy cream

2 tablespoons chopped fresh herbs or 1 herbal tea bag

2 tablespoons sugar

½ teaspoon vanilla extract

Garden and tea herbs can be used to elevate your whipped toppings. A mint or lavender whipped cream on strawberry shortcake or a fruit salad is delightful. Try steeping loose leaf tea herbs or even your favorite tea bag to create even more flavor options.

In an airtight container, infuse the cream and herbs (or tea bag) in the refrigerator for 12 to 24 hours. Strain if using loose leaf herbs. Squeeze the herbs or tea bag to release as much flavor as possible. Place the cold cream in a chilled mixing bowl. Add the sugar and vanilla. Beat with an electric mixer on medium speed until soft peaks form.

VARIATION

Spice it up! Add ¼ teaspoon ground cinnamon, ginger, or nutmeg before beating together.

CHAPTER 8

Savory Infusions

185
Infused Vinegars

186
Infused Vinegars Mix-and-Match Menu

187
Infused Vinegars Recipes
Herb Garden Vinegar 187
Wild Violet Vinegar 187
Spiced Blackberry Vinegar 188
Raspberry Vinegar 189

190
Infused Oils

191
Infused Oil Flavoring Menu

193
Infused Oil Recipes
Infused Olive Oil 193
Rosemary Peppercorn Infused Olive Oil 193
Herbes de Provence Dipping Oil 195
Mediterranean Dipping Oil 195
Cheesy Tomato Dipping Oil 195

196
Marinades

196
Marinade Recipes
Garlic and Herb Marinade 196
Jerk Vibes Marinade 197
Lemon Lilac Marinade 197

198
Infusing Butter and Salt

198
Compound Butters

199
Compound Butter Mix-and-Match Menu

201
Compound Butter Recipes

Garden Butter Log 201
Holiday Butter Balls 203
Homestyle Butter 203

205
Infused Salts

205
Infused Salt Flavoring Menu

207
Infused Salt Recipes

Oregano Salt 207
Calendula and Thyme Finishing Salt 208
Spicy Finishing Salt 209
Botanical Bath Salts 209

Infused Vinegars

Vinegar infusions go back thousands of years. Ancient civilizations used them for culinary and medicinal uses, and even to make perfume. Infused vinegars capture the flavors of fruits, flowers, herbs, and spices, elevating your dishes and medicine cabinet, and allowing you to enjoy the seasons, year round. Use the journal pages at the end of the book to write down your favorite flavor combinations and recipes you create.

Methods and Tools

There are two ways I like to infuse vinegar. The hot method is best for extracting flavors from robust herbs (such as rosemary) as well as fruits and berries. The cold method is ideal for more fragile herbs like basil and edible flowers but can be used to infuse the stronger herbs as well. No matter which method you choose, the ratio is two parts vinegar to one part infusing ingredients.

One to two hours before using, rinse your fresh botanicals (herbs, edible flowers, fruits), pat dry, and air dry on towels. Place the infusing ingredients in a clean jar, filling halfway. Canning or clamp-style jars work great for infused vinegars because they are sealed with rubber. For nonmetallic lids, cork, plastic screw-on caps, or two-piece canning lids all work. If you use an uncoated metal lid, place parchment paper or a paper coffee filter over the jar mouth before closing the lid. I like reusing my store-bought glass vinegar jars. They usually come in pretty shapes and with a plastic cap (and often a pour filter).

- *Cold method* Use room-temperature vinegar to cover the infusing ingredients, leaving at least ½-inch headspace.

- *Hot method* Heat the vinegar in a nonreactive (see page 65) pot to almost boiling, 190° to 195°F. Pour over the infusing ingredients, leaving at least ½-inch headspace.

- *For both methods* Wipe the rim and twist on a nonmetallic lid, then label and date. Place in a dark, cool, and dry place for 2 to 4 weeks. A few times each day (or whenever you remember), roll the jar back and forth to mix the infusion. Taste for flavor after 2 weeks and continue to infuse as needed. The longer it infuses, the deeper the flavor. When you are satisfied with the infusion, strain through a fine-mesh strainer, cheesecloth, or paper coffee filter.

Vinegar

Any vinegar with 5% acidity or higher can be infused. The acidity percentage is usually listed on the label, although you may have to do some googling to research vinegars made outside the United States. Mild, light-flavored vinegar lets the flavors really come through. Use the following flavor profile list as a guide.

Apple cider vinegar Inexpensive, light, and versatile. Delightful paired with orchard fruits (apples and pears) or root vegetables (carrots, turnips, and radishes).

Balsamic vinegar Strong, sweet taste. Pairs well with bold flavors like berries or rosemary. Not ideal for lighter flavor additions, such as flowers. White balsamic is ideal because it won't mask the food's color.

Champagne vinegar A sweet, light vinegar that pairs well with fruit and botanicals. An excellent option for infusions, but it can be expensive.

Distilled white vinegar Inexpensive and sharp in flavor and odor. Can be used with herbs and flowers and will have a more intense flavor.

White/red wine vinegar Affordable and mild. An ideal choice for vinegar infusions. For herbs, fruits, and botanicals that bleed color, use white wine vinegar.

Infused Vinegars Mix-and-Match Menu

Vinegar can be steeped with fresh herbs and other botanicals. The choices are many, including the sturdy stems of lavender, oregano, parsley, and woody chive stalks. Cut or smash fruit before infusing to help release the flavors.

Storage

Strained infused vinegar can be safely stored in a cool, dark location. Herb-infused vinegar is best used within several months but can last a few years! Fruit-infused vinegar is best enjoyed within 3 months. For a longer shelf life, store in the refrigerator and use within 6 to 8 months. Discard vinegar if it is bubbly, cloudy, fizzy, moldy, or slimy, or if it smells or tastes foul.

Edible Flowers	Fruits and Vegetables	Herbs	Spices
Borage	Apple slices or peels	Basil	Chiles
Chive blossoms	Berries	Chive stems	Cinnamon sticks
Lavender	Citrus peels	Lemon verbena	Cloves
Lilacs	Melons	Parsley	Fennel seeds
Nasturtium	Peaches	Sage	Ginger
Violas/pansies	Pears	Tarragon	Lavender stems
Wild violets	Pineapples	Thyme	Peppercorns

Herb Garden Vinegar

I make this every season to capture the flavors of my own herb garden in a bottle. What makes this recipe unique is that it doesn't require specific measurements or ingredients—choose whatever herbs you grow and the flavors you like best. Want it infused with color? Add violas, purple basil, or dark-colored pansies. Feel free to use scraps for this, too! I use the discarded parsley stems when I'm drying parsley. Zero waste!

MAKES 2 CUPS

1 cup fresh herbs and/or edible flowers

2 cups white wine vinegar (5% acidity)

1 · Pack the herbs into a clean jar until half filled. Pour in the vinegar. Twist on a nonmetallic lid. Steep in a cool, dark place for 2 to 4 weeks.

2 · Strain through a fine-mesh strainer set over a bowl. Pour the strained vinegar into a clean glass jar or bottle with a tight-fitting nonmetallic lid. Label, date, and store in a cool, dark place.

Wild Violet Vinegar

This hot pink infusion with white wine or apple cider vinegar is delicious. I like to use the white wine vinegar version in my Wild Violet Peppercorn Vinaigrette (page 281). It's also delicious drizzled over grilled veggies, rice, and pasta.

MAKES ABOUT 2 CUPS

1 cup packed fresh wild violets, rinsed and air-dried

2 cups white wine vinegar or apple cider vinegar (5% acidity)

1 · Pack the violets into a clean glass jar until half filled. Pour in the vinegar, leaving ½-inch headspace. Cover with a nonmetallic lid. Steep in a cool, dark place for 2 to 4 weeks.

2 · Pour the vinegar through a fine-mesh strainer lined with cheesecloth or a paper coffee filter set over a bowl. Pour the strained vinegar into a clean glass jar or bottle with a tight-fitting nonmetallic lid. Label and date. Store in a cool, dark place.

VARIATIONS

Purple Basil Vinegar: Substitute purple basil leaves for the violets and use white wine vinegar.

Chive Blossom Vinegar: Substitute chive blossoms for the violets and use white wine vinegar.

Lavender Vinegar: Substitute lavender buds for the violets and use apple cider vinegar.

Rose Vinegar: Substitute rose petals for the violets and use white wine vinegar or apple cider vinegar.

Savory Infusions

Spiced Blackberry Vinegar

The sweet blackberry flavor of summer teams up with the mulled spices of fall to create a delicious combination that can be enjoyed year round. Here I use the boiling water canning method to extend the shelf life to 1 year. Use only fresh berries.

MAKES 3 PINTS

4 cups fresh blackberries

4 cups apple cider vinegar (5% acidity)

2 (3-inch) cinnamon sticks

1 tablespoon whole cloves

1 tablespoon allspice berries

1 · Using a potato masher or large fork, lightly crush the blackberries with 1 cup of the vinegar in a large nonreactive bowl. Stir in the remaining 3 cups of vinegar, the cinnamon, cloves, and allspice. Cover with plastic wrap. Keep in a cool, dark place and infuse, stirring every day, for 4 weeks.

2 · Strain the mixture through a fine-mesh strainer lined with cheesecloth or a jelly bag into a nonreactive medium saucepan, pressing hard on the solids.

3 · Prepare the pint jars, lids, and boiling water canner (see page 66). Leave the canning rack raised above the water.

4 · Bring the strained vinegar to a simmer (180°F) over medium heat. One at a time, fill each jar with the hot vinegar, leaving ¼-inch headspace. Wipe the rim clean, center the lid, and adjust the band. Put the filled jar in the raised rack inside the canner.

5 · Lower the jars on the rack into the pot, making sure that the simmering water covers the jars by 1 inch. Add additional hot water as needed. Cover and bring the water to a rolling boil over high heat. Set a timer and process for 10 minutes (see page 67 for high-altitude adjustments). Remember that timing does not start until the water comes to a full boil. Raise the canning rack above the water and let the jars stand for 5 minutes. Transfer the jars to a kitchen towel and cool, undisturbed, for 12 to 24 hours. Store in a cool, dark place. For best flavor, use within 1 year.

Raspberry Vinegar

Try this with blueberries or blackberries. You can even add fresh herbs to customize the flavors even further. If you're using frozen raspberries, thaw and drain. Amounts can be doubled or tripled if you want to scale up and make a big batch, using the two-to-one vinegar-to-ingredient ratio.

MAKES ABOUT 2 CUPS

2 cups white wine vinegar or distilled white vinegar (5% acidity)

1 cup fresh or frozen raspberries

5 to 6 fresh raspberries (optional, for garnish)

1 · Bring the vinegar and raspberries to a boil in a nonreactive medium saucepan over high heat. Turn the heat down to medium-low and simmer until the raspberries are tender, about 5 minutes. Remove from the heat and cool.

2 · Strain through a fine-mesh strainer set over a bowl. Transfer to a clean glass jar or bottle with a tight-fitting nonmetallic lid. Label, date, and store in a cool, dark spot for 3 weeks.

3 · After 3 weeks, pour the infused vinegar through a coffee filter or cheesecloth-lined strainer into a clean glass jar or bottle with a tight-fitting nonmetallic lid. Store in a cool, dark place. Strained and stored at room temperature, it's best used within 3 months, or 6 to 8 months in the refrigerator. If you choose to add fresh berries to the bottle as a garnish, store the vinegar in the refrigerator.

ZERO WASTE ALERT!
Use the leftover mash to make Raspberry Basil Vinaigrette (page 281).

Infused Oils

I've turned boring dinners into flavored adventures using infused oils. Roasted potatoes drizzled in rosemary oil. Steak rubbed with an herb-infused oil before grilling. Or used infused oils to make vinaigrettes and marinades. They are also an important ingredient in several homemade beauty products. When making infused oils, no measurements are needed! You can customize to fit your needs. Use less infusion ingredients for pungent flavors like rosemary, lavender, and spices.

Methods and Tools

- Use only dried plant materials. Fresh plants can introduce moisture, which can cause botulism. If starting with fresh herbs, rinse and allow them to air-dry for several days. They should be completely free of moisture before infusing with oil.

- Dark, sterilized glass jars with tight-fitting nonmetallic lids should be used for infusing the oil. Exposure to light compromises the shelf life of the oil, so if you use a clear jar keep the oil in a dark cupboard.

- You'll need a stainless steel double boiler (for heat infusion) and a fine-mesh strainer lined with cheesecloth or paper coffee filters for straining. A wooden spoon or chopstick will help stir the ingredients. A bowl with a pour spout and a funnel may also come in handy. All equipment should be sterilized in boiling water and dried before use.

- Olive oil and canola oil contain fewer polyunsaturated fatty acids than many other vegetable oils and will turn rancid less quickly. Choose a light, extra-light, or mild olive oil rather than extra-virgin. Other options are avocado oil, sunflower oil, and grapeseed oil.

There are two methods for infusing oil:

Long (warm) method This is my favorite method for infusing oil. Although called a warm infusion, the method doesn't use any heat at all. Oils made with this method have a longer shelf life than those made with the heat method.

- Place clean, lightly crushed, dried plant material in a dry, sterilized bottle or jar with a tight-fitting lid, until one-fourth to halfway full.

- Cover with at least 1 inch of room-temperature oil. Using a sterilized dry wooden spoon or chopstick, mix thoroughly until coated with the oil, making sure there aren't any air bubbles. Seal the container.

- Infuse in a cool dark place away from direct sunlight (a cupboard is ideal) for 2 to 4 weeks. Taste after 2 weeks. If it's flavorful enough, continue to the next step. If not, infuse for longer. Once the infusion is fully flavored, it's ready to use.

- You can strain the dried herbs and spices out or leave them in. Removing them will extend shelf life. Also keep in mind that if the flavor ingredients are left in, the oil will continue to infuse.

Quick (heat) method With convenience comes sacrifice. This quick method produces less flavorful oil.

- Set up a double boiler (or one pot sitting snugly on top of another). Add water to the bottom pot until it is one-fourth or half-filled. Bring to a simmer.

- Place the dry ingredients and oil in the top pot of the double boiler and gently stir with a sterilized dry wooden spoon to combine. Place the pot over the simmering water, making sure that the bottom of the pot does not touch the water; be careful not to splash water into the oil.

- Gently warm the oil over medium-low heat, without cooking it, until fragrant, 5 to 8 minutes. Be careful not to overheat. Remove from the heat and let steep while cooling. Once cooled, strain the oil into a new sterilized jar, wipe the rim, and close the lid.

Infused Oil Flavoring Menu

Flavorings for oil are plentiful. The list below outlines just a few. Feel free to use single herbs, flowers, and spices, or create a combination. Remember to use only fully dried ingredients.

Storage

Store the strained, infused oil in a glass bottle (preferably dark) with a tight nonmetallic lid in a cool cupboard, away from direct light or heat. Although infused oil can be stored at room temperature for several weeks to a couple months, they may keep longer if stored in the refrigerator. Keep in mind that chilled oil solidifies, so allow to come to room temperature to liquefy before using. Cold infused oils also last longer than heat infused oils. Actual shelf life can vary depending on the oil, add-ins, and method used. Discard the oil if it is cloudy, the color changes, the consistency becomes thicker or thinner, or it smells foul.

Dried Edible Flowers	Dried Herbs	Spices
Calendula	Basil	Allspice
Citrus blossoms	Bay leaves	Chiles
Pansies	Mint	Cinnamon
Lavender	Oregano	Dried seasonings
Marigold petals	Rosemary	Peppercorns
Nasturtiums	Tarragon	Saffron
Rose petals	Thyme	Star anise

Herb Infused Olive Oil

This infused oil is wonderful on pasta, chicken, bread, grilled vegetables, sandwiches, pizza, and more!

MAKES 1 CUP

1 cup light, extra-light, or mild olive oil

3 to 4 dried bay leaves

3 to 4 dried thyme sprigs

1 tablespoon dried oregano leaves

¼ teaspoon red pepper flakes

1 · Infuse the oil, bay leaves, thyme sprigs, oregano, and red pepper flakes according to the warm method (page 190) or heat method (page 190).

2 · Line a fine-mesh strainer with cheesecloth or a paper coffee filter and set over a bowl or pitcher. Pour in the oil, let it drain, and discard the solids. Decant the oil into a dry, sterilized dark-colored jar or bottle and cover with a nonmetallic lid, dropper top, or cap top. Store in a cool, dark cupboard, or refrigerate for longer storage.

Rosemary Peppercorn Infused Olive Oil

Drizzle over steaks before grilling or on potatoes before roasting.

MAKES 1 CUP

1 cup light, extra-light, or mild olive oil

2 to 3 dried rosemary sprigs

1 tablespoon black peppercorns

1 · Infuse the oil, rosemary, and peppercorns according to the warm method (page 190) or heat method (page 190).

2 · Line a fine-mesh strainer with cheesecloth or a paper coffee filter and set over a bowl or pitcher. Pour in the oil, let it drain, and discard the solids. Decant the oil into a dry, sterilized dark-colored jar or bottle and cover with a nonmetallic lid, dropper top, or cap top. Store in a cool, dark cupboard, or refrigerate for longer storage.

Dipping Oils

Dipping oils always remind me of fancy restaurants on date night. Not gonna lie, I get a little excited when that fresh bread and dipping oil arrives at our table. But these flavored creations can go beyond dipping and can be used in any recipe that calls for oil. We enjoy them on grilled meats and veggies or drizzled over rice and pasta. Dipping oils are easy and require only about 30 minutes of infusing time.

Method and Tools

- Since the oil is the star here, be sure to use a quality oil. Olive oil is the most popular base for dipping oil because of its rounded, full flavor. Use a moderately priced olive oil that has lots of character.
- Because we are using dipping oils right away, fresh herbs can be used, adding both color and deep flavor. Mix finely minced herbs of choice (or one of the homemade dried seasoning blends from chapter 4) with the oil in a shallow bowl and let stand while the flavors bloom and mingle, about 30 minutes. If using garlic, remove before serving.

Storage

These oils are meant to be enjoyed immediately. But if you happen to have some left over, it can be refrigerated for a couple days and brought to room temperature before reusing.

Herbes de Provence Dipping Oil

MAKES ½ CUP

½ cup olive oil

1 tablespoon balsamic vinegar

2 teaspoons Herbes de Provence Seasoning Blend (page 109)

Combine the olive oil, vinegar, and the seasoning blend in a small, shallow bowl. Serve right away.

Mediterranean Dipping Oil

MAKES ½ CUP

½ cup olive oil

1 garlic clove, minced

1 teaspoon Greek Seasoning Blend (page 109)

1 tablespoon finely chopped fresh parsley

½ teaspoon flaky sea salt, such as Maldon

¼ teaspoon red pepper flakes

Combine the oilve oil, garlic, seasoning blend, parlsey, salt, and pepper flakes in a small, shallow bowl. Serve right away.

Cheesy Tomato Dipping Oil

MAKES ½ CUP

½ cup olive oil

¼ cup dehydrated tomatoes (see page 128), cut into small pieces

2 garlic cloves, minced

2 tablespoons freshly grated Parmesan cheese

1 tablespoon chopped fresh parsley

1 tablespoon chopped fresh basil

½ teaspoon red pepper flakes

Herb salt (see page 205) or kosher salt and freshly ground black pepper

Combine the olive oil, tomatoes, garlic, cheese, parsley, basil, and red pepper flakes in a small, shallow bowl. Season with salt and black pepper to taste. Serve right away.

Savory Infusions

Marinades

Marinades are a wonderful way to use infused honey, vinegar, oil, and salt to create flavorful meat and vegetables. Here are a few of my favorite marinades, which can be doubled or tripled if you're cooking for a crowd.

Method and Tools

Because marinades usually contain acidic ingredients that will react with metal, use a glass bowl or shallow baking dish, or a plastic resealable bag instead. Coat whatever you wish to marinate on all sides and cover. Turn the food once or twice while marinating. Refrigerate for at least 30 minutes, but use the following guidelines for maximum flavor:

- Meat (beef, pork, lamb) up to 24 hours
- Poultry up to 8 hours
- Vegetables up to 4 hours
- Seafood up to 2 hours

Storage

You can freeze meat or poultry with a marinade (seafood and vegetables are too delicate for this). Put the food and marinade in a 1-gallon freezer-safe bag. Remove as much air from the bag as possible. Label, date, seal, and freeze for up to 3 months. Thaw in the refrigerator for 8 to 12 hours before cooking.

Garlic and Herb Marinade

I often make this ahead of time and freeze. It is flavorful on just about any kind of meat, poultry, or seafood, and especially good for grilling vegetables. This makes enough for about 1 pound of food.

MAKES ABOUT ¼ CUP

½ cup extra-virgin olive oil

2 tablespoons water

3 to 4 garlic cloves, minced

2 tablespoons finely chopped fresh parsley

2 tablespoons finely chopped fresh basil

2 tablespoon fresh lemon juice

2 tablespoons Herb Garden Vinegar (page 187)

1 tablespoon Italian Seasoning Blend (page 110)

1 teaspoon herb salt (see page 205) or kosher salt

¼ teaspoon red pepper flakes

¼ teaspoon freshly ground black pepper

In a medium bowl, whisk together the olive oil, water, garlic, parsley, basil, lemon juice, vinegar, seasoning blend, salt, red pepper flakes, and black pepper.

Jerk Vibes Marinade

I *love* this marinade! It has hints of sweet and spicy and tastes amazing on both chicken and beef. Use to marinate grilled skirt steak. Add more red pepper flakes to turn up the heat.

MAKES ABOUT ¾ CUP

¼ cup extra-virgin olive oil or Herb Infused Olive Oil (page 193)

¼ cup packed light brown sugar

1 tablespoon fresh lime juice

4 teaspoons garlic powder

2 teaspoons dried thyme

2 teaspoons ground allspice

1 teaspoon ground cinnamon

1 teaspoon salt

¼ teaspoon freshly ground black pepper

¼ teaspoon cayenne pepper

In a medium bowl, whisk together the oilve oil, brown sugar, lime juice, garlic powder, thyme, allspice, cinnamon, salt, black pepper, and cayenne pepper until the brown sugar is dissolved.

Lemon Lilac Marinade

This springtime marinade uses lilac-infused honey and is delicious with chicken or fish. Amounts can be doubled or tripled if you're cooking for a crowd.

MAKES ABOUT 1¼ CUPS

½ cup extra-virgin olive oil

4 garlic cloves, minced

¼ cup fresh lemon juice

¼ cup Lilac Honey (page 215)

4 teaspoons lilac- or lavender-infused white vinegar (see page 185), basil-infused white vinegar (see page 185), or Herb Garden Vinegar (page 187)

1 tablespoon dried dill weed

1 teaspoon herb salt (see page 205) or kosher salt

1 teaspoon ground mustard

½ teaspoon freshly ground black pepper

In a medium bowl, whisk together the olive oil, garlic, lemon juice, honey, vinegar, dill weed, salt, ground mustard, and black pepper.

Savory Infusions

Infusing Butter and Salt

The infusions in the earlier sections use liquid as the base, but now it's time to explore the world of solid infusions. Compound butter, the mixing of butter with herbs and edible flowers, has long been used in European kitchens, but I make them into less familiar combinations that are joyful works of art. I also love to mix salt with fragrant and colorful ingredients that transforms into something both beautiful and delicious.

COMPOUND BUTTERS

Compound butter is butter simply compounded with other ingredients. I use herbs, edible flowers, and even fruit to flavor butter. I leave it soft and malleable for immediate use or shape into logs and refrigerate for later. For individual portions, you can cut a hardened log into pats, shape in silicone molds, or roll into balls, just to name a few options.

- Use to make grilled cheese sandwiches or scrambled eggs.
- Add to baked and mashed potatoes, rice, and pasta.
- Melt on top of steak, popcorn, or grilled vegetables.
- Rub on poultry, under and above the skin, before roasting.

Method and Tools

- A bowl, cutting board, knife, parchment paper, plastic wrap, hand mixer (for whipped butter), and silicone molds (for shaped butter) are all you need to pull together a batch of compound butter. You can shape butter into balls with an ordinary melon baller or cookie scoop.

- Butter sticks work best when you're planning to shape into logs or pats. If the butter is not going to be shaped, use sticks or churned-style butter (also called whipped) sold in the tubs. Choose butter that's salted, unsalted, sweet cream, churn-style, whatever you like. Although making homemade butter (see page 203) is simple and special, I often make my creations using store-bought butter because it's friendlier to my budget.

- The method is always the same, no matter the infusing ingredients: Chop most of the fresh, clean, and air-dried herb leaves and edible flowers into small pieces, setting aside some whole blooms, petals, and sprigs for decoration. Using a fork or spoon, mix with softened butter at room temperature. At this point you can leave the butter in a bowl, place into molds, or roll into a log. In all cases, you'll want to refrigerate the butter until firm to make it easier to unmold and to give the flavors time to infuse.

Storage

The storage life of compound butter depends on the add-in ingredients and whether the butter is fresh or homemade (see page 203). Always tightly wrap the butter.

- Herb compound butter can last in the refrigerator for 1 to 2 months.

- Floral butter will last 2 to 3 weeks. I don't recommend freezing floral butter as the flowers may not thaw well.

- Compound butters made with garlic or berries should be used within 5 days.

- Compound butters made with firm homemade butter can be enjoyed for up to 2 weeks.

- Most compound butters and homemade firm butters can be stored in the freezer for up to 6 months.

Compound Butter Mix-and-Match Menu

IMPORTANT: *As with other foods, be sure you are using organically grown edible flowers for your compound butters. Do not eat anything that may have been treated with chemicals. Rinse ingredients well, pat dry with towels, and completely dry before using.*

Herbs	Flower Petals	Extras	Decorations
Chives	Calendula	Berries	Flower petals, whole
Dill	Chive blossoms	Citrus zest	Herb sprigs
Lemon verbena	Dahlia petals	Garlic	Nuts, chopped
Parsley	Snapdragons	Honey	Parsley, chopped
Rosemary	Tulips	Red pepper flakes	Peppercorns
Thyme	Violas/pansies	Tomatoes (dried)	Seeds

Savory Infusions

Garden Butter Log

Sometimes we need to take a step back to just do something creative. Butter is that for me. This recipe is just a guide for your own kitchen creativity, and once you get the feel of it, there will be no measuring, just art!

MAKES 1 BUTTER LOG

6 fresh thyme sprigs

2 fresh rosemary sprigs

4 to 5 fresh chives, finely chopped

12 to 16 whole pansies or violas (more if using violas only)

4 to 5 calendula flowers

2 sticks butter, at room temperature

2 to 4 black peppercorns (optional)

1 · Rinse the herbs and flowers quickly under cool water. Pat dry with a paper towel.

2 · Remove the leaves from 3 of the thyme sprigs and keep the other 3 sprigs whole. Remove the leaves from both rosemary sprigs; chop half and keep separate from the remaining whole leaves. Finely chop the chives. Remove the petals from half the pansies and roughly chop. Remove all the calendula petals and chop half, leaving the remaining petals whole.

3 · Place the butter into a medium bowl. Add the thyme leaves, chopped rosemary, chopped chives, chopped pansies, and chopped calendula. Stir until evenly mixed.

4 · Lay a sheet of parchment paper on a work surface. Spoon the butter mixture onto the edge closest to you. Roll away from you and shape into a log about 6 inches long. Decorate the top and sides with most of the remaining whole rosemary leaves, whole thyme sprigs, pansies, and whole calendula petals, reserving some for the underside. (One favorite design: Calendula petals in a circle with peppercorns, if using, in the center—see photo on page 200.)

5 · Lay a sheet of plastic wrap on the work surface, smoothing out any creases. Move the log onto the bottom edge of the plastic wrap, closest to you, with the decorated side facing down. Decorate the final side with the remaining herbs and flowers. Use the plastic to tightly roll up the log, trying to keep the plastic wrap flat and free of creases. Twist the ends to seal. Oh, isn't it pretty already?! Refrigerate until firm and sliceable, 2 to 4 hours.

6 · To serve, unwrap the chilled butter onto a butter dish or plate. Slice a few rounds of butter to show off and serve.

Holiday Butter Balls

These look so festive served on a platter with Herb and Cheddar Biscuits (page 314). Use a tub of whipped butter instead of sticks. They'll be super quick and easy to make without any waste.

MAKES ABOUT 18 PIECES

Finely chopped fresh herbs (such as thyme or chives), sesame seeds, poppy seeds, and paprika

8-ounce tub cold whipped butter

1 · Line a plate with wax or parchment paper. Put the herbs, seeds, and paprika in individual small bowls or ramekins. Using a 1-tablespoon melon baller or cookie scoop, dip in water, then scoop and shape butter into a ball. Using a fork or spoon, roll in the coating of choice until completely coated and transfer to a plate.

2 · Refrigerate until the balls are firm, 2 to 4 hours. Serve chilled so they hold their shape.

Homestyle Butter

The best part about making this at home is turning heavy cream into butter *and* buttermilk. Another two for one!

MAKES ABOUT 1 CUP

2 cups heavy cream

½ teaspoon kosher salt or herb salt (see page 205; optional)

1 · In a stand mixer fitted with a whisk attachment, whip the cream. (Alternatively, you can use a high-powered blender, but be sure to cover the lid with a towel to minimize splashing.) Process until the cream separates into solid fat and buttermilk, about 10 minutes.

2 · Pour through a fine-mesh strainer set over a bowl. Using the back of a spoon, gently press the solids to release more buttermilk into the bowl. For salted butter, return the butter to the mixer, add the salt, and mix to incorporate. Transfer the butter and buttermilk to separate covered containers and refrigerate for up to 3 days.

3 · For a firm butter with longer storage, place the mass of butter in a large bowl of ice water. Let stand for 1 minute. Lift out of the ice water and transfer to a double layer of cheesecloth. Wrap the butter in the cheesecloth and twist at the top. Wring the butter to squeeze out any remaining liquid. Repeat this process 3 or 4 times. Shape into a log or ball, wrap tightly in plastic wrap, and store in the refrigerator for up to 2 weeks or in the freezer for up to 6 months.

Savory Infusions

Infused Salts

The seasoned salts on my shelves often catch the eye of visitors and those who follow me on social media. Not only do I love to use these salts to bring flavor to just about anything, I enjoy how they double as home decor. Herbs, edible flowers, and coarse salt are all you need. Once you start, you won't be able to stop! These also make beautiful and inexpensive gourmet gifts, and they can even be the base of a luxurious bath salt! Measuring is optional for this simple kitchen craft, but I give a few basic blend measurement suggestions to get you started. Get creative, mixing and matching to make your own custom salt blends.

Method and Tools

- A plate, platter, or shallow bowl, measuring cups, a fork, cheesecloth, and lidded storage container are about all you need to make infused salts.

- A food processor will be needed when using the fresh method, and a fine-mesh strainer may come in handy.

- Sea salt or kosher salt work best for infusing, but any coarse (or even fine) salt can be used. For extra bling, add flake salt or pink Himalayan salt after the infused salt has dried.

- There are two easy ways I like to infuse salt, preserving as much flavor as possible:

Infused Salt Flavoring Menu

FRESH METHOD

Per 1 cup salt:

½ cup fresh herbs

½ cup edible flowers

DRIED METHOD

Per 1 cup salt:

2 to 3 tablespoons dried herbs

¼ cup dried flower petals

1 to 2 teaspoon ground spices or 2 to 4 whole spices (optional)

NOTE

Avoid heating infused salt in the oven or microwave to dry. Valuable oils are lost in the process, resulting in diminished color and flavor.

Fresh Method	Dried Method
Fresh edible flowers (see Note)	Dried edible flowers
Fresh herbs	Dried herbs, ground or crumbled
Fresh citrus zest, grated	Dehydrated citrus or dried peels, ground
Freeze-dried fruit or vegetable powder	Dehydrated fruit or vegetable powder
Red wine (1½ cups boiled until reduced to about 2 tablespoons glaze; cooled)	Dried pepper flakes or dried celery tops
Spices, ground	Spices, ground or whole

Savory Infusions

Fresh method Use fresh but rinsed, patted dry, and thoroughly air-dried ingredients. Process the salt and fresh ingredients in a food processor until the mixture is thoroughly blended. The color of the freshly prepared salt will be intense but will fade into its final color during drying.

Spread the salt mixture onto a rimmed baking sheet or platter and let it air-dry until there is absolutely no moisture, several hours to overnight (or longer as needed). Scrape the salt a few times with a fork, mashing clumps as they appear. After a few times, the salt will stop clumping. If desired, you can cover with a single layer of cheesecloth or paper towel as the salt dries. Transfer the completely dry salt to a jar with a tight-fitting lid and label clearly. Store in a cupboard or pantry, or on a shelf away from direct sunlight.

Dried method This method uses dried ingredients rather than fresh. Combine salt with dried ingredients in a small bowl. Transfer to a glass jar with tight fitting lid. Allow the salt mixture to infuse for 1 to 2 weeks before using. The longer it sits, the more infused the flavor will become. Remove add-ins (if desired) or leave them in.

For a colorful salt, use pigment-rich edible flowers and herbs, such as calendula, purple basil, marigolds, oregano, dark-colored pansies or violas, and roses. These will bleed natural color into the salt using the fresh method. Simply combine flowers with your favorite herb for a colorful, flavorful salt.

Storage

Infused salts are best stored in glass jars with tight-fitting lids (I use canning jars) away from direct sunlight or a heat source. Properly dried salts can be stored on the shelf for years. Over time, the flavor will begin to diminish.

Oregano Salt

This is, by far, my favorite infused salt. Just one herb. Simple. But it offers so much flavor to our pasta dishes, meat, veggies, and eggs. The salt will take on color from the fresh oregano leaves. I make a pint of this every year, but if you don't think you'll need that much you can cut this recipe in half. Or don't even measure at all; a handful here and there will do the trick.

MAKES ABOUT 1 PINT

2 cups kosher or coarse sea salt

1 cup packed fresh oregano leaves

1 · Process the salt and oregano leaves in a food processor until the mixture is completely combined, about 30 seconds.

2 · Spread the salt mixture on a rimmed baking sheet or platter. Cover with a single layer of cheesecloth. Let stand, stirring occasionally to break up any lumps with a fork, until completely dry. When completely dry, pack the salt into a jar with a tight-fitting lid. Store in a cool, dark place, where it will last indefinitely.

VARIATIONS

Purple Basil Salt: This purple-colored salt has a distinct basil aroma that fades into a sweet tea smell. Substitute purple basil leaves for the oregano.

Pansy and Rosemary Salt: Who else (other than me) needs blue salt on the shelf? Substitute ½ cup packed fresh rosemary leaves and ½ cup packed fresh blue- or purple-colored pansies or viola blooms for the oregano.

Rose Salt: Substitute dark-colored, fragrant rose petals for the oregano. For the best flavor, pinch off the white tips from the rose petals before using, as the tips can impart a bitter taste.

Calendula and Thyme Finishing Salt

The salt will take on color from the petals of the calendula. Stir pink Himalayan salt and dried whole calendula petals into the ground salt mixture for an especially pretty salt. Serve this as a finishing salt in small shallow dishes on the table for dinner parties so guests can appreciate its beauty.

MAKES 1½ TO 2 CUPS

1 cup kosher or coarse sea salt

½ to 1 cup fresh calendula petals

¼ cup fresh thyme leaves

½ cup coarse pink Himalayan salt

1 tablespoon chopped dried calendula petals

1 · Process the salt, fresh calendula petals, and thyme in a food processor until the mixture is completely combined, about 30 seconds.

2 · Spread the salt mixture on a rimmed baking sheet or platter. Cover with a single layer of cheesecloth. Let stand, stirring occasionally to break up any lumps with a fork, until completely dry, 12 to 24 hours, or even longer, as needed. When completely dry, stir in the Himalayan salt and dried calendula petals. Pack the salt into a jar with a tight-fitting lid. Store in a cool, dark place, where it will last indefinitely.

Spicy Finishing Salt

The first time I made this salt was for my hubs on Valentine's Day. It's perfect for date night dinners when you want to spice things up!

MAKES ABOUT 1 CUP

½ cup coarse or fine sea salt

½ cup flaky sea salt, such as Maldon

1 teaspoon red pepper flakes

¼ cup dried rose petals, slightly crushed (optional)

Combine the salts, red pepper flakes, and rose petals (if using) in a small bowl. Transfer to a glass jar with a tight-fitting lid. Allow the salt mixture to infuse for 1 to 2 weeks before using. The longer it sits, the more infused the flavor will become.

A LITTLE ME TIME

Botanical Bath Salts

MAKES ABOUT 1 PINT

Use your salt infusions to make a luxurious bath salt. Follow this recipe as a road map to relax-ville.

1 cup Epsom salt

1 cup herb- or flower-infused coarse sea salt (see page 205)

1 tablespoon baking soda

1 to 2 tablespoons almond, grapeseed, jojoba, or avocado oil (optional)

8 to 12 drops essential oil (specifically for homemade cosmetics and fragrances; optional)

Combine the Epsom salt, infused salt, and baking soda in a medium bowl and whisk well.

If using the oils, whisk the oil of choice and essential oils together in another small bowl, add to the salt mixture, and whisk well. Transfer to a jar with a tight-fitting lid and store in a cool, dark place.

To use, sprinkle a few tablespoons of the bath salts into a hot bath, stir to dissolve, and enjoy a relaxing time-out.

CHAPTER 9
Sweet Infusions

213
Infused Honey

215
Recipes
Chamomile Honey 215

Lilac Honey 215

216
Infused Sugars

218
Infused Sugar Recipes
Fruity Sugar 218

Rose Sugar 218

Infused Sugar Shapes 221

Sugared Botanicals 222

Rose Sugar Body Scrub 222

Sweet infusions can come in many forms. Honey and sugar can both be transformed into delightful ingredients. Syrups for beverages, baking, and good old pancakes always come in handy, and they can turn a standard cocktail or mocktail into a signature drink. Oh, this chapter is going to be sweet!

Flavored Syrups

Flavored Syrup Recipes

Blueberry Basil Simple Syrup 225
Butterfly Pea Flower Simple Syrup 225
Raspberry Simple Syrup 228
Rhubarb Simple Syrup 229
Spiced Blueberry Simple Syrup 229
Strawberry Thyme Simple Syrup 230
Elderberry Syrup 231

Infused Honey

Infusing honey is a simple way to add layers of flavor and elevate your everyday cooking. What's more, herbal honeys can be soothing. Chamomile honey aids in relaxation, while sage honey is great for a sore throat. Both are wonderful in tea, spread on muffins, added to a marinade, or used in baking. Raw or local honey is best for infusing. Wildflower or clove honey are other options but will impart additional flavors. **IMPORTANT:** Children under one should not consume honey.

Methods and Tools

- Plastic containers break down over time, so it's best to use a glass jar or bottle that can handle the life span of honey. Honey can oxidize in metal containers, so avoid them, too. Your bottles or jars need to be cleaned with hot soapy water but do not require sterilization.

- It's best to infuse honey with dried herbs and flowers. Fresh herbs and flowers contain moisture, which can cause the growth of botulinum spores. Using dried plant material (or fresh herbs and flowers that have been air-dried for at least 3 to 5 days) will minimize water activity.

You can infuse honey two different ways.

- **Cold method** This method results in the deepest infusion. Place the flavoring ingredients in a clean, dry glass jar. Cover with honey until the jar is half full. Using a chopstick or skewer, stir the infusing ingredients into the honey. Let the honey settle. This will take several minutes. Once settled, finish filling the jar with more honey, leaving ½-inch headspace. Use a skewer to push down the infusing ingredients as needed. Wipe the rim, add the lid, label, and date. Infuse for

---

Infused Honey Flavoring Menu

Use dried petals, buds, leaves, or whole sprigs. Estimate 3 to 4 tablespoons of the following dried plant material to 1 cup honey, and ½ cup for wilted or freshly dried material.

Edible Flowers	Herbs	Spices
Chamomile	Anise hyssop	Cinnamon sticks
Citrus blossoms	Lemon verbena	Cloves, whole
Elderflower	Mint	Coffee beans
Lavender	Rosemary	Dried citrus slices
Lilacs	Sage	Peppercorns
Rose petals	Tarragon	Red pepper flakes
Wild violets	Thyme	Vanilla bean

Sweet Infusions

2 to 3 weeks at room temperature. Once a day, turn the jar over for a minute or two, or stir, to help the flavorings fully incorporate into the honey. Placing it in a sunny window can speed up the infusing process. Scoop the ingredients out of the honey or strain: Place the jar in a bowl with several inches of hot water and let it stand for 5 minutes to warm, then strain through a fine-mesh strainer into another clean, dry jar with a tight-fitting lid.

- **Heat method** This is an excellent option for quick results still packed with flavor. Warm the honey and flavoring ingredients in a small saucepan over low heat. Stir frequently and do not let the mixture boil. When the honey reaches a thin, syrupy consistency, remove from the heat and let cool at room temperature for 1 hour. Repeat this process of heating and cooling two or three times, or until the desired flavor has been reached. Strain the finished honey into a clean, dry jar with a tight-fitting lid.

Storage

Infused honey will last indefinitely when stored in a cool, dark, and dry cupboard or pantry. Do not refrigerate. Signs of spoilage include mold or a vinegar smell. Hard, foggy, or crystalized honey is sometimes mistaken as honey that has spoiled, but this is natural for honey. Heat the honey to melt the crystals and stir well.

Chamomile Honey

I love the sweet, calming vibes of this home-infused honey. I use it in tea, baked goods, and drizzled on fruit, such as Melon Ball Salad (page 283). It's a delightful infusion that doesn't overpower.

MAKES ABOUT 1 CUP

1 cup raw unfiltered or raw honey

3 to 4 tablespoons dried chamomile flowers

1 · Combine the honey and chamomile and process according to the cold or heat method (page 213).

2 · Infuse for 2 to 3 weeks, turning over (or stirring) once a day. Strain through a fine-mesh strainer into a clean jar. Label and date. The honey can be stored in the pantry or cupboard. Do not refrigerate.

VARIATION
Spiced Honey: Replace the chamomile with 2 dried rosemary sprigs and 1 cinnamon stick.

Lilac Honey

Capturing short-lived lilac blooms in honey is a wonderful way to enjoy their essence through the seasons. Use your lilac honey to make the *best* marinade, Lemon Lilac Marinade (page 197).

MAKES ABOUT 1 CUP

½ cup packed lilac blossoms

1 cup raw honey, as needed

1 · With a damp paper towel, gently wipe the lilac blooms, removing any debris. Leaving the flowers on the stems, place on drying screens and let air-dry for 3 to 5 days. The blooms should be wilted and completely free of moisture before infusing the honey. Remove the blossoms from their stems, discarding as many green parts as possible.

2 · Put the wilted lilacs in a clean glass jar or bottle with a tight-fitting lid. Add enough honey to cover. Allow the honey to settle (this can take some time), then continue to add additional honey to the jar until it is full, leaving ½-inch headspace. Use a skewer to push down the blooms if needed.

3 · Infuse for 2 to 3 weeks, turning over (or stirring) once a day. Strain through a fine-mesh strainer into a clean jar. Label and date. The honey can be stored in the pantry or cupboard. Do not refrigerate.

Sweet Infusions

Infused Sugars

Herb and floral sugars can add an unexpected flavor to baked goods, teas, and desserts. Sugar infused with fruit powder will add vibrant color to yogurt, and even the milk in your cereal! Sugar shapes are perfect for tea and make a lovely gift. And sugared petals and leaves add a sweet touch to decorating baked goods—or turn them into a homemade sugar scrub for spa time.

Granulated cane sugar and coconut sugar work best for most sugar infusions because they're loose and dry. Powdered sugar can be infused with fruit powders for quick, naturally colored frostings or glazes.

Method and Tools

There are really no rules here when it comes to measuring. Eyeballing, grabbing handfuls, whatever is left in the container . . . All will work. But here are a few combinations and measurement suggestions to get you started.

Per 1 cup sugar, add:

- ½ cup fresh herbs, edible flowers, or freeze-dried fruit
- 2 to 3 tablespoons dried herbs
- ¼ cup ground dried flower petals
- 1 teaspoon ground spices or 2 to 4 whole spices
- 1 teaspoon flavored extract
- 1 to 5 drops food coloring (optional)

I infuse sugar four different ways:

- **Quick method** This method blends *fresh* ingredients (herbs, edible flower petals, or fruit powder) with sugar in a food processor until the ingredients are pulverized. Be sure the fresh ingredients have been rinsed well, patted dry, and air-dried completely before processing. Spread out the sugar mixture on a plate or tray and allow it to air-dry preferably overnight, stirring a few times with a fork to break up clumps. When the sugar is completely dry, label and store it in an airtight container away from direct sunlight. My favorite infusing ingredients for this method include brightly colored fresh pansies, violas, and rose petals; fresh purple basil leaves; and fruit/vegetable powders.

- **Long method** This method involves layering *fresh*, clean, and air-dried (1 to 3 hours) herbs or flower petals and sugar in a jar or container with a tight-fitting lid. It takes a little time to infuse, usually 2 to 3 weeks. Keep in a cool, dark cupboard. Shake the jar every day to redistribute the flavors. Taste once a week until the desired flavor is reached. Strain. The sugar will likely be wet from the moisture in the fresh ingredients. Spread out on a plate or tray and let air-dry for several hours or overnight, stirring a few times with a fork to break up clumps. When the sugar is completely dry, label and store it in an airtight container away from direct sunlight. My favorite infusing ingredients for this method include mint, rose petals, and lavender.

- **Dry method** With this method, *dried* ingredients and *ground* spices are added to the sugar. Combine the sugar and whatever you are using to flavor it in a bowl, then transfer to a jar with a tight-fitting lid. The sugar can be used immediately, but it is best to infuse for a few days (or even weeks) to reach optimal flavor. My go-to infusing ingredients for this method include ground cinnamon, apple spice, pumpkin spice, ground dried citrus zest, red pepper flakes, and dried herbs or edible flowers.

- **Addition method** In this method you add *dried* ingredients and *whole* spices to the sugar, allowing them to infuse for at least a few days before using. The longer the ingredients infuse, the deeper the flavor will be. I keep mine in the jar and just keep topping it off with more sugar as I use it. This keeps the flavors going and my jar full. My favorites are cinnamon sugar (using a 3-inch stick) and vanilla sugar (using a split vanilla bean). Remove the ingredients before using in a recipe.

Storage

Store infused sugar in an airtight, moistureproof container in a dark, cool, and dry space. Dry spice sugar mixes have an indefinite shelf life when kept moisture-free. Herb and flower infused sugars will last indefinitely when dried and stored properly. Over time, the flavor and color will diminish. Signs of spoilage include mold or a foul smell.

Fruity Sugar

Add a little color to your life and your pantry with freeze-dried fruit-infused sugar! A little bit of water helps bleed the color of the freeze-dried fruit into the sugar. Use powdered sugar when making glazes or frostings.

MAKES 1 CUP

1 cup sugar

½ cup freeze-dried fruit of choice

¼ teaspoon water

Process the sugar, freeze-dried fruit, and water in a food processor until the color is fully infused and the mixture has a moist and sandy consistency. Spread the sugar onto a rimmed baking sheet or platter. Let stand, stirring occasionally to break up any clumps with a fork, until completely dry, for several hours to overnight. When dry, pack into a jar with a tight-fitting lid. Label, date, and store at room temperature.

Rose Sugar

Rose sugar is delicious sprinkled on muffins, mixed in tea, and dare I say, used on your skin! See page 222 for how to turn this sugar into a pampering body scrub. As always, be sure the roses are organically grown and free of any pesticides or insecticides. For a colored sugar, use the quick method (see page 216).

MAKES 2 CUPS

2 cups sugar

1 cup packed fresh rose petals

Layer the sugar and rose petals in an airtight container. Store in a cool dry spot, shaking the container once a day, until the desired flavor has been reached, 2 to 3 weeks. Strain through a fine-mesh strainer set over a bowl to remove the petals. If the sugar is moist, spread on a plate or platter and allow to air-dry for several hours or overnight, stirring occasionally to break up any clumps with a fork. Pack the sugar into a jar with a tight-fitting lid and store at room temperature.

Infused Sugar Shapes

**MAKES 20 PIECES
(DEPENDING ON THE MOLDS)**

1 cup infused sugar

1 tablespoon water

1 tablespoon fruit or flower powder (optional)

You can turn infused sugar into beautiful shapes with just a silicone mold. They make great gifts or table decorations. Some sugar infusions are already colored. If you want additional color, add a little fruit or floral powder into the mix.

Blend the sugar, water, and powder, if using, in a food processor to a wet sand consistency, adding a little more water as needed. Pack the sugar into the molds and let stand at room temperature until completely dry and solid. This can take several hours or up to a few days. Unmold onto parchment paper and let air-dry again overnight before storing in an airtight container.

Sugared Botanicals

These candied petals use meringue powder instead of the traditional fresh egg whites and because of that, they'll last several months stored in an airtight container. They are beautiful on cakes, cupcakes, pies, and ice cream, or as a garnish for any other desserts. Refer to the complete lists of edible flowers (page 99) and herbs (page 90) for a wider range of options, but a few of my favorite herbs are basil, mint, and sage leaves. For flowers, I like to use rose petals, English daisies, violas, pansies, and violets.

MAKES ABOUT 40 PETALS OR LEAVES *(depending on the size)*

2 tablespoons water

2 teaspoons meringue powder

1 cup superfine sugar

40 flower petals or herb leaves

1 · In a small bowl, stir the water and meringue powder together until the powder is dissolved.

2 · Working with one petal or leaf at a time, use a small, food-grade paintbrush or pastry brush to evenly brush the meringue mixture all over the petals or leaves. Working over a plate, sprinkle the superfine sugar on top to coat. Transfer to a wire cooling rack and let stand at room temperature until completely dried; this can take up to 1 to 2 days.

3 · Carefully transfer the candied petals and leaves to an airtight container or jar with a tight-fitting lid. Store in a cool, dry place.

A LITTLE ME TIME

Rose Sugar Body Scrub

MAKES ABOUT 1 CUP

1 cup Rose Sugar (page 218)

2 to 4 tablespoons grapeseed oil, as needed

1 teaspoon vitamin E oil (optional)

Roses reduce redness and relieve dry skin. Grapeseed oil is loaded with antioxidants that help skin disorders and rashes. It's also known to minimize clogged pores and clear acne, too. A good one for the teenagers in the house! Vitamin E oil is optional here but will moisturize your skin.

In a small bowl, mix the sugar and 1 tablespoon of the grapeseed oil at a time, stirring until the desired consistency is reached. Add the vitamin E oil, if using. Transfer the scrub to an airtight container. The scrub can be stored at room temperature for up to 2 months or in the refrigerator for up to 6 months. Discard if there are any signs of spoilage, such as a foul smell or mold.

Flavored Syrups

Basic simple syrup is equal parts sugar and water. You can take it to the next level with all kinds of fresh or dried herbs, spices, fruits, and flowers. I use flavored syrups for beverages but also for baking, candies, and even tea. Thicker syrups, often made with fruits and served as a topping for waffles and pancakes, use a ratio of two parts sugar to one part water.

Raw cane or granulated sugar works best, but simple syrups can be made using equal amounts of other sweeteners, including honey, molasses, maple syrup, brown sugar, demerara sugar, coconut sugar, or agave.

Method and Tools

- For both simple and fruit syrups, the ingredients are simmered together to marry the flavors. Be sure to use a nonreactive saucepan (see page 65).

- Dried herbs can be used in place of fresh in any simple syrup recipe. Just reduce the amount by half.

Storage

Most flavored simple syrups, refrigerated in an airtight container, will last for about a month. But those made with flower powders spoil more quickly, lasting 2 to 3 weeks. Discard syrup if mold appears or a foul smell is present. Canned fruit syrups are best used within 1 year.

Flavored Simple Syrup Menu

Fresh or dried ingredients are fair game, as are powdered, freeze-dried, and frozen foods.

ZERO WASTE ALERT!

When you make fruit-flavored syrup, you will have leftover fruit mash as a bonus. Use the mash from berries to flavor your tea, infuse water, top ice cream, add to smoothies or ice pops, mix into cake batters, or make a quick jam (see page 46), or use in desserts like Strawberry Thyme Bars (page 325).

Herbs	Edible Flowers	Spices	Fruits and Vegetables
Basil	Apple blossoms	Chiles	Berries
Lemon balm	Butterfly pea flowers	Cinnamon sticks	Carrots
Lemon verbena	Elderflowers	Coffee	Cucumbers
Mint	Freesia	Peppercorns	Melons
Rosemary	Rose petals	Star anise	Peaches
Thyme	Wild violets	Vanilla beans	Rhubarb

Blueberry Basil Simple Syrup

This simple syrup makes a delicious Blueberry Basil Mocktail (page 238) or just splash some in your favorite lemonade. Our favorite way to use it, though, is to make the delicious, deep purple fruit leathers on page 132.

MAKES ABOUT 1½ CUPS

2 cups fresh or frozen blueberries

1½ cups water

1 cup raw honey, or herb- or flower-infused honey (see page 213)

15 fresh basil leaves

Grated zest of 1 lemon

1 · Bring the blueberries, water, and honey to a boil in a medium saucepan over medium-high heat, stirring often to dissolve the sugar and honey. Add the basil and lemon zest and turn the heat down to low. Simmer, stirring occasionally, until the berries are completely collapsed, about 10 minutes. Remove from the heat and cool completely.

2 · Set a fine-mesh strainer over a bowl, line with cheesecloth, and strain the syrup. Transfer to a jar with a tight-fitting lid. Refrigerate until chilled before using, about 2 hours. The syrup can be refrigerated for up to 1 month.

Butterfly Pea Flower Simple Syrup

This simple syrup uses flower powder, and boy is it beautiful! It is a fun syrup for cocktails and mocktails. It's also delicious in lemonade and iced tea, or as part of a homemade blue soda (see page 238)! Add a splash of lemon juice and watch the color change to a magenta. So fun!

MAKES 1¼ CUPS

1 cup sugar

1 cup water

1 teaspoon butterfly pea flower powder

1 · Bring the sugar, water, and flower powder to a boil in a small saucepan over high heat. Turn the heat down and simmer, stirring occasionally, until the sugar and powder have dissolved, about 5 minutes. Remove from the heat and cool completely.

2 · Set a fine-mesh strainer over a bowl, line with cheesecloth, and strain the syrup. Transfer to a jar with a tight-fitting lid. Refrigerate until chilled before using, about 2 hours. The syrup can be refrigerated for 2 to 3 weeks.

Sweet Infusions

Raspberry Simple Syrup, p. 228

Butterfly Pea Flower Simple Syrup, p. 225

Blueberry Basil Simple Syrup, p. 225

Rhubarb Simple Syrup, p. 229

Raspberry Simple Syrup

This recipe is easy to customize using herb- or flower-infused sugars. Rose, chamomile, or basil sugar work nicely, too. Make this using fresh, in-season raspberries or frozen berries in the off season.

MAKES ABOUT 1½ CUPS

2 cups fresh or frozen raspberries

1 cup sugar or herb- or flower-infused sugar (see page 216)

1 cup water

1 · Bring the raspberries, sugar, and water to a boil in a medium saucepan over medium-high heat. Turn the heat down to low and simmer until the raspberries are soft and the liquid is deep red, about 10 minutes. Place a fine-mesh strainer over a bowl and strain the fruit mixture, pressing down gently to release the juices. Discard the solids. Let the syrup cool completely.

2 · Transfer to a jar with a tight-fitting lid. Refrigerate until chilled before using, about 2 hours. The syrup can be refrigerated for up to 1 month.

VARIATION
Spiced Raspberry Syrup: This syrup is delicious for wintertime spirits. Add ½ teaspoon ground cinnamon and ½ teaspoon ground nutmeg to the syrup after straining.

Simple Syrup Snow Cones

MAKES 1 SERVING

1 cup shaved ice

¼ cup simple syrup of your choice

Edible flower or herb leaf

For many years, my hubs and I put on a Fourth of July carnival for the kids in the backyard, complete with games and carnival fare like good ol' snow cones. Traditional flavors like strawberry and blueberry are delicious, but I encourage you to get adventurous and try floral and herb-infused syrups. Making them for adults only? Add a splash of your favorite spirit. You can find shaved ice machines, both electric and hand-cracked, easily online, but a blender will also do the trick.

Scoop up the shaved ice into a compact ball and put into a bowl or a paper snow-cone cup, just like the good old days. Then pour the syrup over the ice and serve immediately. Add a fresh edible flower or herb leaf before serving just to be "extra."

Rhubarb Simple Syrup

This is my very favorite thing we make from the garden in spring. It's a vibrant shade of red, and its sweet-and-sour flavor makes it both delightful and beautiful to serve. I don't even like rhubarb, and yet I love this syrup!

MAKES ABOUT 2 TO 3 CUPS

4 cups chopped rhubarb

2 cups sugar

2 cups water

1 • Bring the rhubarb, sugar, and water to a boil in a medium saucepan over medium-high heat, stirring to dissolve the sugar. Turn the heat down to medium-low and simmer until the rhubarb is falling apart, about 10 minutes. Remove from the heat and cool completely.

2 • Set a fine-mesh strainer over a bowl, line with a double layer of cheesecloth, and strain the rhubarb mixture, pressing gently on the solids with a spoon to extract the liquid. Reserve the solids for another use (see Zero Waste Alert). Let the syrup cool completely.

3 • Transfer to a jar with a tight-fitting lid. Refrigerate until chilled before using, about 2 hours. The syrup can be refrigerated for up to 1 month.

ZERO WASTE ALERT!
Use the leftover rhubarb mash in smoothies, ice pops, or oatmeal. You can also add it to muffins as you would any berry. Or turn it into the Quick Rhubarb Jam (page 48).

Spiced Blueberry Simple Syrup

Elevate breakfast with homemade fruit syrups! This recipe will work with whatever berry is in season.

MAKES ABOUT 1 CUP

2 cups fresh or frozen blueberries

1 cup pure maple syrup

2 teaspoons fresh lemon juice

1 teaspoon ground cinnamon

½ teaspoon ground nutmeg

1 • Bring the blueberries, syrup, lemon juice, cinnamon, and nutmeg to a boil in a medium saucepan over medium heat, stirring occasionally. Turn the heat down to medium-low and simmer, stirring occasionally, until the blueberries are soft, 15 to 20 minutes. Remove from the heat.

2 • Using a potato masher, thoroughly mash the blueberries. For a smooth syrup, place a fine-mesh strainer over a bowl, pour in the berry mixture, and let it drain. Discard the solids (or use to make tea!). Serve warm or cool to room temperature. To store, transfer to an airtight container. The syrup can be refrigerated for up to 1 month.

Sweet Infusions

Strawberry Thyme Simple Syrup

Strawberry and thyme are a summery match made in heaven. After hulling and slicing the berries, save the tops for a batch of Zero-Waste Strawberry Top Simple Syrup (see Variation below).

MAKES ABOUT 2 TO 3 CUPS

4 cups fresh or frozen hulled and sliced strawberries

2 cups sugar

2 cups water

5 to 6 fresh thyme sprigs

1 · Bring the strawberries, sugar, water, and thyme to a boil in a medium saucepan over medium-high heat, stirring often to dissolve the sugar. Turn the heat down to medium-low and simmer until the berries are soft and the syrup is deep red, about 15 minutes.

2 · Place a fine-mesh strainer over a bowl. Pour the strawberry mixture into the strainer and let it slowly drain, without pressing, until the fruit looks relatively dry and the syrup has completely been collected in the bowl, about 30 minutes. (If you press the fruit, the syrup will become cloudy.) Discard the solids. Let the syrup cool completely.

3 · Transfer to a jar with a tight-fitting lid. Refrigerate until chilled before using, about 2 hours. The syrup can be refrigerated for up to 1 month.

VARIATION
Strawberry Top Simple Syrup: Substitute 4 cups strawberry tops (greens with bits of red flesh) for the sliced berries.

Simple Syrup Glaze
MAKES ABOUT 1 CUP

1½ cups powdered sugar

1 tablespoon flavored simple syrup of choice (page 224)

½ teaspoon almond or vanilla extract

1 to 3 tablespoons heavy cream

Drizzle over cakes, doughnuts, quick breads, and muffins.

Whisk together the sugar, simple syrup, and extract. Add the cream, 1 tablespoon at a time, until the desired consistency is reached.

Elderberry Syrup

Elderberry syrup is a potent syrup used mainly to boost the immune system and fight colds and flus. But it can also be drizzled on pancakes, used in baked goods recipes, added to smoothies or tea, or even turned into elderberry gummies (see page 331).

The suggested daily dose is ½ to 1 teaspoon for kids under 12 and 1 tablespoon for adults. When fighting a cold, take the normal dose every 3 to 4 hours until symptoms disappear. My family likes to put the measured syrup into 6 to 8 ounces of hot water for a soothing tea.

MAKES ABOUT 1½ CUPS

3 cups water

1 cup fresh elderberries or ½ cup dried

1 (3-inch) cinnamon stick

3 to 4 whole cloves

1 cup raw honey or flower- or herb-infused honey (see page 213; for extra medicinal and flavor benefits)

2 tablespoons grated fresh ginger (optional)

1 · Place the water, elderberries, cinnamon stick, and cloves in a medium saucepan, cover, and bring to a boil over medium-high heat. Uncover, turn the heat down to medium-low, and simmer until the berries are soft, about 45 minutes. Remove from the heat and let cool slightly.

2 · Set a fine-mesh strainer over a bowl, line with cheesecloth, and pour the mixture through. Gently mash the berries with a spoon, being careful not to crush any seeds (or skip mashing entirely). Discard the solids. Stir the honey into the strained syrup until dissolved. Transfer to jars with tight-fitting lids. The syrup can be refrigerated for up to 3 months.

HOW TO HANDLE ELDERBERRIES

Unripe berries, stems, and seeds are toxic. Only the mature black berries and flowers are edible. Berries must be cooked to eat safely. Mash gently, if at all, and be careful to not break the seeds. Use a fork or your fingers to easily separate berries from stems. Be sure to rinse the berries well before using. It's okay if you have some of the dried blooms in the mixture, as they will get strained out or dried in the dehydration process.

Serving the Seasons

PART THREE

Cooking for a family of eight was not easy. In fact, when the kids were very little (three under three, plus three more) it often felt like a chore. But I learned ways to make it enjoyable. The key is in preparing your mind and space so you're ready to create. Turn on music and light a candle. Gather utensils, chop ingredients, and measure seasonings in advance. Before you know it, you're feelin' good, surrounded by little bowls of ingredients, ready to make magic!

Recipes That Use What You've Preserved!

236
I'll Cheers to That!
Sunshine Mocktail 236
Blueberry Basil Mocktail 238
Easy Homemade Soda 238
Strawberry, Lime, and Thyme Cooler 239
Summer Sunset Mocktail 239
North Pole Hot Chocolate 240
Whipped Toppers 240

242
Snack Shack
Cheddar Cheese Ball 242
Herb and Dried Tomato Cheese Spread 243
Rustic Herb and Garlic Crackers 245
Pretty in Pink Deviled Eggs 246

248
Off to a Good Start
Lemon Lilac Doughnuts 248
Pumpkin Spice Pancakes 250
Apple Cinnamon Oatmeal 250
Lavender Orange French Toast 251
Avocado Garden Toast 253
Ham and Cheese Garden Quiche 254
Totally Twisted Yogurt 257
Lavender Granola 257
Smart Start Smoothie 258
Tropical Dreams Smoothie 261
Tickled Pink Smoothie Bowl 261

262
Soups & Sandwiches
Creamy Roasted Tomato Soup 262
Vegetable and Bean Soup 263
Fresh Pea Soup 264
Vegetable, Beef, and Farro Soup 267
Teatime Sandwiches 268
Candied Bacon Chicken Sandwich 268
Rosemary Candied Bacon 271
Turkey-Stuffed Lettuce Wraps 273

274
Salad Bar
Garden Wraps with Sweet Chili Sauce 274
Sweet Chili Sauce 276
Cucumber Rose Garden Salad 279
Herb Croutons 279
Chive Blossom Vinaigrette 280
Garlic Scape Vinaigrette 280
Raspberry Basil Vinaigrette 281
Wild Violet Peppercorn Vinaigrette 281
Melon Ball Salad with Chamomile Honey 283
Picnic Potato Salad 283

Dinner Menu

Pacific Northwest Crab Cakes 284
Homestead Tartar Sauce 285
Stuffed Zucchini 285
Potato Roses 286
Glazed Carrots 288
Honey-Glazed Pork Loin 289
Go-To Spice Rub 289
Slow-Cooked Dried Beans 290
Vegetable Rice 290
Rainbow Rice 291
Scalloped Potatoes 291
Homemade Herb Pasta 293
Pantry Tomato Sauce 296
Tomato Basil Pasta Salad 296
Roasted Marinara Sauce 297
Spinach Parm Pasta 299
Creamy Garlic Scape Sauce 299
Herby Pizza Dough 300
Pizza Assembly and Baking 301
Pizza Sauce 301
Garden Focaccia 302

Hit the Sauce

Barbecue Sauce 303
Orange Spice Cranberry Sauce 304
Kickin' Ketchup 304

The Bread Box

Quick Honey Wheat Bread 305
Lemon, Lilac, and Poppy Seed Bread 307
Lavender Cornbread 308
Rose Scones 310
Banana Bread 311
Minty Strawberry-Orange Sauce 311
Chocolate, Tahini, and Banana Muffins 313
Herb and Cheddar Biscuits 314
Rosemary Baguettes 317

Sweet Tooth

Floral Sugar Cookies 318
Botanical Graham Crackers 322
Ice Cream Sandwiches with Botanical Graham Crackers 322
Raspberry Jam Thumbprint Cookies 324
Strawberry Thyme Bars 325
Botanical Candy Bars 327
Chocolate Raspberry Truffles 328
Berry Quick Cheesecake 329
Homemade Elderberry Candies 331
Chocolate Zucchini Bundt Cake 332
Garden Mint Chocolate Ganache 333
Rosemary Citrus Bundt Cake with Orange Glaze 334
Jam Pocket Pies 337
Blueberry Basil Lilac Crumb Pie 338
Peach Slab Pie 339
Grandma's Pie Dough 340

I'll Cheers to That!

Whether mocktails or cocktails for date nights in the dining room, homemade sodas for a backyard picnic, or decadent hot chocolate for the holidays, a drink in hand is a reason to cheer.

Sunshine Mocktail

MAKES 4 TO 6 SERVINGS

Ring in the summer solstice with this sunshine in a cup! Go for the paper umbrella—you deserve it!

Mango Strawberry Puree
1 cup fresh or thawed frozen mango chunks

1 cup sliced fresh or thawed frozen strawberries

¼ cup water

Per Serving
1 cup lemon-lime soda, such as Sprite

2 tablespoons Rhubarb Simple Syrup (page 229) or Strawberry Simple Syrup (see chart page 224)

½ teaspoon fresh lemon juice

Ice cubes (optional)

Dehydrated lemon slice (page 120) or fresh strawberry, for garnish

Paper cocktail umbrella, for decoration

1 · Make the puree: In a blender, puree the mango, strawberries, and water. Cover and refrigerate until ready to use.

2 · For each serving, stir ¼ cup of the puree, the soda, syrup, and lemon juice in a fancy glass. Add ice and garnish as desired. Don't forget the umbrella!

Blueberry Basil Mocktail

Only mocktails for me! But who needs alcohol when you have drinks like this? Okay, if you raised your hand, this would be delicious with gin or vodka—add ¾ cup of either spirit to the pitcher for a boozy version. See the Note for how to create a fun sugar rim for your drink.

MAKES 6 SERVINGS

1 cup fresh blueberries

6 large basil leaves, chopped

⅓ cup fresh lemon juice

1 cup Blueberry Basil Simple Syrup (page 225)

2 cups sparkling water, seltzer, or lemon-flavored soda

2 cups regular ice cubes or Fancy Pants Ice with flowers (page 166)

Basil sprigs, lemon wedges, and violas, for garnish (optional)

Using a wooden spoon, crush the blueberries and basil together in a pitcher to release their juices. Add the lemon juice, syrup, and sparkling water and stir to combine. To serve, add the ice to the pitcher and stir well to chill. Serve over ice and garnish with a sprig of basil, a lemon wedge, and/or a fresh viola, if desired.

NOTE
To give your glass a flavorful sugar rim, spread about ½ cup basil-infused sugar or other infused sugar (see page 216) in a saucer, about ¼ inch deep. Rub and moisten the glass's edge with the juice from a lemon, lime, or orange wedge. Place the glass, open end down, in the sugar. Twist it a few times to coat the moistened edge, then remove, gently shaking off any excess sugar.

Easy Homemade Soda

With homemade syrups, making your own pop is a cinch. Here is a basic recipe to get you started on the path of creating custom sodas with natural flavors.

MAKES 1 SERVING

Additional flavorings, such as fresh fruit, fresh herbs, fruit juice, and/or vanilla extract (optional)

2 to 3 tablespoons flavored simple syrup (see pages 224 to 231)

1 cup cold seltzer or sparkling water (plain or flavored)

Regular ice cubes or Fancy Pants Ice (page 166)

Fresh or dehydrated citrus slices, fresh herb sprigs, and/or edible flowers, for garnish

If using fruits as an additional flavorings, muddle them in a tall glass first. Add the flavored syrup of your choice with the cold seltzer and stir to combine. Add ice. Garnish as desired and serve.

Strawberry, Lime, and Thyme Cooler

I love this combination of flavors. It brings me back to so many sweet summer nights, sipping coolers in the warm night air, watching the kids run barefoot by the moon's glow. It sure is special when the senses work in harmony like that. If you wish, give the glass a sugar rim (see Note page 239) with thyme-infused sugar (see page 216).

MAKES 1 SERVING

5 to 6 freeze-dried strawberry slices (page 26) or 1 or 2 fresh or frozen hulled strawberries

¼ cup Strawberry Thyme Simple Syrup (page 230)

¾ cup water

2 tablespoons fresh lime juice

Ice cubes

Lime slice and fresh thyme sprigs, for garnish

Place the strawberries in a tall glass or 1-pint glass jar. Pour in the syrup, water, and lime juice, and stir to combine. Add ice. Garnish with the lime and thyme and serve.

Summer Sunset Mocktail

Kick back and watch the sunset with this refreshing mocktail in hand. It is easy to turn this into a spirited drink for those who indulge. See the suggestions in the tequila variation below or make the champagne version.

MAKES 4 SERVINGS

2½ cups fresh orange juice

1 cup Raspberry Simple Syrup (page 228)

½ cup fresh lemon juice

1 teaspoon vanilla extract

2 cups seltzer or sparkling water

Ice cubes

Orange slices and edible flowers, for garnish (optional)

1 · Stir together the orange juice, syrup, lemon juice, and vanilla in a pitcher. Refrigerate to blend the flavors for 10 minutes. Add the seltzer.

2 · For each serving, add ice to a short glass and fill. Garnish with orange slices and edible flowers, if desired, and serve.

VARIATIONS

Summer Sunset Champagne Cocktail: Replace the seltzer with champagne or sparkling wine.

Tequila Sunset Cocktail: Add ¾ to 1 cup silver tequila or rum (or gin or vodka) to the pitcher with the orange juice.

North Pole Hot Chocolate
with Whipped Toppers

This is what I imagine hot chocolate at Santa's house tastes like. Rich, creamy, and decadent, it is perfect for snow days and holidays.

MAKES 4 TO 5 SERVINGS

1 tablespoon dried mint leaves

5 cups whole milk, divided

1 cinnamon stick

1 (7-ounce) jar marshmallow creme

½ cup semisweet chocolate chips

1 teaspoon vanilla extract

Whipped Toppers (optional; recipe follows) or fresh whipped cream

1 · Put the mint leaves in a tea ball, cloth tea bag, or infuser. Heat 3½ cups of the milk, the mint leaves, and cinnamon stick in a medium saucepan over medium heat, stirring often to avoid scorching, until small bubbles appear around the edges. Remove from the heat and let cool for 10 minutes.

2 · Remove the cinnamon and mint. (If flecks of mint are showing, you can strain the milk through a fine-mesh strainer if you like.) Return to low heat, add the marshmallow creme, and whisk until the creme melts. Add the remaining 1½ cups of milk and the chocolate chips. Whisk until the chocolate is melted and fully incorporated. Remove from the heat and whisk in the vanilla.

3 · Ladle into mugs and add a whipped topper (if using) to each.

Whipped Toppers

Use these frozen or freeze-dried cuties to crown your hot chocolate. Freeze-dried toppers are also nice in a gift basket with a packet of hot chocolate, a bag of sprinkles, and a pretty mug. Use the toppers on other hot beverages (such as flavored coffees), ice cream, or warm desserts, or just let them melt in your mouth as a sweet treat.

MAKES ABOUT 24 TOPPERS

1 (6.5-ounce) can dairy whipped topping

Colored sprinkles, for garnish

Make and freeze the toppers using either of the following methods:

Standard freezer: Line a rimmed baking sheet with parchment paper and put in the freezer for at least 4 hours. Squirt about 24 swirls of the whipped topping on the lined trays, leaving a small space in between. Top with the sprinkles. Return the loaded pan to the freezer and freeze until solid, 4 to 6 hours. Transfer to an air-tight container or resealable freezer bag. (The toppers can be frozen for up to 6 months.)

Freeze-dryer: After freezing for 4 to 6 hours in a standard freezer as directed above, freeze-dry the toppers according to the manufacturer's instructions.

Preserving the Seasons

Snack Shack

Nothing gets the party started like a Cheddar Cheese Ball (this page)! Rustic Herb and Garlic Crackers (page 245) are the perfect match. Place them on a platter along with fruit, colorful veggies, and meats and decorated with edible flowers, and now your party is the talk of the town. The snack section always spreads joy!

Cheddar Cheese Ball

MAKES 8 TO 10 SERVINGS

Hubs is from Wisconsin, so we're a family of cheeseheads. This cheddar cheese ball makes an appearance at our house during the holidays and on game days. Go Pack, go!

1 pound cream cheese, cut into chunks

2 cups finely shredded smoked cheddar cheese

8 tablespoons (1 stick) unsalted butter, cut into chunks

2 tablespoons whole or 2% milk

2½ teaspoons steak sauce

1 tablespoon chopped fresh parsley or 2 teaspoons dried

2 teaspoons chopped fresh oregano or 1 teaspoon dried

Toppings (optional): pressed edible flowers, seeds, chopped fresh herbs, or chopped nuts

Rustic Herb and Garlic Crackers (page 245) or use store-bought

1 · Place the cream cheese, cheddar cheese, and butter in a large bowl and let stand at room temperature to soften for 20 minutes. Add the milk, steak sauce, parsley, and oregano and beat with a wooden spoon or electric mixer at medium speed until the mixture is combined and creamy.

2 · Transfer the cheese mixture to a sheet of parchment paper. Use the parchment to help form it into a ball or a log. Transfer the shaped cheese from the parchment to a sheet of plastic wrap and wrap tightly. For a log, twist the ends tightly to help keep the log in shape. Chill for a minimum of 12 and up to 24 hours.

3 · Just before serving, unwrap and decorate with flowers, or roll in herbs, nuts, seeds, or flower petals, if desired. Let stand at room temperature for 15 minutes before serving with crackers.

Herb and Dried Tomato Cheese Spread

This is the perfect spread for Teatime Sandwiches (page 268). Or shape into a log and decorate with flowers and herbs for a beautiful platter presentation. Rustic Herb and Garlic Crackers (page 245) also pair well with this spread.

MAKES 6 TO 8 SERVINGS

- 8 ounces cream cheese, cut into chunks
- 4 tablespoons (½ stick) unsalted butter, cut into chunks
- 1 tablespoon finely snipped dehydrated tomatoes (see page 128)
- 1 tablespoon finely chopped scallion
- 1 tablespoon finely chopped fresh parsley
- 1 teaspoon finely chopped fresh basil
- ¼ teaspoon salt
- ⅛ teaspoon freshly ground black pepper

Place the cream cheese and butter in a large bowl and let stand at room temperature to soften for 20 minutes. Beat with a wooden spoon or an electric mixer at medium speed until the mixture is combined and creamy. Add the tomatoes, scallion, parsley, basil, salt, and pepper and mix well. Heap the mixture onto a sheet of plastic wrap and wrap tightly. Chill for at least 4 and up to 24 hours to chill and blend the flavors. If using as a sandwich filling, let stand at room temperature for 30 minutes to soften until spreadable.

VARIATION

Herb and Dried Tomato Cheese Log: Pile the cheese mixture onto parchment paper and use the paper to help shape into a log. Decorate the top and sides of the log with fresh herb leaves and edible flowers. Carefully transfer the log, decorated side down, to a sheet of plastic wrap. Decorate the remaining side with herbs and flowers. Wrap tightly, twisting the ends to tighten the log shape. Refrigerate for at least 4 and up to 24 hours.

Rustic Herb and Garlic Crackers

Once you make your own homemade crackers, you will never buy store-bought again. They are easy to make, and the flavoring possibilities are endless.

MAKES ABOUT 100 CRACKERS

1½ cups all-purpose flour, plus more for rolling

1½ cups whole wheat flour

2 teaspoons Italian Seasoning Blend (page 110)

1 teaspoon garlic powder

1 teaspoon salt

1 cup water

¼ cup extra-virgin olive oil, plus more for brushing

Herb salt (see page 205) or kosher salt

1 · Preheat the oven to 375°F.

2 · Whisk the all-purpose and whole wheat flours, Italian seasoning, garlic powder, and salt together in a large bowl. Gradually stir in the water and oil to make a rough dough. Knead the dough in the bowl with your hands until it comes together, but do not overwork the dough. Divide the dough into four equal portions, and shape each into a thick disk.

3 · Working with one portion of dough at a time, on a lightly floured surface, roll out the dough until about ⅛-inch thick. Thin is the key! Using a 2-inch round cookie cutter, cut out crackers, then transfer them to two ungreased rimmed baking sheets. Brush the tops lightly with oil and sprinkle each with a pinch of herb salt.

4 · Bake until lightly browned, 9 to 11 minutes. Cool on the baking sheets for 2 minutes, then transfer to a wire cooling rack to cool completely. Repeat with the remaining dough. The crackers can be stored in an airtight container at room temperature for 4 to 6 weeks.

VARIATION

Tomato Basil Crackers: Omit the Italian seasoning. Add 2 tablespoons tomato powder (see page 113) and 1 teaspoon dried basil to the flour mixture.

Pretty in Pink Deviled Eggs

Soaking the cooked egg whites in a natural food coloring and topping them with edible flowers makes this party favorite almost too pretty to eat!

MAKES 12 SERVINGS

6 hard-boiled eggs, peeled and cut in half lengthwise

2 tablespoons beet powder (see page 113)

1 tablespoon distilled white vinegar

3 cups boiling water

¼ cup mayonnaise

1 teaspoon ground mustard

½ teaspoon Greek Seasoning Blend (page 109)

Salt and freshly ground black pepper

Edible flowers, chopped fresh herbs (especially chives), or seeds, for garnish

1 · Line a rimmed baking sheet with parchment paper and place a cooling rack on top. Remove the yolks from the egg whites and set aside in a small bowl. In a medium glass bowl, stir together the beet powder and vinegar. Add the boiling water, stirring until the powder dissolves. Add the egg whites and let stand until they reach the desired color, checking every 30 seconds. Keep in mind that the longer they soak, the more they will take on the beet flavor as well. Drain the egg whites and transfer to the rack to drain.

2 · Using the back of a fork, mash the yolks into a fine crumble. Add the mayonnaise, mustard, and Greek seasoning and mix to combine. Season with salt and pepper. Transfer the yolk mixture to a resealable plastic bag and snip off one corner. Use the bag to pipe the yolk mixture into the whites to give them a fancy-pants look. (Or just spoon the yolk mixture into the whites.) Cover and refrigerate until ready to serve, up to 8 hours. Just before serving, garnish with edible flowers, herbs, or seeds.

Off to a Good Start

Mornings were always a fire drill when the kids were younger. Five kids to get fed, dressed, and off to three different schools with a baby on my hip. I deserved that Avocado Garden Toast (page 253)! I bet you do, too.

Lemon Lilac Doughnuts

MAKES 20 DOUGHNUTS

These are a delightful spring treat. I use a doughnut baking pan so these are cakey and don't require frying.

Doughnuts
Nonstick cooking oil spray
1 (15.25-ounce) box yellow cake mix
1 (3.4-ounce) instant lemon pudding mix
1 cup cool lilac botanical water (see page 165)
4 large eggs
½ cup vegetable oil
1 teaspoon lemon extract
½ cup fresh lilac blossoms

Lilac blossoms, pansies, violas, and candy sprinkles, for decorating (optional)

Glaze
1 cup freeze-dried blueberries or blackberries
2 cups powdered sugar
4 tablespoons (½ stick) unsalted butter, melted
1½ teaspoons vanilla extract
2 tablespoons 2% milk, as needed

1 · Make the doughnuts: Preheat the oven to 350°F. Grease a doughnut pan with 20 molds with the oil spray.

2 · In a large bowl, combine the cake mix, pudding mix, lilac water, eggs, oil, and lemon extract with an electric mixer on medium speed for 2 minutes, scraping down the sides of the bowl as needed. Fold in the lilac blossoms. Transfer the batter to a pastry bag without a tip (or a 1-gallon resealable plastic bag with one corner snipped off) and pipe the batter into the molds. (Or spoon the batter into the molds with a dessert spoon.)

3 · Bake until the doughnuts are golden brown and a wooden toothpick inserted in the center comes out clean, 15 to 18 minutes. Let cool in the pan on a cooling rack for 5 minutes. Remove from the pans and cool completely on the rack.

4 · Make the glaze: Grind or smash the freeze-dried berries into a powder. Strain through a fine-mesh strainer if needed. In a medium bowl, whisk the powdered sugar and berry powder until combined. Stir in the butter and vanilla. Add enough milk as needed for a glaze about the consistency of thick heavy cream. One at a time, dip a doughnut upside down into the glaze, letting the excess glaze drip off into the bowl. Return the doughnuts to the cooling rack. Decorate, if desired, with fresh edible flower blossoms and sprinkles. Let the glaze set for about 1 hour. (The doughnuts can be stored in an airtight container, layers separated by parchment or waxed paper, for up to 5 days.)

Off to a Good Start

Pumpkin Spice Pancakes

Here's a tasty way to use pumpkin puree. If using frozen puree, thaw then drain (if needed) in a cheesecloth-lined strainer to remove excess liquid.

MAKES ABOUT 10 PANCAKES

1 cup whole wheat flour

¾ cup all-purpose flour

3 tablespoons light brown sugar

1 tablespoon baking powder

1 teaspoon pumpkin pie spice

¼ teaspoon salt

1¾ cups milk (dairy or oat)

⅔ cup pumpkin puree, homemade (strained) or store-bought

1 large egg

3 tablespoons vegetable oil, plus more for the griddle

Softened butter and warmed maple syrup, for serving

1 · In a large bowl, whisk together the whole wheat and all-purpose flours, brown sugar, baking powder, pumpkin pie spice, and salt. In a medium bowl, whisk together the milk, pumpkin puree, egg, and oil. Pour into the flour mixture and stir just until combined.

2 · Heat a griddle over medium-high heat until a sprinkle of water on the surface immediately turns into skittering balls. (If using an electric griddle, preheat to 375°F.) Brush the griddle with oil. Using about ⅓ cup for each pancake, pour the batter onto the griddle. Cook until the tops are covered with small holes and the underside is golden brown, 2 to 3 minutes. Flip the pancakes and cook until the other side is golden brown. Serve hot, with the butter and syrup.

Apple Cinnamon Oatmeal

I make this in a big batch on a Sunday morning and then freeze individual servings in muffin cups for the week ahead. Single servings can easily be reheated in the microwave for a quick breakfast before work or school.

MAKES 8 SERVINGS

10 cups water

1½ teaspoons salt

2½ cups steel-cut oats (not quick-cooking)

8 dried apple rings, scissor-snipped into small pieces

¾ cup light brown sugar

4 tablespoons (½ stick) unsalted butter, cut into ½-inch cubes

1 tablespoon ground cinnamon

1 teaspoon vanilla extract

Milk of your choosing, for serving

1 · Bring the water to a boil in a large saucepan over high heat. Stir in the salt. Stir in the oats and dried apples. Return to a boil. Turn the heat down to low, cover, and simmer, stirring often, until the oats are tender, about 30 minutes.

2 · Remove from the heat and let stand for 5 minutes. Add the brown sugar, butter, cinnamon, and vanilla and stir until the sugar and butter are melted. Ladle into bowls and serve warm, with milk.

Preserving the Seasons

VARIATION

Make-Ahead Oatmeal: Spray a standard muffin pan with nonstick oil spray. Using an ice cream scoop, drop portions of the oatmeal into the cups. Cover with plastic wrap and freeze until firm, 3 to 4 hours. Remove the oatmeal from the cups and transfer to a resealable freezer bag. Freeze for up to 3 months. To reheat, put one or two mounds into a microwave-safe bowl. Cover with plastic wrap and microwave on high (100%) power until thawed and hot, 2 to 3 minutes. Stir well. If the oatmeal seems too thick, stir in milk as needed.

Lavender Orange French Toast

The comforting flavors in this French toast will surely get your day going on a positive note. Drizzle homemade blackberry simple syrup (see page 224) over the top for extra yum!

MAKES 9 SERVINGS

3 dehydrated orange slices (see page 120)

1 tablespoon dried lavender buds

6 large eggs

2 cups 2% milk

½ cup packed light brown sugar

1 teaspoon vanilla extract

½ teaspoon ground cinnamon

Melted butter or nonstick cooking oil spray, for the griddle

18 slices brioche

Powdered sugar, for garnish

Softened butter and your favorite syrup (warmed), for serving

1 · Using a mortar and pestle, or a spice/coffee grinder, pulverize the orange slices and lavender buds. You should have about 2 tablespoons.

2 · Heat a griddle over medium heat. (If you have an electric griddle, heat it to 375°F.) Whisk the eggs in a large bowl. Add the milk, brown sugar, ground orange-lavender mixture, vanilla, and cinnamon and whisk until the sugar is dissolved.

3 · Brush the griddle with melted butter or grease with oil spray. In batches, dip the bread in the egg mixture, letting it soak for a few seconds. Place on the griddle. Cook until the underside is golden brown, 2 to 3 minutes.

Turn onto the second side and cook until golden, 2 to 3 minutes more. Sift powdered sugar on top and serve hot with softened butter and syrup.

VARIATION

Baked Lavender Orange French Toast: Preheat the oven to 350°F. Grease a 9-by-13-inch baking dish with oil spray. Cut the brioche into 1- to 2-inch cubes and spread evenly in the dish. Evenly pour the egg mixture over the brioche. Stir the pieces, making sure all of them are coated in the mixture. Bake until golden brown, 20 to 25 minutes.

Off to a Good Start

Avocado Garden Toast

I love this weekend breakfast/art project! It begins with a walk around the gardens to collect my toppings and ends with a delicious and nutritious start to my day. My stomach and soul are both filled. Depending on your mood, go savory with avocado, or sweet with jelly or jam.

MAKES 2 SERVINGS

Toppings—see below (optional)

2 ripe avocados (see Note), halved, peeled, and pitted

1 tablespoon Herb Infused Olive Oil (page 193)

2 teaspoons fresh lemon juice

½ teaspoon Greek Seasoning Blend (page 109)

Salt and freshly ground black pepper

2 large slices crusty sourdough or whole wheat bread, toasted, if desired

1 · Gather the toppings from your garden, rinse, and let air dry.

2 · Mash the avocados in a medium bowl with a fork. Stir in the oil, lemon juice, and Greek seasoning. Season with salt and pepper to taste.

3 · Spread the avocado mash on the bread to create the background for your design. Using the topping inspirations, decorate a garden-like still life on the spread. Serve immediately.

TOPPING INSPIRATIONS

- *For flowers:* Use thinly sliced radishes and cucumber, and halved cherry tomatoes as the center of flowers with fresh petals from zinnias, dahlias, or calendula arranged around them. Or whole flowers like pansies, violas, chamomile, and daisies.

- *For flower leaves:* Use fresh mint leaves, flat leaf parsley, basil leaves, wild violet leaves.

- *For flower stems:* Use fresh chives or scallions.

- *For grass:* Use fresh dill, parsley, carrot greens, or lettuce leaves.

NOTE

To substitute freeze-dried avocado for fresh, grind enough to measure 1 cup and transfer to a bowl. Stir in cool water, 1 tablespoon at a time, to reach the desired consistency.

VARIATION

Sweet Garden Toast: Substitute your favorite jam or jelly for the avocado.

Ham and Cheese Garden Quiche

I love this recipe because it's semi-homemade and a beautiful food creation in half the time, with half the dirty dishes. Winning! Have the time to make it from scratch? Use Grandma's Pie Dough (page 340).

MAKES 8 SERVINGS

1 (14.1-ounce) package refrigerated pie crusts (2 crusts)

4 large eggs

1½ cups half-and-half or light cream

½ cup chopped leafy greens (such as kale, chard, or spinach)

½ cup seeded and diced red or orange bell pepper (see Note)

½ teaspoon dried thyme

¼ teaspoon salt

⅛ teaspoon freshly ground black pepper

⅛ teaspoon grated nutmeg

1½ cups shredded cheddar or Swiss cheese

1 tablespoon all-purpose flour, plus more for the crust

¾ cup (½-inch) diced ham

1 large egg white, lightly beaten

Edible flowers, herb sprigs, and/or whole, small leafy greens, for garnish

1 • Preheat the oven to 450°F.

2 • Line a 9-inch pie plate with one pie crust, pressing the top edge of the crust onto the top edge of the plate. Cover the pie crust with a double thickness of aluminum foil, pressing the foil against the crust. Place on a baking sheet. Bake for 8 minutes. Remove the foil and continue baking until the crust is set, about 4 minutes more. Remove from the oven and lower the temperature to 325°F.

3 • In a medium bowl, whisk together the eggs, half-and-half, chopped greens, bell pepper, thyme, salt, black pepper, and nutmeg. Toss the cheese and flour in another bowl to coat the cheese. Stir into the egg mixture, followed by the ham. Pour into the partially baked crust. Place the second crust on a lightly floured work surface. Using a small cookie cutter, cut out the desired shapes. Brush the edge of the pie crust with the egg white and adhere the cutouts to the edges. Brush the cutouts again with the egg white. Decorate the top of the filling with edible flowers, herb sprigs, and whole greens in a garden design. Loosely cover the crust edge with strips of aluminum foil.

4 • Bake until the filling is lightly browned and set when the quiche is gently shaken, 45 to 50 minutes. Let cool for 5 minutes on a wire cooling rack. Slice and serve warm.

NOTE

Substitute ½ cup thawed frozen, ¼ cup rehydrated dried, or ½ cup refreshed freeze-dried peppers for fresh.

Totally Twisted Yogurt

Morning yogurt, with a twist! Use flower, fruit, or vegetable powders to color and flavor your favorite yogurt. Here's how we often enjoy it, but get creative using whatever you've put up.

MAKES 1 SERVING

1 cup nonfat vanilla Greek yogurt

1 teaspoon freeze-dried or dehydrated blueberry powder (see page 113) or ½ teaspoon butterfly pea flower powder

1 kiwi, sliced

4 to 6 fresh blueberries

½ teaspoon poppy seeds

2 to 3 tablespoons Lavender Granola (recipe below), for sprinkling

Edible flowers, such as violas or pansies, for garnish

1 tablespoon your favorite herb-infused honey (see page 213), for drizzling

Stir the yogurt and blueberry powder together in a bowl. Top with the kiwi, blueberries, and poppy seeds.

Sprinkle with the granola, garnish with the flowers, and drizzle with the honey.

Lavender Granola

This is a deliciously crunchy yet chewy grab-and-go snack. It's also good with yogurt and ice cream.

MAKES 4 TO 5 CUPS

4 cups old-fashioned (rolled) oats

2 cups unsweetened coconut flakes

2 tablespoons flax seeds

½ cup honey or infused honey (see page 213)

½ cup packed light brown sugar

½ cup sunflower butter

1 tablespoon unsalted butter

1 teaspoon dried lavender buds

½ teaspoon ground cinnamon

1 teaspoon vanilla extract

1 · Preheat the oven to 300°F. Line a rimmed baking sheet with parchment paper.

2 · Mix the oats, coconut, and flax seeds on the prepared sheet and spread evenly. Bake, stirring occasionally, until the mixture begins to brown around the edges, about 12 minutes. Remove from the oven but leave the oven on. Let the oat mixture cool.

3 · Heat the honey, brown sugar, sunflower butter, unsalted butter, lavender, and cinnamon in a medium saucepan over medium heat, stirring often, until combined and the butter is melted. Remove from the heat and stir in the vanilla.

4 · Transfer the oat mixture to a large bowl and set the baking sheet aside. Add the honey mixture and mix well to coat. Return to the lined baking sheet and spread with an oiled silicone spatula. Return to the oven and bake, stirring occasionally, until the granola is golden brown, 12 to 15 minutes. Cool completely. Break up the granola into smaller pieces. Transfer to an airtight container and store at room temperature for up to 6 months.

You're So Smooth!

Having preserved fruit on hand makes whipping up a smoothie in any season a snap. They're also a super sneaky way to add vegetables, protein powders, seeds, and other "good for you" things that make the kids give you the side-eye.

Did you know there's a system to a smooth smoothie? Who knew?! The key is in layering the ingredients in the blender.

- Start with liquid first.
- Add protein, vegetable, or fruit powders and sweeteners.
- Next up are the leafy greens.
- Then soft ingredients, like yogurt.
- Follow with fruit, seeds, and/or nuts.
- Top with ice.

Smart Start Smoothie

This smoothie was the one sure way I could get my kids to have spinach. Once they realized they liked spinach in smoothies, they were willing to try it in other things. Who knew a smoothie would be the gateway to liking veggies?

MAKES 2 SERVINGS

2 cups fresh orange juice

2 to 3 frozen spinach cubes (see page 33) or ½ cup packed fresh baby spinach

½ cup plain Greek yogurt or 1 cup Freeze-Dried Yogurt Drops (page 155)

1 apple, peeled, cored, and coarsely chopped

1 banana, sliced, or 1 cup frozen banana slices

Ice cubes (optional)

In this order, place the orange juice, spinach cubes, yogurt, apple, banana, and a few ice cubes (if using) into a blender and process until smooth. Pour into glasses and serve cold.

Tropical Dreams Smoothie

Enjoy this refreshing smoothie while you sit outside with the sun shining on you and the kids squawking like tropical birds in the background. Almost like being there . . .

MAKES 2 TO 3 SERVINGS

1 cup coconut water

1 cup fresh orange juice

2 tablespoons carrot powder (see page 113)

2 tablespoons sugar or raw honey

1 cup frozen strawberries

1 cup frozen mango chunks

1 cup fresh, frozen, or canned pineapple

1 cup ice cubes

In this order, put the coconut water, orange juice, carrot powder, sugar, strawberries, mango, pineapple, and ice cubes in a blender and process until smooth. Pour into glasses and serve chilled.

Tickled Pink Smoothie Bowl

Let your creativity loose with smoothie bowls.

MAKES 2 SERVINGS

½ cup milk (dairy, oat, coconut, or nut)

¼ cup fresh orange juice

1 cup nonfat vanilla yogurt

2 cups frozen strawberries

Toppings
6 to 8 freeze-dried strawberry slices, crumbled

¼ cup pomegranate seeds

1 teaspoon flax seeds

Edible flowers (optional)

In this order, put the milk, orange juice, yogurt, and strawberries in a blender and process until smooth. Divide into bowls. Distribute the toppings equally over the smoothies, decorating them in a fairy food kind of way. Serve immediately.

Off to a Good Start

Soups & Sandwiches

Fun fact: Hubs dreams of a food cart where he can serve up sandwiches and hang with the locals. I have dreams of eating sandwiches. Soups, which I also enjoy eating, are an easy way to use canned, dried, freeze-dried, and frozen foods. Serve with Herb and Cheddar Biscuits (page 314) or Garden Focaccia (page 302).

Creamy Roasted Tomato Soup

MAKES 2 TO 4 SERVINGS

Nothing screams sweater weather like tomato soup. I make mine using my roasted marinara and it never disappoints. Serve it with a crusty grilled cheese sandwich made using an herb compound butter (see page 198) and the crowd will go wild! This soup also makes an excellent creamy sauce for pasta.

2 cups Roasted Marinara Sauce (page 297)

½ cup heavy cream

Salt and freshly ground black pepper

Fresh basil leaves, torn (optional)

Bring the marinara sauce to a boil in a small saucepan over medium-high heat. Stir in the cream and turn the heat down to medium-low. Simmer, stirring occasionally, until hot, 2 to 3 minutes. Season with salt and pepper. Top with torn basil leaves, if using. Remove from the heat and let stand for a few minutes before serving.

Vegetable and Bean Soup

Time to put that pretty jar of dehydrated vegetable and bean soup mix from chapter 5 to good use! This soup is also a great excuse to clean out the refrigerator! During the last 10 minutes of cooking, stir in baby spinach, corn kernels, chopped kale leaves, or slices of cooked ham or sausage. Bring up the heat by adding red pepper flakes.

MAKES 6 SERVINGS

1 quart Zero-Waste Vegetable Broth (page 163) or store-bought vegetable or chicken broth

3 cups water, divided

1 cup Vegetable and Bean Dried Soup Mix (page 136)

¼ teaspoon dried marjoram

¼ teaspoon dried thyme

1 (14.5-ounce) can diced tomatoes or 1 pint home-canned tomatoes cut into ½-inch pieces

1 cup egg noodles

Kosher salt or herb salt (see page 205) and freshly ground black pepper

Pinch of red pepper flakes (optional)

1 · Bring the broth, 2 cups of the water, the soup mix, marjoram, and thyme to a boil in a medium saucepan over high heat. Turn the heat down to medium-low and simmer for 30 minutes.

2 · Stir in the tomatoes and their juice, the remaining 1 cup of water, and the noodles. Increase the heat to high and return to a boil. Turn the heat back down to medium-low and simmer until the vegetables and beans are very tender, 15 to 20 minutes. If the soup seems too thick, add additional broth or water, ½ cup at a time, until it reaches the desired consistency. Season with salt and pepper and red pepper flakes (if using) to taste and serve.

Fresh Pea Soup

Instead of dried peas for this soup, I use fresh-out-of-the-garden peas. When I have some on hand, I also use my homemade vegetable broth. Serve this soup with a warm homemade baguette (see page 317) smothered in your favorite herb compound butter (see page 198).

MAKES 8 SERVINGS

1 tablespoon extra-virgin olive oil or Herb Infused Olive Oil (page 193)

1 medium yellow onion, chopped

1 cup (½-inch) fresh, frozen, or freeze-dried diced carrots or ½ cup dehydrated, refreshed

1 cup fresh, frozen, or freeze-dried chopped celery or ½ cup dehydrated, refreshed

3 garlic cloves, minced

1 tablespoon fresh thyme or 1 teaspoon dried

½ teaspoon salt, plus more as needed

¼ teaspoon freshly ground black pepper, plus more as needed

4 pounds shell peas, shelled (4 cups peas, pods reserved to make more broth)

2 quarts Zero-Waste Vegetable Broth (page 163) or store-bought vegetable or chicken broth

3 yellow potatoes, such as Yukon Gold (about 1 pound), peeled and cut into ½-inch cubes

8 ounces cooked ham, cut into ½-inch dice

1 · Heat the oil in a large, heavy saucepan over medium heat. Add the onion, half the carrots, the celery, garlic, thyme, salt, and pepper and cook, stirring occasionally, until the vegetables start to soften, about 2 minutes. Stir in the peas and cook for 2 minutes. Add the broth and bring to a boil. Turn the heat down to medium-low and simmer for 10 minutes. Remove the pot from the heat. Using an immersion blender, puree the soup to the desired consistency.

2 · Add the potatoes, ham, and the remaining carrots to the soup and return to a simmer over medium heat. Turn the heat down to medium-low, cover, and simmer, stirring occasionally to avoid scorching, until the potatoes and carrots are tender, 15 to 20 minutes. Season with salt and pepper. Let cool for about 15 minutes before serving. (The completely cooled soup can be stored in airtight containers in the refrigerator for up to 5 days or in the freezer for up to 3 months.)

Vegetable, Beef, and Farro Soup

This is pure comfort in a bowl. Serve for lunch or dinner on rainy days, sunny days, crisp cool days, or any days!

MAKES 10 TO 12 SERVINGS

2 tablespoons extra-virgin olive oil, divided

1½ to 2 pounds boneless beef chuck, cut into 1- to 2-inch chunks

Salt and freshly ground black pepper

1 large onion, chopped

1 cup diced carrots

1 cup diced celery

4 garlic cloves, minced

½ teaspoon dried rosemary

½ teaspoon dried thyme

3 tablespoons Homemade Tomato Paste (page 113) or store-bought

3 (32-ounce) containers beef broth, divided

2 teaspoons low-sodium soy sauce

2 teaspoons Worcestershire sauce

¾ cup dehydrated mushrooms (page 126) or store-bought dried mushrooms

1½ cups organic farro

1 cup fresh, frozen, or freeze-dried zucchini, diced, or 2 cups dehydrated

2 cups packed stemmed kale or chard leaves, coarsely chopped

Chopped fresh parsley, for garnish

1 · Heat 1 tablespoon of the oil in a large Dutch oven over medium-high heat. Add the beef and season lightly with salt and pepper. Cook, stirring occasionally, until browned, about 3 minutes. Transfer the meat and juices to a plate.

2 · Add the remaining 1 tablespoon of oil to the pot. Add the onion, carrots, and celery and season lightly with salt and pepper. Cook until the vegetables begin to soften, about 2 minutes. Stir in the garlic, rosemary, thyme, and tomato paste and cook until the garlic is fragrant, about 1 minute. Add about ½ cup of the broth and stir to scrape up the browned bits at the bottom of the pot. Add the remaining broth in the container and one more container, along with the soy sauce, Worcestershire sauce, and mushrooms. Return the beef and any collected juices to the pot.

3 · Bring to a boil, then turn the heat down to medium-low, cover, and simmer for 1 hour. Add the farro and zucchini and simmer for 30 minutes. Stir in the kale and the remaining container of broth and simmer until the beef and farro are tender, about 10 minutes. Season with salt and pepper to taste. Remove from the heat and let stand for 10 to 15 minutes. Ladle into bowls, sprinkle with the parsley, and serve warm.

Teatime Sandwiches

Serve these super-easy open-faced tea sandwiches at your next tea party or get-together. They look fancy, taste delicious, and take no time at all to put together. If you have some time, make Rosemary Baguettes (page 317) to use here. Oh, so good!

MAKES 6 TO 8 SERVINGS

Herb and Dried Tomato Cheese Spread (page 243), at room temperature

16 slices crusty bread

Toppings: thinly sliced cucumbers, thinly sliced radishes, thinly sliced cherry tomatoes, microgreens, pancetta, tiny carrot sticks, whole viola flowers

Flaky sea salt, such as Maldon (optional)

Spread the cheese mixture evenly over each bread slice. Cut in half or use a cookie cutter to cut into desired shapes. Decorate with the toppings of your choice. Sprinkle with flaky salt, if desired, and serve.

Candied Bacon Chicken Sandwich

This scratch-made sandwich goes perfect with a bowl of homemade soup and a big pair of socks! Or a potato salad and a picnic blanket. Either way, it's so good!

MAKES 4 SANDWICHES

2 (10- to 12-ounce) boneless, skinless chicken breast halves

Garlic and Herb Marinade (page 196)

4 slices provolone or Swiss cheese

4 slices Garden Focaccia (page 302), cut in half horizontally

1 cup mayonnaise

Rosemary Candy Bacon (page 271)

1 medium tomato, sliced

1 cup microgreens

1 · Pound the chicken breasts with a mallet or the back of a large metal spoon until about ½ inch thick, trimming any fat. Place in a plastic bag and cover with the marinade. For the best flavor, marinate in the refrigerator for 4 to 6 hours.

2 · Preheat the oven to 375°F.

3 · Transfer the chicken to a small baking dish. Discard the remaining marinade. Bake until an instant-read thermometer inserted in the thickest part of the chicken reads 170°F, 25 to 30 minutes. Top each breast with 2 slices of cheese and bake until the cheese melts, about 2 minutes. Cool slightly. Cut each chicken portion in half crosswise to make 4 pieces total.

4 · Spread the bottom halves of the focaccia generously with the mayonnaise. Top each with a piece of chicken, 1 or 2 pieces of rosemary bacon, a tomato slice, and a quarter of the microgreens. Cover with the top halves of the focaccia. Cut each sandwich in half and serve.

Preserving the Seasons

Rosemary Candied Bacon

MAKES 8 SLICES

½ cup packed light brown sugar

8 thick slices bacon

½ teaspoon coarsely chopped dried rosemary

This bacon is beyond decadent. But it sure is a treat on the weekends or holidays and it rocks BLTs, burgers, and salads. Use applewood or maple-smoked pepper bacon for the best flavor.

1 · Preheat the oven to 400°F. Line a rimmed baking sheet with parchment paper.

2 · Rub half the brown sugar over the bacon. Flip the bacon and rub the other side with the remaining sugar. Sprinkle with the rosemary. Transfer the bacon, rosemary-side up, to the prepared pan.

3 · Bake, watching carefully to make sure the sugar does not burn, until the bacon is browned, 12 to 15 minutes. Let cool on the pan for 5 minutes. Serve warm.

Turkey-Stuffed Lettuce Wraps

These are good either warm or cold, but serve them the same day that you're cooking the filling. For easy wrapping, use a wide lettuce with a tender vein, such as red or green leaf varieties. Replace the fresh scapes with Quick-Pickled Garlic Scapes (page 60) if you made some.

MAKES 4 TO 6 SERVINGS

1 tablespoon extra-virgin olive oil

1 small onion, chopped

½ cup (½-inch) diced fresh or thawed frozen red or green bell peppers (see Note)

3 garlic scapes, chopped, or 1 garlic clove, minced

Salt and freshly ground black pepper

1 pound ground turkey

¼ teaspoon dried oregano

¼ teaspoon dried rosemary

¼ teaspoon dried thyme

2 tablespoons sweet teriyaki sauce

4 to 6 wide, tender lettuce leaves

4 to 6 long, whole chives

4 to 6 edible flowers, such as pansies (optional)

1 · Heat the oil in a medium saucepan over medium-high heat. Add the onion, bell pepper, and garlic scapes and season lightly with salt and pepper. Cook, stirring often, until the onion is translucent, 2 to 3 minutes. Add the turkey, oregano, rosemary, and thyme. Cook, stirring occasionally, until the turkey is no longer pink, about 5 minutes. Stir in the teriyaki sauce and cook until slightly reduced and the mixture thickens, 1 to 2 minutes. Season with salt and pepper. Remove from the heat and let cool slightly.

2 · Spoon a portion of the turkey mixture onto the narrow end of a lettuce leaf. Fold up the bottom and then roll up, tucking in the sides, to make a packet. Using a chive, tie the packet closed. Slip a pansy under the chive, if desired. You now have yourself one delicious gift from the garden and grocery store.

NOTE

If you don't have fresh or frozen peppers, hit the pantry and use ¼ cup dried bell peppers, rehydrated, or ½ cup freeze-dried peppers, refreshed.

Salad Bar

We make salads using whatever greens are in the garden or on sale, topped with what's available in the garden or refrigerator that day. But the real star is the vinaigrette. Try dressing up your greens with one of the following delicious "salad potions." Beyond the greens at the salad bar, you'll find fruit and potato salads, too.

Garden Wraps with Sweet Chili Sauce

MAKES 4 SERVINGS

Just a regular salad wrapped up into perfection! You can find rice paper wrappers in many grocery stores and online. Use the recipe below to get you inspired, but do consider including whatever you have on hand in the garden or from the store or farmers' market.

1 (20- to 24-count) package rice paper rounds (also known as spring roll wrappers)

Edible flowers, as needed

Basil leaves, as needed

2 cups fresh or refreshed freeze-dried shredded red cabbage

2 cup shredded leaf lettuce

1 cup finely chopped rainbow chard leaves and stems

1 to 2 carrots, cut into thin sticks

1 fresh or thawed frozen yellow bell pepper, seeded and cut into thin sticks

1 fresh or thawed frozen red or orange bell pepper, cut into sticks

1 cucumber, peeled and thinly sliced

2 cups microgreens or broccoli sprouts

2 to 3 fresh or refreshed freeze-dried radishes, thinly sliced

Sesame seeds, for garnish (optional)

Sweet Chili Sauce (page 276), for serving

1 · Fill a large bowl with warm water and place it near a clean cutting board or flat work surface. Working one at a time, submerge a rice paper round in the water and let it soak, turning a few times until pliable, about 15 seconds. Remove from the water and place on the cutting board with the lower edge of the round hanging over the bottom edge of the board.

2 · For each roll, the first ingredients will be the visible "pretty side," so start by arranging a few flowers and basil leaves in the center of the round. Top with thin layers of the cabbage, lettuce, chard, carrots, bell peppers, cucumber, microgreens, and radishes. Do not overfill the roll. (You will quickly get an idea of how many vegetables you need with your first roll or two.)

3 · Bring up the edge closest to you to partially cover the vegetables. Fold in the sides toward the center and roll up from the bottom, applying pressing to compact the vegetables and make a tight roll. Transfer to a large platter, leaving room in the center for a bowl for the sauce. The wraps can be loosely covered with plastic wrap and refrigerated for up to 2 hours.

4 · Sprinkle with sesame seeds, if desired. Pour the chili sauce into the bowl and serve, with the sauce for dipping.

Salad Bar

Sweet Chili Sauce

MAKES 2 CUPS

1 cup long red chiles (such as Thai, jalapeño, or cayenne), finely chopped with seeds

1 cup sugar

1 cup water plus 2 tablespoons cold water

½ cup rice wine vinegar

3 garlic cloves, peeled and diced

1 tablespoon cornstarch

1 · Using food-safe gloves, remove the stem end and chop the chiles, measuring as you chop until you have 4 ounces.

2 · Combine the sugar, 1 cup of the water, the vinegar, garlic, and chiles in a small saucepan. Bring to a boil over medium heat, stirring until the sugar is dissolved. Turn the heat down to medium and simmer rapidly for 10 to 12 minutes.

3 · In a small bowl, mix the cornstarch and the remaining 2 tablespoons of cold water. Turn the heat down to low and stir in the cornstarch mixture. Stirring constantly, cook for 3 minutes as the sauce thickens. Remove from the heat and cool completely. Use right away, or store in an airtight container in the refrigerator for up to 3 months. For the best flavor, allow the sauce to warm to room temperature before serving.

Cucumber Rose Garden Salad

An art project on a plate! Create your own garden scene using your favorite salad ingredients, drizzled with wild violet vinaigrette and let this deliciously whimsical plate spoil your senses. It's also a fun way to get the kiddos excited to eat vegetables. This is designed to be a starter salad, but by all means, load up the vegetables!

MAKES 2 SERVINGS

2 large cucumbers, unpeeled

6 lettuce leaves

8 chives

2 basil leaf tops

½ yellow bell pepper, top and bottom cut off and pepper sliced open so it lays flat

1 large radish, cut into 8 very thin rounds

1 strawberry, cut crosswise into 4 rounds

8 violas with their stems

½ cup Herb Croutons (recipe follows)

½ cup crumbled feta cheese

¼ cup Wild Violet Peppercorn Vinaigrette (page 281)

1 · Make the cucumber roses: Cut one cucumber crosswise into six 1-inch sections. Use a spoon or melon baller to hollow out the seedy centers to make cucumber cups. Using a mandoline, cut the remaining cucumber into ¹⁄₁₆-inch-thick rounds. Overlap 6 cucumber rounds. Starting from one end, roll up the slices to create a "rose," and insert into a cucumber cup to hold it in shape. Repeat to make 5 more roses. Refrigerate until ready to use.

2 · For each salad, place 2 lettuce leaves in a V shape on a dinner plate and a third leaf vertically in the middle. Arrange 4 chives, starting at the base of the lettuce to act as flower stems. Cover the base of the lettuce and chives with 3 cucumber roses. Place a basil top next to the roses. Using a mini cookie cutter, cut out 2 shapes from the yellow bell pepper. Add 2 of the yellow pepper cutouts on top of 2 radish rounds as the flower centers. Add 2 strawberry slices on top of the remaining chives. Add the violas to your garden, scatter a few croutons on the plate, and sprinkle with 2 tablespoons feta. Drizzle 2 tablespoons vinaigrette over the top of the salad. Repeat with the remaining ingredients.

Herb Croutons

MAKES ABOUT 2 CUPS

I save the ends of our bread loaves to make these zero-waste croutons. Another win for the pantry!

2 tablespoons extra-virgin olive oil or Herb Infused Olive Oil (page 193)

1 teaspoon Italian Seasoning Blend (page 110)

½ teaspoon garlic powder

½ teaspoon herb-infused salt (see page 205) or kosher salt

8 slices bread, cut into ½-inch cubes

1 · Preheat the oven to 375°F.

2 · Whisk the oil, Italian seasoning, garlic powder, and salt in a large bowl. Add the bread cubes, turning until evenly coated.

3 · Spread in a single layer on a rimmed baking sheet. Bake for 8 minutes. Flip the cubes and continue baking until crisp and golden, 8 to 10 minutes more, watching carefully during the last 5 minutes to avoid burning. Cool completely on the baking sheet.

4 · Use right away, or transfer to an airtight container and store in a cool, dark, place for up to 1 month.

Chive Blossom Vinaigrette

This delicious vinaigrette features the popular pink vinegar infusion enjoyed by gardeners every spring. After using the blossoms, put the woody stems to good use by adding to Zero-Waste Vegetable Broth (page 163).

MAKES ABOUT ½ CUP

¼ cup extra-virgin olive oil

¼ cup Chive Blossom Vinegar (page 187)

2 tablespoons raw honey or your favorite infused honey (see page 213)

½ teaspoon Dijon mustard

Pinch of salt

Freshly ground black pepper

Shake the oil, vinegar, honey, and mustard together in a jar with a tight-fitting lid until the dressing is combined and thickened. Season with salt and pepper and shake again. Use immediately or refrigerate for up to 1 week. Shake well before using.

Garlic Scape Vinaigrette

This recipe takes advantage of garlic scape powder, basil-infused vinegar, and infused honey. Of course, plain versions are always an option.

MAKES ABOUT 1¼ CUPS

¾ cup sunflower oil

¼ cup basil-infused vinegar (see page 186)

¼ cup water

2 tablespoons garlic scape powder (see page 113)

1 tablespoon infused honey (see page 213) or raw honey

1 tablespoon Dijon mustard

½ teaspoon salt

Cracked black pepper

Shake the oil, vinegar, water, garlic scape powder, honey, mustard, salt, and pepper in a jar with a tight-fitting lid until incorporated. Use immediately or refrigerate for up to 1 week. Shake well before using.

Raspberry Basil Vinaigrette

This zero-waste recipe calls for the raspberry mash after making raspberry-infused vinegar. But if you don't have that, a handful of fresh berries will do the trick. Might even be sweeter! Although nothing is sweeter than zero waste.

MAKES ABOUT 1 CUP

½ cup extra-virgin olive oil

¼ cup raspberry mash from Raspberry Vinegar (page 189) or ½ cup fresh raspberries, mashed

2 tablespoons basil-infused vinegar (see page 186) or distilled white vinegar

2 tablespoons herb-infused honey (see page 213) or raw honey

1 teaspoon fresh lime juice

1 teaspoon spicy brown mustard (not Dijon)

1 teaspoon dried basil, crushed

¼ teaspoon herb-infused salt (see page 205) or sea salt

¼ teaspoon freshly ground black pepper

Shake the oil, raspberry mash, vinegar, honey, lime juice, mustard, basil, salt, and pepper in a jar with a tight-fitting lid until incorporated. Let stand for 15 to 30 minutes to infuse the flavors. Use immediately or refrigerate for up to 1 week. Shake well before using.

Wild Violet Peppercorn Vinaigrette

Oh, this one is so pretty! It also has a delightful flavor that will have you looking forward to these weeds popping up every spring.

MAKES ABOUT ⅓ CUP

¼ cup sunflower oil

2 tablespoons Wild Violet Vinegar (page 187)

1 tablespoon wild violet–infused honey (see page 213) or raw honey

1 teaspoon fresh lemon juice

Pinch of salt

Freshly ground black pepper

Shake the oil, vinegar, honey, lemon juice, salt, and pepper in a jar with a tight-fitting lid until incorporated. Use immediately or refrigerate for up to 1 week. Shake well before using.

Melon Ball Salad *with* Chamomile Honey

Serve this simple, sweet, colorful dish in a beautiful bowl and let it double as table decor.

MAKES 6 TO 8 SERVINGS

½ ripe cantaloupe, seeded

½ ripe honeydew melon, seeded

1 seedless baby watermelon

3 tablespoons Chamomile Honey (page 215) or raw honey

2 tablespoons fresh lime juice

Fresh mint leaves, for garnish

1 · Using a melon baller, scoop balls from the melons, placing the balls in a large bowl. Cover and refrigerate until chilled, or up to overnight.

2 · Whisk the honey and lime juice in a small bowl. Just before serving, pour over the melon balls and toss gently. Spoon into individual bowls, garnish with mint leaves, and serve.

Picnic Potato Salad

This recipe takes advantage of our seasonal chive blossom vinegar and home-style pickles. I love it when that happens!

MAKES 8 TO 12 SERVINGS

2½ to 3 pounds Yukon Gold potatoes, peeled

Salt

1 cup mayonnaise

1 tablespoon yellow mustard

1 tablespoon Chive Blossom Vinegar (page 187)

1 teaspoon dried basil

1 teaspoon dried oregano

½ teaspoon garlic powder

¼ teaspoon freshly ground black pepper

6 hard-boiled eggs, peeled and cut into ½-inch dice

3 to 4 scallions, chopped

⅓ cup diced Homestyle Pickles (page 85) or store-bought

1 · Put the potatoes in a large saucepan and add enough water to cover by 1 inch. Add a generous pinch or two of salt to the water. Bring to a boil over high heat. Turn the heat down to medium-low and simmer until the potatoes can be easily pierced with the tip of a sharp knife, 20 to 30 minutes. Drain the potatoes and let cool.

2 · In a large bowl, stir together the mayonnaise, mustard, vinegar, 1½ teaspoons salt, the basil, oregano, garlic powder, and pepper. Cut the potatoes into bite-size cubes (you should have about 7 cups). Add the potatoes, eggs, scallions, and pickles to the bowl and mix well. Cover and refrigerate for at least 4 hours or up to 4 days. Serve chilled.

Dinner Menu

I love a hearty main dish, and side dishes straight from the garden, the grocery, pantry, or the freezer are always a winner when there are vegetables on the table. Rice and beans are vessels of flavor with so many possibilities.

Pacific Northwest Crab Cakes

MAKES 6 CRAB CAKES

Of all the things I cook for my husband, this is one of his favorites. These are small but mighty. Serve a few alongside a large garden salad and top with tartar sauce. You'll be full before you know it! These also make an excellent appetizer. If you don't have fresh bell peppers, frozen (thawed) or dehydrated and freeze-dried (refreshed) can be used.

1½ cups panko

1 cup (8 ounces) cooked crabmeat

1 large egg, beaten

¼ cup finely diced yellow bell pepper

¼ cup finely diced orange bell pepper

2 tablespoons finely chopped fresh flat-leaf parsley or 1 tablespoon dried

1 tablespoon spicy brown mustard

1 tablespoon minced shallots

1 teaspoon finely chopped fresh dill or ½ teaspoon dried dill

½ teaspoon Homemade Celery Salt (page 148)

½ teaspoon sweet paprika

½ teaspoon garlic scape powder (see page 113) or ¼ teaspoon garlic powder

¼ teaspoon salt

⅛ teaspoon freshly ground black pepper

¾ cup sunflower or vegetable oil

Homestead Tartar Sauce (page 285) or store-bought, for serving

1 · In a medium bowl, stir together the panko, crabmeat, egg, bell peppers, parsley, mustard, shallots, dill, celery salt, paprika, garlic scape powder, salt, and pepper until evenly mixed. Using your hands, divide into 6 portions and shape into cakes about ½ inch thick. Transfer to a plate. Cover and chill in the refrigerator for 30 minutes.

2 · Heat the oil in a large skillet over medium-high heat until the oil is shimmering. Add the crab cakes and cook until the underside is golden brown, about 2 minutes. Flip the cakes and cook to brown the other side, about 2 minutes more. Serve hot with tartar sauce.

Homestead Tartar Sauce

This sauce takes advantage of your homemade pickles, fresh and dried herbs, dehydrated onion powder, and celery salt. Wow, go you! You can also use all store-bought items too—no matter how you get there, you're doing it!

MAKES ABOUT ¾ CUP

⅔ cup mayonnaise

¼ cup finely chopped Homestyle Pickles (page 85)

2 teaspoons finely chopped fresh parsley or 1 teaspoon dried

1 teaspoon fresh lemon juice

½ teaspoon dried dill

¼ teaspoon onion powder

¼ teaspoon Homemade Celery Salt (page 148)

Whisk the mayonnaise, pickles, parsley, lemon juice, dill, onion powder, and celery salt together in a small bowl. Cover and refrigerate for at least 2 hours or up to 2 weeks.

Stuffed Zucchini

Zucchini is best when harvested small. But that doesn't mean those big mamas aren't delicious! I use half a giant zucchini to make this recipe and the other half to make Chocolate Zucchini Bundt Cake (page 332). That's dinner *and* dessert thanks to an overgrown zucchini!

MAKES 4 TO 5 SERVINGS

Nonstick cooking oil spray

1 large overgrown zucchini or 4 small zucchini, ends trimmed

1 tablespoon extra-virgin olive oil

Herb-infused salt (see page 205) and freshly ground black pepper

1 cup diced bacon

1 small white or yellow onion, chopped

½ cup diced fresh, thawed frozen, or refreshed freeze-dried bell peppers (any color) or ¼ cup dehydrated, refreshed

1 teaspoon Italian Seasoning Blend (page 110)

½ teaspoon garlic powder

1 cup Roasted Marinara Sauce (page 297) or store-bought

½ cup Italian-style dried breadcrumbs

¼ cup freshly grated Parmesan

½ cup shredded mozzarella

1 · Preheat the oven to 400°F. Grease a 9-by-13-inch baking dish with the oil spray.

2 · Cut the zucchini in half lengthwise. Scoop out the seeds and stringy flesh, leaving a ½-inch-thick shell. (Feed the discards to your backyard chickens!) Put the zucchini halves in the prepared baking dish, cut side up, drizzle with the oil, and season with the herb salt and pepper.

3 · Cook the bacon in a large skillet over medium-high heat, stirring occasionally, until it has rendered some fat and is beginning to brown, 3 to 5 minutes. Stir in the onion, bell peppers, Italian seasoning, and garlic powder. Continue cooking until the bacon is browned and the onion is softened, about 5 minutes. Stir in the marinara sauce and bring to a simmer. Turn the heat down to low and simmer, stirring occasionally, to blend the flavors, about 5 minutes. Remove from the heat. Stir in the breadcrumbs and Parmesan. Spoon into the prepared zucchini halves. Cover with the mozzarella.

4 · Bake until the sauce is bubbling and the mozzarella is golden brown, 25 to 30 minutes. Let stand for 5 minutes, then slice and serve.

Potato Roses

This is a perfect side dish for date night dinners or a fancy party on a budget. A mandoline or plastic vegetable slicer will make slicing the potatoes quick and easy. If you don't have one, just take your time to slice the potatoes as thinly and evenly as possible. Serve plain or with Kickin' Ketchup (page 304).

MAKES 12 ROSES

4 small to medium Yukon Gold potatoes, scrubbed, trimmed, and cut into 1/16-inch-thick rounds

¾ cup (1½ sticks) unsalted butter, melted

2 teaspoons garlic powder

1½ teaspoons Italian Seasoning Blend (page 110)

½ teaspoon herb-infused salt (see page 205) or kosher salt, plus more for serving

1 · Preheat the oven to 400°F. Brush 12 mini-muffin cups with some of the melted butter.

2 · Mix the remaining melted butter, garlic powder, Italian seasoning, and salt in a small bowl.

3 · For each rose, overlap 10 potato rounds into a row on the work surface, placing each round about halfway over the next one. Brush with some of the seasoned melted butter. Starting with the first round and holding them all together as you go, carefully roll up the slices to create a rose shape. Use your fingers to grab the first round to secure the bundle.

4 · Stand each rose in a muffin cup and splay the slices to separate the "petals." Repeat with the remaining potatoes until you have a dozen roses. Brush the remaining seasoned melted butter over the potato roses.

5 · Bake until the potatoes are tender, and the edges are browned, 30 to 35 minutes. Season each with a pinch of salt. Loosen the roses from the cups and serve hot.

Glazed Carrots

This recipe works well with frozen carrot sticks. No need to thaw first! You can also use store-bought carrot sticks or even baby-cut carrots. The goal is a uniform size so they cook evenly.

MAKES 6 SERVINGS

1 pound fresh or frozen carrots, peeled and cut into sticks, 3 to 4 inches long and ½-inch thick

4 to 5 fresh thyme sprigs

¼ cup herb compound butter (see page 198) or unsalted butter

¼ cup packed light brown sugar

¼ teaspoon herb-infused salt (see page 205)

⅛ teaspoon freshly ground black pepper

1 · Place the carrot sticks and thyme sprigs in a medium saucepan and add just enough water to cover. Bring to a boil over medium-high heat. Cook until the carrots are tender, 10 to 15 minutes. Drain the carrots and discard any bare thyme sprigs, leaving any sprigs with leaves.

2 · Melt the butter, sugar, salt, and pepper in the same saucepan and cook, stirring, to dissolve the sugar. Add the carrots and thyme sprigs to the saucepan, turning until evenly coated. Cook until the carrots are glazed, about 3 minutes. Discard the thyme sprigs. Transfer to a bowl and serve immediately.

Honey-Glazed Pork Loin

This is a Sunday kind of dinner for us. I like to prepare big dishes in the hopes there will be leftovers for the week ahead. Use leftover pork loin in sandwiches, tacos, or soups.

MAKES 8 SERVINGS

1 recipe Go-To Spice Rub (recipe below)

1 (4½-pound) boneless pork loin

1 tablespoon extra-virgin olive oil

Honey-Garlic Glaze

¼ cup rosemary-infused honey (see page 213) or raw honey

2 tablespoons low-sodium soy sauce

2 tablespoons spicy brown mustard

1 tablespoon light brown sugar

1 tablespoon Herb Infused Olive Oil (page 193) or extra-virgin olive oil

4 garlic cloves, minced

1 · Preheat the oven to 375°F. Line a rimmed baking sheet with aluminum foil.

2 · Evenly rub the spice mixture all over the pork. Heat the oil in a large skillet over medium-high heat. Add the pork and cook, turning occasionally, until browned, 6 to 8 minutes. Transfer to the prepared baking sheet, fat-side up.

3 · Make the glaze: Whisk the honey, soy sauce, mustard, brown sugar, oil, and garlic together in a small bowl. Brush half the glaze all over the meat. Bake for 30 minutes. Brush with the remaining glaze and tent with foil. Continue baking until an instant-read thermometer inserted in the center of the loin reads 145°F for medium, about 1½ hours. (I like to cook mine to 160°F, about 2 hours.)

4 · Rest the meat for 10 minutes. Slice and serve.

Go-To Spice Rub

MAKES ABOUT 2½ TABLESPOONS

In a small bowl, stir together 2 teaspoons sweet paprika, 1 teaspoon garlic powder, 1 teaspoon ground thyme, 1 teaspoon ground rosemary, 1 teaspoon kosher salt, ½ teaspoon onion powder, and ¼ teaspoon freshly ground black pepper.

Use immediately or transfer to an airtight container and store in a cool, dry place for up to 3 months.

Slow-Cooked Dried Beans

Cool weather is always my sign to break out a pot and start slow cooking dry beans. It's a filling comfort food that takes some time but always satisfies. Older beans should soak for several hours to overnight before cooking to help soften.

MAKES 5 TO 6 CUPS COOKED BEANS

1 pound (2 cups) dry beans

2 teaspoons salt

½ cup diced onion

2 carrots, diced

2 garlic cloves, peeled

1 teaspoon dried thyme

1 bay leaf

6 cups fresh water

Salt and freshly ground black pepper

1 · Sort the beans, removing any that are shriveled. Rinse in a fine-mesh strainer under cold water.

2 · Put the beans in a Dutch oven. Add enough water to cover by about 1 inch. Bring to a boil over high heat and boil for 2 minutes. Remove from the heat, cover, and let stand for 1 hour.

3 · Drain and rinse. Discard the soaking liquid. Rinse the pot. Return the beans to the pot and add the salt, onion, carrots, garlic, thyme, bay leaf, and water. Bring to a boil, then turn the heat down to low, cover partially, and gently simmer, stirring occasionally, until fork-tender and creamy, 1 to 2 hours. Older or large beans may take longer to cook.

4 · Remove the bay leaf. Season with salt and pepper to taste. Serve hot or cold, whole or mashed, or use in other recipes. Store leftovers in an airtight container in the refrigerator for up to 3 days.

Vegetable Rice

Make this quick side on those busy weeknights when you don't have time to chop vegetables but still want to serve up a healthy dish. It takes full advantage of our dehydrated vegetable pantry selection.

MAKES 4 TO 6 SERVINGS

1 tablespoon extra-virgin olive oil

½ cup chopped fresh or freeze-dried onion

2 garlic cloves, minced

½ teaspoon Herbes de Provence Seasoning Blend (page 109) or Greek Seasoning Blend (page 110)

4 cups Zero-Waste Vegetable Broth (page 163) or store-bought vegetable broth

1 cup water

1 packed cup mixed dried vegetables (such as bell peppers, mushrooms, carrots, and broccoli)

2 cups long-grain white rice

Heat the oil in a large skillet over medium heat. Add the onion and garlic and cook, stirring often, until the onion softens, about 1 minute. Stir in the seasoning blend. Add the broth and bring to a boil. Stir in the dried vegetables, rice, and water and return to a boil.

Cover tightly and turn the heat down to low. Simmer until the rice is tender and has absorbed the liquid, 15 to 20 minutes. Fluff the rice with a fork, transfer to a bowl, and serve hot.

Rainbow Rice

When Minute Rice becomes wait-a-minute rice! With naturally pigmented powders, you can create vibrant magical colored rice that packs a healthy boost. My kids liked choosing their own colors, so this recipe is for 2 servings. Double the recipe if everyone wants the same.

MAKES 2 SERVINGS

1 cup water

1 cup instant long-grain white rice (I use Minute Rice, but any brand or type of rice will work—just follow the package or rice cooker instructions)

½ teaspoon butterfly pea flower powder for blue rice or 1 teaspoon ground turmeric for yellow/orange rice or 1 teaspoon beet powder for pink rice

Herb Infused Olive Oil (page 193; optional)

Herb compound butter (see page 198; optional)

Salt and freshly ground black pepper

Bring the water to a boil in a small pot. Add the rice and your choice of pigment powder and stir until evenly coated. Remove from the heat, cover, and let stand for 5 to 10 minutes. Fluff with a fork. If desired, drizzle with oil or add a pat of butter, and season with salt and pepper. Serve hot.

Scalloped Potatoes

This recipe uses dehydrated potato slices and skips the rehydrating step since we're cooking in liquid. The results are soft and creamy potato slices in the middle with a crunchy potato or two on top. Around here, the crunchy bites are gold!

MAKES 6 SERVINGS

Nonstick cooking oil spray

4 cups dehydrated potato slices (see page 127)

2 cups boiling water

1¾ cups 2% milk

¼ cup freeze-dried onions (see page 30) or 2 tablespoons dried onion flakes

3 tablespoons all-purpose flour

1 tablespoon freeze-dried chives

1½ teaspoons salt

1 teaspoon dried thyme

1 teaspoon dried marjoram

1 teaspoon garlic powder

½ teaspoon ground mustard

½ teaspoon freshly ground black pepper

1 cup heavy cream

1 · Preheat the oven to 375°F. Grease a 9-by-13-inch baking dish with cooking spray.

2 · Spread the potato slices evenly in the dish. Pour the boiling water evenly over the potatoes. Stir gently, keeping the potatoes in a single layer, to coat evenly with the water.

3 · Mix the milk, onions, flour, chives, salt, thyme, marjoram, garlic powder, mustard, and pepper in a medium bowl. Pour the milk mixture evenly over the potatoes. Cover with aluminum foil and bake for 30 minutes. Uncover and pour the cream evenly over the potatoes and bake uncovered until the top is golden brown, 20 to 25 minutes more. Cool slightly and serve hot.

Homemade Herb Pasta

Homemade pasta is easy and inexpensive to make. With a variety of flower and vegetable powders, juices, and dried seasonings at your disposal, keeping pasta night exciting is simple. Use a pasta machine, if you have one, or roll it by hand. Want it plain? Omit the herbs.

MAKES ABOUT 14 OUNCES

2 cups all-purpose flour, plus more for kneading and rolling

3 large eggs

2 tablespoons Herb Infused Olive Oil (page 193) or extra-virgin olive oil

3 tablespoons minced fresh herbs (such as basil, oregano, parsley, and/or chives) or 1½ tablespoons dried

1 · Pour the flour onto a clean work surface, shape it into a mound, and make a well in the center. Crack the eggs into the well. Add the oil and herbs. Using a dinner fork, mix the ingredients together to combine. With the fork, slowly stir along the edges of the well to bring in the flour, eventually incorporating the ingredients into a rough dough. If the dough is too wet and very sticky, sprinkle in additional flour, 1 tablespoon at a time. If it seems too dry and crumbly, do the same with water. Finish the dough by kneading by hand until it is smooth and no longer sticky, about 10 minutes. Shape into a ball and cover with a kitchen towel. Rest the dough at room temperature for 30 minutes.

2 · Cut the dough into quarters and cover with the towel. On a lightly floured work surface, working with one dough quarter at a time and keeping the remainder covered until needed, roll out the dough until your hand is visible when you slip it underneath the dough.

3 · Starting at the bottom edge of the pasta sheet closest to you, fold up 2 inches of the pasta. Continue folding up the sheet in 2-inch increments until you reach the top—this makes the dough easier to cut evenly. Using a sharp knife, cut the dough vertically into strips, as follows:

- Spaghetti: 1/16-inch wide
- Linguine: ⅛-inch wide
- Fettuccine: ¼-inch wide

4 · Pick up the strips, shake them apart, then toss in a dusting of flour on the work surface. Lay the strips as flat as possible on parchment paper, a clean work surface, or baking sheets. (You can also hang the strips from a pasta drying rack or hanger.) Repeat with the remaining dough. Let the pasta strips dry at room temperature until they feel leathery and flexible, about 1 hour. Cook right away or store in resealable plastic bags in the refrigerator for up to 2 days. To freeze the pasta, line a rimmed baking sheet with parchment paper. Twirl the pasta into the desired portions on the baking sheet. Freeze until firm, about 2 hours. Transfer to a resealable freezer bag and freeze for up to 9 months.

5 · To cook, fill a large saucepan with water, add 1 teaspoon salt, and 1 teaspoon olive oil, and bring to a boil. Add the fresh pasta and cook for 3 to 5 minutes, or 7 to 10 minutes for frozen pasta.

VARIATIONS

Flower Pasta: Use 2 cups all-purpose flour, 3 large eggs, 2 tablespoons extra-virgin olive oil, and 3 tablespoons fresh flower petals or 2 tablespoons dried.

Powder Pasta: Use 2 cups all-purpose flour, 3 large eggs, 2 tablespoons extra-virgin olive oil, and 1 tablespoon butterfly pea flower, hibiscus, beet, or tomato powder.

Veggie Pasta: Use 2 cups all-purpose flour, 2 large eggs, ¼ cup vegetable juice (beet, carrot, or spinach), and 1½ tablespoons extra-virgin olive oil.

Dinner Menu

Pantry Tomato Sauce

This sauce highlights the flavor of the fragrant sweetness of dehydrated tomatoes. Adjust the salt and sugar in your sauce to your preference.

MAKES 3 CUPS

2½ packed cups (about 2½ ounces) dehydrated tomatoes (see page 128)

5 cups hot water

2 tablespoons extra-virgin olive oil

1 large yellow onion, chopped

4 garlic cloves, minced

1 tablespoon sugar, plus more as needed

2 teaspoons dried oregano

2 teaspoons dried basil

1 teaspoon salt

¼ teaspoon freshly ground black pepper

1 · Put the tomatoes in a medium bowl and add the hot water. Be sure the tomatoes are submerged—I put a bowl or small plate on top to weigh them down. Let stand until the tomatoes soften, 10 to 20 minutes. Do not drain.

2 · Heat the oil in a large saucepan over medium heat. Add the onion and cook, stirring occasionally, until softened, about 3 minutes. Stir in the garlic and cook until fragrant, about 1 minute. Add the tomatoes and their soaking liquid, the sugar, oregano, basil, salt, and pepper. Bring to a boil over high heat. Using an immersion blender, puree. (Or puree in batches in a blender with the lid ajar and return to the saucepan.)

3 · Turn the heat down to low and simmer to blend the flavors and thicken, about 10 minutes. Season with additional salt, sugar, and pepper to taste. Serve immediately. Serve or cool, cover, and refrigerate for up to 1 week or freeze for up to 1 month.

Tomato Basil Pasta Salad

I like this pasta dish served cold, but some of our kids love to heat it up. Either way, it's a tasty way to use dehydrated tomatoes.

MAKES 8 SERVINGS

1 cup dehydrated tomatoes (see page 128)

Boiling water, as needed

Salt

1 pound farfalle or penne pasta

1 tablespoon olive oil

1 shallot, chopped (about ½ cup)

3 garlic cloves, minced

½ cup chopped fresh basil

Freshly ground black pepper

1 cup mayonnaise

1 teaspoon Worcestershire sauce

¼ teaspoon dried oregano

½ cup grated Parmesan cheese, plus more for serving

3 tablespoons scallions, chopped

1 · Put the tomatoes in a small bowl and add enough boiling water to cover. Let stand until the tomatoes are rehydrated, about 10 minutes. Drain. Coarsely chop the tomatoes, if desired.

2 · Bring a large pot of water and a generous pinch of salt to a boil over high heat. Add the pasta and cook according to the package directions, stirring occasionally, until tender. Drain well.

3 • Heat the oil, tomatoes, shallot, and garlic in a medium skillet over medium heat, stirring occasionally, until the shallot is softened, about 2 minutes. Remove from the heat. Stir in the basil and season lightly with salt and pepper.

4 • Whisk the mayonnaise, Worcestershire sauce, ½ teaspoon salt, ¼ teaspoon pepper, and the oregano in a large bowl. Add the pasta, tomato mixture, Parmesan, and scallions and mix well. Serve warm, with additional Parmesan passed on the side. Or let cool for about 1 hour, cover with plastic wrap, and refrigerate to blend the flavors and chill the salad, at least 4 and up to 12 hours. Serve chilled or reheat in a microwave and serve warm.

Roasted Marinara Sauce

You can use home-canned, store-bought canned, or fresh tomatoes here. Roasting the tomatoes makes the sauce next-level good. Use as the base for the Creamy Roasted Tomato Soup (page 262). It's also delicious on pizza and pasta or as a dipping sauce for homemade focaccia (see page 302).

MAKES 4 CUPS

2 (28-ounce) cans whole tomatoes, 2 quarts home-canned tomatoes (see page 75), or 2 pounds ripe fresh or thawed frozen tomatoes, cut into quarters lengthwise

4 garlic cloves, smashed under a knife and peeled

3 tablespoons extra-virgin olive oil, divided

1 teaspoon herb-infused salt (see page 205) or kosher salt, plus more as needed

½ teaspoon freshly ground black pepper, plus more as needed

1 large yellow onion, chopped

1 tablespoon sugar, plus more as needed

1 tablespoon chopped fresh basil or 1 teaspoon dried

1 tablespoon chopped fresh oregano or 1 teaspoon dried

1 • Preheat the oven to 400°F.

2 • Spread the tomatoes in a 9-by-13-inch baking dish. Reserve the juices from canned tomatoes for later. Add the garlic. Drizzle with 2 tablespoons of the oil. Sprinkle with the salt and pepper. Roast, stirring occasionally, until the tomatoes have shrunk and the edges are beginning to char, 1 to 1¼ hours.

3 • Remove the roasted garlic cloves, let cool until easy to handle, and coarsely chop.

4 • Heat the remaining 1 tablespoon of oil in a large saucepan over medium heat. Add the onion and a pinch of salt and pepper. Cook, stirring occasionally, until softened, about 3 minutes. Add the roasted garlic and cook for 1 minute. Carefully transfer the roasted tomatoes and their juices, as well as any reserved juices, to the pot. Bring to a simmer. Remove from the heat. Using an immersion blender, puree.

5 • Return to low heat and stir in the sugar, basil, and oregano. Cover and simmer over low heat, stirring often, to blend the flavors, about 10 minutes. Taste and add more salt, pepper, and sugar to taste. Serve hot. Leftovers can be cooled, covered, and refrigerated for up to 1 week or frozen for up to 3 months.

Spinach Parm Pasta

This is another quick weekday favorite. It uses frozen spinach. Stick it in the refrigerator in the morning to thaw, and it will be ready at dinnertime. Go, us!

MAKES 6 SERVINGS

2 cups frozen chopped spinach, thawed

8 tablespoons (1 stick) unsalted butter

1 large shallot, chopped (about ½ cup)

3 garlic cloves, minced

1 teaspoon dried thyme

½ cup finely grated Parmesan cheese, plus more for serving

Salt and freshly ground black pepper

1 pound Homemade Herb Pasta (page 293) or store-bought, cooked until al dente

1 · Drain the spinach in a fine-mesh strainer, pressing hard on the spinach with a wooden spoon or your hands to remove excess liquid. Heat the butter in a large saucepan over medium heat, until it is halfway melted, about 1 minute. Add the shallot and cook, stirring occasionally, until softened, 1 to 2 minutes. Stir in the garlic and thyme and cook until fragrant, about 1 minute. Stir in the spinach and cook, stirring often, until heated through, about 2 minutes. Remove from the heat and mix in the Parmesan. Season with salt and pepper.

2 · Add the pasta to the sauce and stir until combined. Serve hot, with additional Parmesan passed on the side.

Creamy Garlic Scape Sauce

I usually toss this sauce with cooked cavatappi or homemade fettucine, but you can use it to sauce other dishes, such as sautéed chicken breasts.

MAKES ENOUGH TO COAT 1 POUND PASTA

1½ teaspoons garlic scape powder (see page 113) or ¾ teaspoon garlic powder

1 teaspoon Italian Seasoning Blend (page 110)

½ teaspoon ground nutmeg

½ teaspoon salt

⅛ teaspoon freshly ground black pepper

8 tablespoons (1 stick) unsalted butter, cut into chunks

2 cups heavy cream

1 cup freshly grated Parmesan cheese

Chopped fresh parsley, for garnish (optional)

1 · In a small bowl, stir together the garlic scape powder, Italian seasoning, nutmeg, salt, and pepper.

2 · Heat the butter in a large saucepan over low heat. When the butter is half-melted, add the cream. Cook, whisking occasionally, until the butter is melted and the cream is hot, about 2 minutes. Whisk in the seasoning mix and cook for 1 minute. Remove the sauce from the heat and gradually whisk in the Parmesan. Garnish with parsley, if desired.

Herby Pizza Dough

My homemade dough paired with pizza sauce transforms at-home pizza night into mama's pizzeria! This is the easiest homemade pizza dough ever—you can use it right away without kneading or a bulk-rise. That's my kind of recipe! The dough can also be transformed into bread sticks or focaccia (see page 302) or used to make homemade hot pockets. You can also make ahead (see step 3).

MAKES 1 LARGE THICK-CRUST, 2 MEDIUM DEEP-DISH, OR 4 INDIVIDUAL PIZZAS

- 1 cup plus 1 tablespoon warm (110° to 115°F) water
- 1 tablespoon sugar
- 1 (¼-ounce) package active dry yeast (2¼ teaspoons)
- 2 tablespoons extra-virgin olive oil, plus more if refrigerating
- 2 teaspoons Italian Seasoning Blend (page 110)
- 1 teaspoon salt
- 3 cups bread flour, plus more for rolling

1 · Pour the warm water into a large bowl and sprinkle in the sugar and yeast. Let stand for 5 to 10 minutes, or until you see some movement in the liquid, then stir to dissolve the yeast. Add the oil, Italian Seasoning Blend, and salt. One cup at a time, stir in the flour and mix to make a rough dough. Finish by bringing the dough together with your hands. The dough will feel firm. If it is too wet, and very sticky work in more flour, one tablespoon at a time. If the dough seems too dry and crumbly, sprinkle with water, one tablespoon at a time, and work it in.

2 · For one pizza, shape into one ball; for two pizzas, make two balls. Leave on the flat surface and cover with a kitchen towel. Let stand while preheating the oven to relax the dough, 20 to 30 minutes. Follow the method on the next page for assembly and baking.

3 · Not using right away? Place the dough in a large bowl and drizzle 1 tablespoon oil on top, turning to coat, with smooth side up. Cover tightly with plastic wrap and refrigerate for up to 3 days. To freeze, slip the oil-coated dough into a 1-gallon resealable freezer bag and freeze for up to 1 month. Thaw overnight in the refrigerator. Let the chilled dough stand at room temperature for 30 minutes to 1 hour before rolling out.

Pizza Assembly and Baking

Yellow or white cornmeal, for sprinkling

Pizza Sauce (recipe follows)

Toppings (as desired): cooked vegetables (such as sliced mushrooms, bell peppers, zucchini, broccoli, broccoli rabe, or chopped spinach), sliced Italian meats (salami, pepperoni, prosciutto, cooked sliced meatballs), and sliced black olives

Shredded low-moisture mozzarella cheese

1 · Preheat the oven to 450°F with a rack in the top third of the oven.

2 · **For a single large pizza,** lightly sprinkle cornmeal on a 12- to 14-inch pizza pan. On a lightly floured work surface, pat, stretch, and roll out the entire ball of dough into a 12- to 14-inch round. Fit the dough into the prepared pan, stretching it in place as needed. Spread about ⅔ cup Pizza Sauce over the dough, leaving a ½-inch border. Add toppings as desired, then sprinkle with 1 cup mozzarella. Bake until the crust is browned, 10 to 12 minutes. Slice and serve.

3 · **For 4 individual pizzas,** preheat the oven to 450°F with racks in the top third and center. Cut the dough into four equal portions and shape each into a ball. Lightly sprinkle cornmeal on four 9-inch cake pans. On a lightly floured work surface, pat, stretch, and roll out each ball into a 10-inch round. As they are rolled, transfer the round to the prepared pans creating an edge. Spread about ¼ cup Pizza Sauce over the bottom of the dough. Add toppings as desired and sprinkle each with ⅓ cup mozzarella. Bake, switching the positions of the pans from top to bottom after 5 minutes, until the crust is browned, 8 to 10 minutes. Slice and serve.

Pizza Sauce

MAKES ABOUT 1 CUP

¼ cup dehydrated tomato powder (see page 113)

¼ cup plus 6 to 8 tablespoons water

1 teaspoon dried oregano

1 teaspoon dried basil

1 teaspoon dried thyme

1 teaspoon garlic powder

Salt and freshly ground black pepper

1 tablespoon olive oil

This pizza sauce is packed with flavor, just like real pizzeria sauce. Plus, the kids can mix the ingredients themselves, making homemade pizza night even more fun. See the variation using tomato paste.

Whisk the tomato powder and ¼ cup of the water in a medium bowl to make a paste. Whisk in the oregano, basil, thyme, garlic powder, salt, and pepper, followed by the oil. Whisk in enough water, 1 tablespoon at a time, to reach a sauce consistency. Let the sauce stand for 5 minutes to thicken slightly.

VARIATION

Tomato Paste Pizza Sauce: Substitute ¼ cup store-bought tomato paste for the dehydrated tomato powder and dilute with about ½ cup water to reach sauce consistency.

Garden Focaccia

This easy take on traditional focaccia uses homemade pizza dough. You can make it a showstopper by arranging a topping of edible flowers, vegetables cut out like flowers, and herbs in a garden scene. For the best effect, present the whole focaccia at the table before slicing so everyone can see your "garden." Or keep it plain to use for sandwiches like the Candied Bacon Chicken Sandwich (page 268) or to serve alongside soup or salad.

MAKES 8 TO 12 SERVINGS

Olive oil, for the bowl, baking pan, and topping

Flour, for kneading

Herby Pizza Dough (page 300)

Toppings
Herb-infused salt (see page 205)

1 small red onion or shallot, cut into thin rings, for flowers

Cherry or grape tomato halves, for flowers

Fresh chives or parsley, for grass

Red, yellow, or orange bell peppers, cut into flower shapes with small cookie cutters

Rehydrated dried tomato slices, for flowers

Rehydrated dried mushroom slices, as themselves

Fresh edible flowers and herb sprigs, as needed or desired

1 · Generously oil a large bowl. Knead the pizza dough on a lightly floured work surface until smooth, 6 to 8 minutes. Shape the dough into a taut ball. Add to the bowl, coat with oil, and leave smooth side up. Cover the bowl with plastic wrap or a moistened kitchen towel. Let rise in a warm place until doubled in volume, 1 to 1½ hours.

2 · Generously oil a 9-by-13-inch baking pan. Punch down the dough. Transfer to the pan and pat and stretch it to fit, being sure to fill the corners. (You may have to restretch the retracted dough in the corners after 5 minutes.) Cover with plastic wrap or a moistened kitchen towel and let rise in a warm place until it looks puffy, about 1 hour.

3 · Preheat the oven to 400°F.

4 · Press your fingertips all over the top of the dough, leaving indentations about ½ inch deep. Brush with oil, sprinkle with salt, and decorate with the desired toppings. Brush the toppings with oil. Bake until golden brown, 15 to 20 minutes. Let cool slightly. Remove from the pan, cut, and serve warm or cooled to room temperature.

Hit the Sauce

Making your own condiments at home is easy! Add new flavors to some of your old favorites by using infused vinegars, oils, butter, salt, honey, and sugar. Keep track of the recipes you create in the journal pages at the back of the book

Barbecue Sauce

MAKES ABOUT 2 CUPS

I make this barbecue sauce when we're grilling meats and baking chicken. It's also delicious added to a big pot of Slow-Cooked Dried Beans (page 290) during the last 20 minutes of cooking.

1 cup Kickin' Ketchup (page 304) or store-bought

⅓ cup steak sauce

⅓ cup packed light brown sugar

¼ cup herb-infused honey (see page 213) or raw honey

1 tablespoon purple basil vinegar (see page 186)

2 teaspoons dried rosemary

1 teaspoon dried thyme

Stir together the ketchup, steak sauce, brown sugar, honey, vinegar, rosemary, and thyme in a medium saucepan. Bring to a boil, stirring occasionally, over medium-high heat. Turn the heat down to low, cover, and simmer to blend the flavors for about 2 minutes. Let cool. Use the sauce right away or store in an airtight container in the refrigerator for up to 1 week.

Orange Spice Cranberry Sauce

This wonderful recipe uses oranges, rosemary, and cinnamon to fill the house with the sweet smell of the holidays.

MAKES ABOUT 3 CUPS

1 cup fresh orange juice

1 cup cinnamon-infused sugar (see page 216)

1 (12-ounce) bag fresh or thawed frozen cranberries (3 cups)

1 tablespoon crushed dehydrated orange slices (see page 120)

¼ teaspoon dried rosemary

1 · Bring the orange juice and sugar to a boil in a medium saucepan over high heat. Stir in the cranberries, crushed orange, and rosemary and return to a boil.

2 · Turn the heat down to low and simmer, stirring occasionally, until the juices are syrupy, about 10 minutes. Remove from the heat and let cool to room temperature.

Use right away or store in an airtight container in the refrigerator for up to 2 weeks. To freeze, transfer to a freezer-safe container, leaving a ½-inch headspace, cover, and freeze for up to 6 months. Thaw in the refrigerator overnight before serving.

Kickin' Ketchup

Ketchup with a kick! The flavor is a mash-up of plain ketchup and cocktail sauce, a delicious choice for hamburgers, fries, Potato Roses (page 286), and seafood. I like to use rosemary as my flavor infusion for the vinegar, honey, and salt. Thyme is good too!

MAKES 1 CUP

1 cup water

⅓ cup Herb Garden Vinegar (page 187) or apple cider vinegar

⅓ cup herb-infused honey (see page 213) or raw honey

6 tablespoons dehydrated tomato powder (see page 113)

1½ teaspoons herb-infused salt (see page 205) or kosher salt

½ teaspoon onion powder

¼ teaspoon garlic powder

¼ teaspoon ground allspice

⅛ teaspoon cayenne pepper

In a small saucepan whisk together the water, vinegar, honey, tomato powder, salt, onion powder, garlic powder, allspice, and cayenne. Bring almost to a boil over medium heat, whisking often. Turn the heat down to low and simmer, whisking occasionally, until the mixture thickens, about 10 minutes. Remove from the heat and cool completely. Use right away or store in an airtight container in the refrigerator for up to 3 weeks.

The Bread Box

Bread is my weakness and quick is my superpower. Combine them together and you get a delicious selection of breads you'll surely keep bookmarked. I'm pretty sure the scent of heaven is the smell of fresh rising bread. I don't always have time to make bread from scratch, but when I do, I'm always glad that I did.

Quick Honey Wheat Bread

MAKES 1 LOAF

This quick bread recipe is one of my favorites. It's perfect for butter, jam, and honey and delicious served warm, cold, or toasted. Once you've made your first jam of the season, you'll want to make this, too!

Vegetable oil, for the pan

2 cups whole wheat flour

2 teaspoons dried marjoram

1 teaspoon baking powder

1 teaspoon baking soda

1 teaspoon salt

2 cups 2% or whole milk

1 large egg, lightly beaten

3 tablespoons herb-infused honey or floral-infused honey (see page 213)

2 tablespoons unsalted butter, melted

1 · Preheat the oven to 350°F. Lightly oil a 9-by-5-inch loaf pan.

2 · Whisk the flour, marjoram, baking powder, baking soda, and salt together in a large bowl and make a well in the center. Whisk the milk, egg, honey, and melted butter in a medium bowl and pour into the well. Stir to combine. Do not overmix. Spread evenly in the prepared pan.

3 · Bake until a wooden toothpick inserted in the center comes out clean, 50 to 60 minutes. Cool in the pan on a wire cooling rack for 10 minutes. Remove from the pan and let cool on the rack. Serve warm or cooled to room temperature. Wrap leftovers loosely in parchment paper, then slip into a resealable plastic bag and store at room temperature for up to 4 days.

Lemon, Lilac, and Poppy Seed Bread

Use your lilac-infused sugar from chapter 9 to make a glaze for this sweet quick bread. Or feel free to replace the lilac sugar with rose, lavender, or even plain sugar.

MAKES 1 LOAF

1½ cups all-purpose flour

1 teaspoon baking powder

½ teaspoon salt

8 tablespoons (1 stick) unsalted butter, at room temperature, plus more for the pan

1 cup sugar

2 large eggs, at room temperature

½ teaspoon almond extract

½ cup 2% or whole milk

Finely grated zest of 1 lemon

1 teaspoon poppy seeds

¼ cup fresh lemon juice

¼ cup lilac-infused sugar (see page 216)

1 · Preheat the oven to 350°F. Lightly butter an 8-by-4-inch loaf pan.

2 · Sift the flour, baking powder, and salt together in a medium bowl. In another medium bowl, beat the butter and sugar with an electric mixer set on high speed until light and fluffy, about 3 minutes. One at a time, beat in the eggs until absorbed. Add the almond extract. With the mixer on low speed, add the flour in thirds, alternating with two additions of the milk, scraping down the sides of the bowl as needed with a silicone spatula. Fold in the lemon zest and poppy seeds. Spread in the prepared pan.

3 · Bake until the loaf is golden brown and a wooden toothpick inserted in the center comes out clean, 50 to 55 minutes. Transfer to a wire cooling rack and let cool for 5 minutes. Using a wooden skewer, poke several holes all over the top of the loaf.

4 · Whisk the lemon juice and lilac sugar until the sugar is mostly dissolved. Drizzle the mixture over the warm loaf. Let cool for 10 minutes more. Remove the loaf from the pan and let cool completely on the rack. Slice and serve warm or cool to room temperature. Wrap leftovers tightly in plastic wrap and store at room temperature for up to 3 days.

Lavender Cornbread

This slightly sweet cornbread is delicious served warm topped with floral compound butter (see page 198) and extra lavender honey.

MAKES 8 TO 10 SERVINGS

1 cup all-purpose flour

¾ cup yellow cornmeal

2½ teaspoons baking powder

1 teaspoon dried lavender or 2 teaspoons fresh

1 teaspoon salt

1 cup 2% or whole milk

2 large eggs, beaten

¼ cup lavender-infused honey (see page 213)

¼ cup vegetable oil

1 tablespoon unsalted butter

1 · Preheat the oven to 400°F.

2 · Whisk the flour, cornmeal, baking powder, lavender, and salt in a medium bowl. Whisk the milk, eggs, honey, and oil in a second bowl. Pour the milk mixture into the flour mixture and stir just until combined.

3 · Put the butter in a 10- to 11-inch cast-iron skillet or a 9-inch round cake pan. Place in the oven until the butter melts, 2 to 3 minutes. Remove from the oven and swirl to coat the bottom and sides of the pan. Spread the batter into the hot pan and return to the oven. Bake until golden brown and a wooden toothpick inserted in the center comes out clean, 15 to 20 minutes. Cool slightly. Cut into wedges and serve warm.

VARIATION

Calendula Cornbread: Replace the lavender with 2 teaspoons dried calendula petals (or 1 tablespoon fresh) and the lavender-infused honey with calendula-infused honey.

Rose Scones

This recipe uses dried rose petals and rose-infused sugar. Serve as is or with floral compound butter (see page 198) and floral-infused honey (see page 213) or Rose Jelly (page 83).

MAKES 8 SCONES

1 cup 2% or whole milk

¼ cup dried rose petals

2½ cups all-purpose flour, plus more for kneading

1 tablespoon baking powder

½ teaspoon salt

8 tablespoons (1 stick) cold unsalted butter, cut into ½-inch cubes

⅓ cup Rose Sugar (page 218)

Turbinado sugar or additional Rose Sugar, for sprinkling

1 · Preheat the oven to 425°F.

2 · Heat the milk and dried rose petals in a small saucepan over medium heat until small bubbles appear around the edges. Remove from the heat and cool until lukewarm. Strain and measure ⅔ cup of the rose-infused milk. Reserve the remaining infused milk for brushing before baking.

3 · Whisk the flour, baking powder, and salt together in a large bowl. Add the butter and stir until coated. Using a pastry blender, cut in the butter until most of the butter is pea-sized. Stir in the rose sugar. Make a well in the center, add the rose milk, and use a fork to stir just until it forms a rough, soft dough.

4 · Turn out the dough onto a lightly floured work surface. Knead just a few times, until the dough holds together. Pat the dough into a 6-inch round. Using a sharp knife, cut into 8 equal wedges. Place the wedges, in the order they were cut from the round, on an ungreased rimmed baking sheet, leaving about ⅛ inch in between. Brush the tops and edges with the reserved rose milk and sprinkle turbinado or more rose sugar on top. Bake until risen and golden brown, 14 to 16 minutes. Transfer to a wire cooling rack and cool until warm, then serve.

VARIATION

Lavender Scones: Substitute 1 tablespoon dried lavender for the rose petals and lavender-infused sugar (see page 216) for the rose sugar.

Banana Bread

Use your thawed frozen bananas from chapter 1 to make this homemade favorite, or substitute very ripe fresh bananas. As this makes two loaves, if you have a smaller family than mine, you may want to freeze one loaf for another time. It's delicious sliced and topped with Minty Strawberry-Orange Sauce (page 311) and a dollop of Herbal Whipped Cream (page 180).

MAKES 2 LOAVES

Nonstick cooking oil spray

3 cups thawed frozen banana slices (page 22) or 3 overripe fresh bananas

2½ cups all-purpose flour

1 cup sugar or your favorite floral-infused sugar (see page 216)

¾ cup 2% dairy or oat milk

3 tablespoons vegetable oil

1 tablespoon plus ½ teaspoon baking powder

1 large egg

1 teaspoon salt

1 teaspoon vanilla extract

1 · Preheat the oven to 350°F. Lightly grease two 8½-by-4½-inch loaf pans with the oil spray.

2 · In a large bowl, beat the bananas, flour, sugar, milk, oil, baking powder, egg, salt, and vanilla with an electric mixer on medium speed until just until combined (the batter will be slightly lumpy). Divide equally between the prepared pans.

3 · Bake until a wooden toothpick inserted in the center comes out clean, about 1 hour. Let cool completely on a wire cooling rack. Invert and unmold the breads, slice, and serve. Wrap leftovers in plastic wrap and store at room temperature for up to 3 days, or freeze for up to 6 months and thaw before serving.

Minty Strawberry-Orange Sauce

This simple strawberry sauce is good on toast, baked Brie, ice cream, pancakes, or our favorite way, on top of sliced Banana Bread (above) with a dollop of Herbal Whipped Cream (page 180).

MAKES ABOUT 1 CUP

1 pound fresh or thawed frozen strawberries, hulled and halved

2 tablespoon mint-infused sugar (see Note)

2 dehydrated orange slices, ground to a powder in a spice/coffee grinder

Mash the strawberries in a medium bowl with a potato masher. Stir in the sugar and ground orange. Let stand for at least 10 minutes and up to 1 hour before serving. The sauce can be covered and refrigerated for up to 2 days.

NOTE

Don't have mint-infused sugar on hand? That's okay! Crush 2 tablespoons sugar with 5 or 6 fresh mint leaves or 1½ teaspoons dried mint in a small bowl with a spoon as a substitute.

The Bread Box

Chocolate, Tahini, and Banana Muffins

The rehydrated bananas in these muffins enhance the flavors of the chocolate and tahini, creating a rich, decadent muffin. Get your glass of milk ready! You will need a jumbo muffin tin and jumbo liners for this recipe.

MAKES 8 JUMBO MUFFINS

1 cup dehydrated banana slices

1 cup boiling water

¾ cup all-purpose flour

½ cup whole wheat flour

¼ cup natural cocoa powder

1½ teaspoons baking powder

½ teaspoon baking soda

½ teaspoon salt

1 cup packed light brown sugar

¼ cup tahini

4 tablespoons (½ stick) unsalted butter, at room temperature

2 large eggs, room temperature

½ cup sour cream

1½ teaspoons vanilla extract

¼ cup semisweet chocolate chips

1 · Combine the dehydrated bananas and boiling water in a small bowl and let stand until the bananas are soft, about 30 minutes. Do not drain. Using a fork or a potato masher, mash the bananas with the water (or puree in a blender).

2 · Preheat the oven to 425°F. Line 8 jumbo muffin cups with paper liners.

3 · Whisk the all-purpose and whole wheat flours, cocoa powder, baking powder, baking soda, and salt in a medium bowl. Beat the brown sugar, tahini, and butter in a large bowl with an electric mixer set at high speed until the mixture is combined and creamy, about 2 minutes. One at a time, beat in the eggs, beating well after each addition. Beat in the banana mash, sour cream, and vanilla. Fold the dry ingredients into the wet mixture until combined. Do not over mix. Divide the batter evenly among the muffin cups. Sprinkle the chocolate chips over the muffins.

4 · Bake for 5 minutes. Turn the oven temperature down to 350°F. Continue baking until the muffins have risen and a wooden toothpick inserted in the center comes out clean, about 15 minutes more.

NOTE

For smaller muffins, line 16 to 18 standard muffin cups with paper liners. Reduce the baking time by about 5 minutes.

Herb and Cheddar Biscuits

These biscuits are perfect served at breakfast, lunch, or dinner. Melted butter brushed on before baking makes the biscuits turn golden brown and helps glue on any edible garnishes.

MAKES 12 BISCUITS

3 cups all-purpose flour, plus more for rolling

1 tablespoon baking powder

1 tablespoon sugar

1 teaspoon salt

1 teaspoon dried thyme

1 teaspoon dried rosemary

¾ teaspoon cream of tartar

½ teaspoon garlic powder

1 cup finely shredded sharp cheddar cheese

1 cup (2 sticks) cold unsalted butter, ¾ cup (1½ sticks) cut into ½-inch cubes and ¼ cup (½ stick), melted

1 cup 2% or whole milk

Fresh edible flowers or herb leaves, for garnish (optional)

1 · Preheat the oven to 450°F.

2 · In a large bowl, whisk together the flour, baking powder, sugar, salt, thyme, rosemary, cream of tartar, garlic powder, and cheese. Add the cold cubed butter and toss to coat with the flour mixture. Using a pastry cutter, cut in the butter until the mixture resembles coarse breadcrumbs. Make a well in the center, pour in the milk, and stir just until combined. Do not overmix.

3 · Turn out the dough onto a lightly floured surface and fold and press the dough over on itself six times. Pat out the dough into a rectangle, ½- to ¾-inch thick. Using a 2½-inch round biscuit cutter dipped in flour, cut out biscuits and place them, 1 inch apart, on an ungreased rimmed baking sheet. Gather up the dough scraps and gently press into a circle about ¾-inch thick. Cut out more biscuits and add to the sheet. Repeat until all the dough is used.

4 · Bake until the biscuits are golden brown, 10 to 14 minutes. Remove from the oven and brush the tops of the biscuits with the melted butter. If desired, top with fresh or pressed flowers and herbs, then brush again with melted butter to "glue" them on. Serve hot, warm, or at room temperature.

Rosemary Baguettes

While most home-baked bread recipes seem difficult, this one is super easy and yields 4 baguettes you'll be proud of! You can also shape them into 2 larger loaves to use as sandwich bread (see Note).

MAKES 4 LOAVES

5½ cups all-purpose flour, divided, plus more for kneading

2 (¼-ounce) packages active dry yeast (4½ teaspoons)

2 teaspoons dried rosemary, coarsely crushed, plus more for topping (optional)

1½ teaspoons salt

2 cups hot (120°F) tap water

Vegetable oil, for greasing

Yellow cornmeal, for dusting

1 large egg white beaten with 1 tablespoon water

Finely chopped rosemary, for garnish (optional)

Poppy seeds, for garnish (optional)

Rosemary herb-infused salt (see page 205), for garnish (optional)

1 • Combine 2 cups of the flour with the yeast, rosemary, and salt in the bowl of a stand mixer. Add the hot water and mix on low speed for 30 seconds. Scrape the sides of the bowl at medium-high speed for 3 minutes.

2 • Remove the bowl from the mixer. Using a sturdy wooden spoon, stir in the remaining 3½ cups of flour. Turn out the dough onto a lightly floured work surface. Knead the dough until stiff, smooth, and elastic, about 8 minutes. (Check the arm workout off your to-do list!)

3 • Lightly oil a large bowl. Shape the dough into a ball, place in the bowl, and turn to coat with oil, leaving it smooth side up. Cover with plastic wrap or a moistened kitchen towel. Let rise in a warm place until the dough is doubled in volume, 1 to 1½ hours.

4 • Punch the dough down and turn it out onto a lightly floured work surface. Cut the dough into 4 equal pieces. Shape each into a ball, place on the work surface, and cover loosely with plastic wrap or a moistened towel. Let rest for 10 minutes.

5 • Lightly oil 2 rimmed baking sheets and dust with cornmeal. Roll one dough ball into a 14-by-5-inch rectangle, with the long side facing you. Roll up into a tight cylinder and pinch the seam closed. Pinch the tips into points and pull them slightly to taper the dough. Transfer to the prepared baking sheet. Repeat with the remaining dough, placing two loaves, well apart, on each pan.

6 • Brush with about half the egg wash. Let rise in a warm place until almost doubled in volume, about 45 minutes.

7 • Preheat the oven to 375°F. Using a sharp knife, cut 4 diagonal slashes, about ¼ inch deep and 1 inch apart, in a row on top of each loaf. Bake for 20 minutes. Remove from the oven, brush again with the egg wash, and, if desired, sprinkle with rosemary, poppy seeds, and/or herb salt. Continue baking until the loaves are shiny and golden brown and sound hollow when tapped on the bottom with your knuckles, 8 to 10 minutes. Carefully transfer the loaves to wire cooling racks to cool completely. Store at room temperature, tightly wrapped in plastic wrap or foil, and stored in a paper or cloth bag. Will last 2 to 3 days.

NOTE

To make 2 larger loaves, divide the dough into 2 balls. Roll each one out into a 15-by-10-inch rectangle. Continue as directed in step 4.

Sweet Tooth

For years I'd make treat platters with cookies, bars, and candies during the holidays for friends, neighbors, teachers, and my husband's coworkers. I always had a crew of happy helpers just waiting to crack an egg or stir the batter. Yes, kids are messy, but the time is so short. Put on the aprons and make messes. Create sweet treats and memories together.

Floral Sugar Cookies

MAKES ABOUT 4 DOZEN COOKIES

These fun garden-inspired sugar cookies use floral-infused sugars and are decorated with fresh flowers. Instead of using whole flower heads, consider using just the petals to design your own flower creations. Note that your yield will vary depending on the size of your cutters. Be sure to cut out cookies of approximately the same size so they bake evenly and at the same time.

- 2½ cups all-purpose flour
- 1 teaspoon baking powder
- 1 teaspoon salt
- 1 cup floral-infused sugar (such as rose, lilac, or lavender; see page 216)
- ¾ cup (1½ sticks) unsalted butter, at room temperature
- 2 large eggs, at room temperature
- 1 teaspoon almond extract
- Fresh edible flowers, petals, and sprinkles, for decorating

1 · Whisk the flour, baking powder, and salt together in a medium bowl.

2 · Beat the sugar and butter in a large bowl with an electric mixer set at medium speed until light and fluffy, 2 to 3 minutes, scraping down the sides of the bowl as needed. One at a time, beat in the eggs, beating until the first egg is absorbed before adding another. Beat in the almond extract. Reduce the speed to low. Gradually beat in the flour mixture until combined.

3 · Gather the dough into a thick disk and wrap tightly in plastic wrap. Refrigerate until chilled, at least 1 hour. (The dough can be refrigerated for up to 2 days. Let stand at room temperature for 30 minutes before rolling.)

4 · Preheat the oven to 400°F. Line a rimmed baking sheet with parchment paper.

5 • On a lightly floured work surface, roll out the dough ¼-inch thick. Using a 3-inch round cookie cutter, cut out cookies and place them about 1 inch apart on the prepared baking sheet. Gather up the scraps, press together, and roll and cut them out until all the dough is used up. Decorate the cookies with the edible flowers.

6 • Bake until the edges are lightly browned, 6 to 8 minutes. Let cool on the baking sheet for 2 minutes. Transfer to a cooling rack to cool completely. The cookies can be stored in an airtight container at room temperature for up to 3 weeks.

Sweet Tooth

Botanical Graham Crackers

This is a fun way to use your floral-infused honey with delicious options for dandelion, chamomile, lavender, rose, or wild violet graham crackers. I make 3-inch-square crackers, but you can cut out other shapes if you adjust the baking time accordingly.

MAKES ABOUT 42 CRACKERS

2 cups whole wheat flour, plus more for rolling

1 teaspoon ground cinnamon

1 teaspoon baking soda

½ teaspoon salt

1 cup packed light brown sugar

8 tablespoons (1 stick) unsalted butter, at room temperature

⅓ cup floral-infused honey (such as chamomile, dandelion, rose, lavender, elderberry flower, or wild violet; see page 213)

3 tablespoons oat milk or 2% dairy

2 teaspoons vanilla extract

1 · Whisk the flour, cinnamon, baking soda, and salt together in a medium bowl.

2 · In the bowl of a stand mixer set at medium speed, beat the brown sugar and butter until light and fluffy, scraping down the sides of the bowl as needed, 2 to 3 minutes. Reduce the speed to low. Gradually add the flour mixture and mix until combined, about 2 minutes. Beat in the honey, milk, and vanilla to make a soft, sticky dough. (The dough can also be made in a medium bowl using a handheld mixer with a strong motor.)

3 · Divide the dough in half. Shape each into a thick disk and wrap tightly in plastic wrap. Refrigerate until chilled, at least 1 hour. (The dough can be refrigerated for up to 1 week. Let stand at room temperature for 30 minutes before rolling.)

4 · Preheat the oven to 350°F.

5 · Generously flour the work surface. Unwrap one portion of dough and sprinkle more flour on top. Rub a rolling pin with flour. Roll out the dough, working from the center toward the edges, changing directions with each roll and adding more flour underneath and on top of the dough as needed to avoid sticking, until the dough is ⅛- to ¼-inch thick.

6 · Using a 3-inch-square cutter, cut out squares and place ½-inch apart on an ungreased rimmed baking sheet. Using a bamboo skewer, poke four rows of five holes in the center of each cracker. Repeat with the remaining dough. Gather up the scraps, press together, and roll and cut out more squares until all the dough is used up.

7 · Bake until the crackers are darkened and almost firm, 10 to 12 minutes. Cool on the baking sheet for 2 minutes. Transfer to a cooling rack and cool completely. The crackers can be stored in an airtight container at room temperature for up to 3 weeks.

ICE CREAM SANDWICHES WITH BOTANICAL GRAHAM CRACKERS

Let your favorite ice cream soften slightly for 10 minutes. For each sandwich, using an ice cream scooper, place a large ball of ice cream on a graham cracker. Top with a second graham cracker, and lightly apply pressure to press together. Use a butter knife to clean up the edges. Tightly wrap each sandwich in plastic. Freeze for at least 4 hours.

If decorating, just before serving, place mini chocolate chips, sprinkles, edible flowers, or chopped nuts in small bowls. Unwrap each sandwich and press the exposed ice cream on all four sides into the decorations. Serve immediately.

Raspberry Jam Thumbprint Cookies

Once we've made our jam for the year, the kids know these giant thumbprint cookies are just around the corner. A perfect after-school treat that tastes like Christmas!

MAKES ABOUT 25 COOKIES

Nonstick cooking oil spray

1½ cups old-fashioned (rolled) oats

¾ cup packed light brown sugar, divided

2 cups whole wheat flour

1 cup all-purpose flour

2 teaspoons baking powder

1 teaspoon salt

1 cup (2 sticks) unsalted butter, at room temperature

2 large eggs, at room temperature

2 teaspoons vanilla extract

2 teaspoons almond extract

½ cup turbinado sugar

1 cup (1 half-pint jar) Grandma's Raspberry Freezer Jam (page 47), Spiced Raspberry Jam (page 79), or store-bought

1 · Preheat the oven to 350°F. Line 2 rimmed baking sheets with parchment paper and grease with the oil spray.

2 · Process the oats and ¼ cup of the brown sugar in a food processor until the oats are finely ground, about 20 seconds. Add the whole wheat flour, all-purpose flour, baking powder, and salt and pulse until combined, 15 to 20 seconds.

3 · Using an electric mixer set at medium speed, beat the butter and remaining ½ cup of brown sugar in a large bowl until light and fluffy, scraping down the sides of the bowl as needed, 2 to 3 minutes. One at a time, beat in the eggs, beating until the first egg is absorbed before adding another. Beat in the vanilla and almond extracts. Gradually stir in the flour mixture until combined.

4 · Roll portions of the dough between your hands into about 25 balls the size of Ping-Pong balls. Put the turbinado sugar in a small bowl. Roll each ball in the sugar and arrange them about 1 inch apart on the prepared baking sheets. Using your thumb or the bottom of a tablespoon, press to make an indentation in the center of each ball. Reshape the sides if they crack for the jam to sit in. Stir the jam to loosen it, then spoon into the indentations.

5 · Bake until the cookies are lightly golden and the jam has set, 13 to 15 minutes. Let the cookies cool on the baking sheets for 2 minutes. Transfer them to a wire cooling rack and cool completely. The cookies can be stored in an airtight container at room temperature, separating the layers with parchment paper, for up to 1 week.

Strawberry Thyme Bars

Zero waste alert! These delicious fruit bars are made using the discarded pulp from the Strawberry Thyme Simple Syrup (page 230). Talk about turning trash into treasure! Didn't make the syrup but you need these in your life? I got you! Replace the berry mash with 1½ cups strawberry jam, or whatever jam is your jam! See the additional variation below.

MAKES 24 BARS

- 1¼ cups all-purpose flour
- 1¼ cups old-fashioned (rolled) oats
- ½ cup sugar
- ½ teaspoon baking soda
- ¼ teaspoon salt, plus a pinch
- ¾ cup (1½ sticks) unsalted butter, cut into tablespoons, at room temperature
- 2 teaspoon vanilla extract
- 1½ cups strawberry mash from Strawberry Thyme Simple Syrup (page 230), thyme sprigs removed
- 1 tablespoon cornstarch

1 · Preheat the oven to 350°F. Line the bottom and two short sides of a 9-by-13-inch baking pan with parchment paper, letting the short sides hang over the ends to act as handles.

2 · Stir the flour, oats, sugar, baking soda, and the ¼ teaspoon of salt in a medium bowl. Add the butter and vanilla. Use a fork to mix and mash the ingredients together into a crumbly mass. Measure and reserve half of the mixture for the topping. Press the remaining crumb mixture firmly and evenly into the bottom of the pan for the crust.

3 · Stir the strawberry mash, cornstarch, and the remaining pinch of salt together in a medium bowl. Spread evenly over the crumb crust. Sprinkle with the reserved crumb mixture. Bake until the topping is golden brown, 30 to 40 minutes. Let cool completely in the pan on a wire cooling rack. Lift up on the parchment paper handles to remove the pastry in one piece. Cut into 24 bars. The bars can be refrigerated in an airtight container for up to 2 weeks.

VARIATION

Blackberry Basil Bars: Make the same crust as above. For the filling, combine 2 cups fresh blackberries, ½ to ¾ cup sugar (depending on the sweetness of your berries), 1 teaspoon ground cinnamon, 2 teaspoons fresh basil (or 1 teaspoon dried), 1 tablespoon cornstarch, and a pinch of salt. Stir to combine, mashing the berries slightly.

Botanical Candy Bars

Create your own magical candy bar blends using dried herbs, flowers, fruits, spices, seeds, and nuts. If you wish, use fruit or flower powders to add natural color to your bars instead of food coloring. These bars are a great way to use up that last bit of an ingredient from a jar. Here are a few suggestions to get you inspired.

MAKES 6 MINI CANDY BARS

Base
1 cup white baking chips
1 tablespoon refined coconut oil

Coloring Options
¼ cup fruit powder, such as blueberry, strawberry, raspberry, mango, or peach

2 teaspoons flower powder, such as butterfly pea, hibiscus, marigold, calendula, or rose

1 to 3 drops plant-based food gel or paste

Stir-In Options
1 to 2 tablespoons finely chopped nuts, such as almonds, walnuts, pecans, or pistachios

1 to 2 tablespoons finely snipped or chopped dehydrated blueberries (see page 120) or strawberries (see page 122)

1 to 2 teaspoons crushed or ground dried herbs, such as mint, lemon balm, chamomile, or lavender (see page 88)

1 tablespoon seeds, such as poppy, sesame, pepitas, sunflower, or flax

½ to 1 teaspoon flavored extract, added gradually while stirring to avoid the mixture from hardening.

Decorating Options
Candy sprinkles, decorative sugar, Flower-fetti (page 110), or any of the seeds, nuts, or dehydrated fruits listed

Special tools: silicone mini candy molds with cavities about 3½ by 1½ inches

1 · Make the base: Put the baking chips and coconut oil in a microwave-safe bowl. Microwave on medium (50%) power, in 20- to 30-second intervals, stirring after each, until the chips are smooth and melted.

2 · Mix in your choice of coloring and stir-ins.

3 · For added stability, place a silicone candy mold on a rimmed baking sheet. Pour equal amounts of the mixture into the cavities. Tap the sheet on the counter to even out the candy bars. Decorate as desired. Let stand at room temperature for several hours or overnight to completely set. Remove the bars from the molds. The bars can be stored in an airtight container at room temperature for up to 6 months.

Chocolate Raspberry Truffles

If you're a chocolate lover, you will appreciate this melt-in-your-mouth homemade treat. It is an annual tradition on our holiday candy platter.

MAKES ABOUT 24 TRUFFLES

1¾ cups (10½ ounces) milk chocolate chips

1 cup semisweet chocolate chips

1 cup coarsely crushed freeze-dried raspberries (see page 144)

¾ cup heavy cream

1 teaspoon vanilla extract

Optional coatings: edible flower petals and powders, dehydrated or freeze-dried fruit powders, chopped nuts or seeds, cocoa, or powdered sugar

1 · Mix the milk chocolate and semisweet chocolate chips and the crushed raspberries in a heatproof medium bowl. Heat the cream in a medium saucepan over medium heat, stirring often, until just boiling. Pour evenly over the chocolate mixture. Let stand until the chips soften, about 1 minute. Stir until the chips melt and the mixture is smooth. Stir in the vanilla.

2 · Cover with plastic wrap and refrigerate until firm enough to scoop, about 1 hour. (The truffle mixture can be refrigerated, covered, for up to 3 days. Let stand at room temperature to soften slightly, about 30 minutes, before shaping.)

3 · Line a rimmed baking sheet with wax or parchment paper. Using a 1½-inch-diameter scoop, make balls of the chocolate mixture, and put them on the prepared sheet. Refrigerate until firm, about 20 minutes.

4 · Roll the truffles in the desired coating(s). Or, if you prefer truffles plain, you can skip the coating step.

5 · To store, refrigerate in an airtight container for up to 2 weeks.

Berry Quick Cheesecake

Here's a much easier and less expensive take on cheesecake. This recipe uses fruit powder to add a little excitement and a lot of flavor. Serve with chilled Scented Blackberry Sauce (recipe follows.)

MAKES 8 SERVINGS

Graham Cracker Crust
1¼ cups graham cracker crumbs

¼ cup sugar

5 tablespoons unsalted butter, melted

Filling
½ cup packed freeze-dried raspberries, blackberries, or strawberries

1 (14-ounce) can sweetened condensed milk

1 (8-ounce) package cream cheese, softened

3 tablespoons fresh lemon juice

1 teaspoon vanilla extract

1 cup heavy cream, whipped (2 cups whipped cream)

1 · Make the crust: Mix the crumbs, sugar, and butter in a medium bowl until the crumbs are moistened. Press firmly and evenly into a 9-inch pie plate. Refrigerate until set, at least 30 minutes. If you prefer a baked crust, bake in a preheated 350°F oven until the crust smells toasty, 6 to 8 minutes. Cool completely.

2 · Make the filling: Using a mortar and pestle, finely crush the berries. (Or put the berries in a resealable plastic bag and crush under a heavy saucepan.) In a large bowl, mix the condensed milk, cream cheese, crushed berries, lemon juice, and vanilla with an electric mixer on medium speed, scraping down the sides of the bowl, until smooth. Fold in the whipped cream. Spread the filling evenly in the crust.

3 · Cover with plastic wrap and refrigerate until chilled and set, at least 4 hours or overnight. Slice and serve chilled.

Scented Blackberry Sauce

MAKES ABOUT 1 CUP

3 cups fresh or thawed frozen blackberries

2 tablespoons floral- or herb-infused sugar (see page 216)

This quick and easy sauce is delicious on cheesecake or ice cream. I also like to drizzle it on dessert plates before plating and serving. Get even more creative by using different flower- or herb-infused sugars to customize your sauce. Rose, lilac, mint, or basil sugar are all great options.

Stir the berries and sugar in a small bowl and let stand for 15 minutes. Press on the berries with a large spoon or fork to release the juices. Press through a fine-mesh strainer set over a bowl for a smooth sauce. Use immediately or cover and refrigerate for 1 to 2 hours until chilled, or up to 5 days.

VARIATION
Raspberry Sauce: Substitute raspberries for the blackberries.

Homemade Elderberry Candies

These homemade candies are not like store-bought gummies. They are more tender, partly because they don't include the junky preservatives. They include just three ingredients, one of which is homemade syrup. Elderberry gummies are not only tasty; they're good for you! Take one a day to help keep the germs away. Pop a couple a day if the bug has already hit. Your little homemade candy may just help you feel better!

MAKES ABOUT 85 PIECES

2 (¼-ounce) envelopes unflavored powdered gelatin (2 tablespoons)

½ cup fresh orange juice

1 cup Elderberry Syrup (page 231)

Equipment: silicone mini candy pan, food-safe liquid dropper (both sold at craft and hobby stores and online)

1 · Sprinkle the gelatin over the orange juice in a small bowl. Let stand until the gelatin softens, about 5 minutes.

2 · Heat the syrup in a small saucepan over medium heat, stirring often, until hot—do not boil. Turn the heat down to low. Stir the gelatin mixture, then whisk into the saucepan. Heat, stirring almost constantly, until the gelatin is completely dissolved, about 2 minutes. Remove from the heat.

3 · For added stability, place a silicone mini candy pan on a rimmed baking sheet. Using a food-safe liquid dropper, fill the molds with the gelatin mixture. Let stand for at least 30 minutes to a few hours. I often forget about them and let them stand all day long. It's fine—don't sweat it.

4 · Pop the candies out of the molds onto a sheet of parchment paper. Transfer to an airtight container, separating the layers with parchment paper. To store, refrigerate for up to 2 weeks.

VARIATION

Fruity Jelly Candies: Replace the elderberry syrup with other fruit flavors of simple syrup. Strawberry and raspberry are delicious options.

Chocolate Zucchini Bundt Cake

Cake is one of my favorite ways to use zucchini. First, I know the kids will eat it, and second, zucchini makes an incredibly moist cake. Add a little pudding to the mix and this cake becomes a delicious slice of heaven! Drizzle the slightly warm cake with Garden Mint Chocolate Ganache (page 333) or Simple Syrup Glaze (page 230), or cool completely and dust with powdered sugar before serving.

MAKES 12 SERVINGS

Nonstick cooking spray

1 (15.25-ounce) box devil's food cake mix

1 (3.9-ounce) box instant chocolate pudding mix

4 large eggs

1 cup water

⅓ cup vegetable oil

1 cup shredded fresh or thawed frozen zucchini (see Note)

½ cup mini semisweet chocolate chips

Powdered sugar, for dusting

1 · Preheat the oven to 350°F. Grease a 10-inch Bundt pan with oil spray.

2 · Mix the cake mix, pudding mix, eggs, water, and oil in a large bowl with an electric mixer set at medium speed for 2 minutes, scraping down the sides of the bowl as needed. Fold in the zucchini and chocolate chips. Scrape into the prepared pan and smooth the top.

3 · Bake until a wooden toothpick inserted in the center of the cake comes out clean, 40 to 45 minutes. Transfer to a wire cooling rack. Loosen the cake from the sides and tube with a butter knife. Let cool for 20 minutes. Put the cooling rack over the cake. Invert the pan and rack together to unmold the cake onto the rack. Cool completely.

4 · Dust with powdered sugar. Slice and serve. Wrapped in plastic wrap, the cake can be stored at room temperature for up to 3 days.

Garden Mint Chocolate Ganache

Steeping a packed ¼ cup of fresh mint in cold cream for 12 to 24 hours before using will make a strong infusion to help compete with the richness of the chocolate. But I usually have dried mint handy, which imparts deeper flavors using a heat infusion.

MAKES ABOUT 2 CUPS

1 cup heavy whipping cream

1 tablespoon crushed dried mint

12 ounces milk chocolate or semisweet chocolate

In a small saucepan, heat the cream until almost boiling. Remove from the heat and add the mint. Cover and steep for 20 to 30 minutes. Strain. Reheat the cream until hot. Place the chocolate chips in a bowl and pour the hot cream on top. Do not stir. Let sit for 5 minutes. Stir until smooth. Cool for 10 to 15 minutes before drizzling over your cake.

NOTE

If using frozen shredded zucchini, it must be properly prepped. First, thaw completely. Then, using your hands, squeeze well to wring out any excess moisture. Spread out on a rimmed baking sheet and let air-dry for a few hours. Measure after squeezing out the liquid. Sopping wet shredded zucchini will ruin the texture of the cake, so don't skip this step.

Rosemary Citrus Bundt Cake *with Orange Glaze*

Another boxed cake mix with a twist! Semi-homemade is nothing to be ashamed of. Boxed cakes are how my girls learned to follow recipes and bake. Soon they were changing and adding ingredients and creating their own signature bakes. They're also budget friendly, and cleanup is a cinch. Orange and rosemary is a delightful combination. This recipe honors those flavors.

MAKES 12 SERVINGS

Cake
Nonstick cooking spray
2 dehydrated orange slices (see page 120), coarsely chopped
1 teaspoon dried rosemary or 2 teaspoons finely chopped fresh
1 (15.25-ounce) box yellow cake mix
1 (3.4-ounce) box instant vanilla pudding mix
4 large eggs
½ cup water
½ cup fresh orange juice
½ cup vegetable oil
½ teaspoon vanilla extract

Orange Glaze
5 tablespoons (½ stick plus 1 tablespoon) unsalted butter
2 cups powdered sugar
2 tablespoons fresh orange juice
1 teaspoon vanilla extract
1 tablespoon hot water, as needed

1 · Make the cake: Preheat the oven to 350°F. Grease a 10-inch Bundt pan with the oil spray.

2 · Pulverize the orange slices in a coffee/spice grinder or with a mortar and pestle. Add the rosemary and pulse or stir to combine. Beat the cake mix, pudding mix, eggs, crushed orange mixture, water, orange juice, oil, and vanilla in a large bowl with an electric mixer set on low speed for 30 seconds. Increase the mixer speed to high and mix, scraping down the sides of the bowl as needed, for 2 minutes. Scrape into the prepared pan and smooth the top.

3 · Bake until a wooden toothpick inserted in the center of the cake comes out clean, 40 to 45 minutes. Transfer to a wire cooling rack. Loosen the cake from the sides and tube with a butter knife. Cool for 20 minutes. Place a wire cooling rack over a sheet of parchment paper. Invert onto the rack.

4 · Make the glaze: Melt the butter in a medium saucepan over medium heat. Remove from the heat. Add the powdered sugar, orange juice, and vanilla and whisk until smooth, adding the hot water, as needed, to make a glaze thick enough to drizzle.

5 · Drizzle the glaze over the slightly warm cake. Scrape up the icing on the parchment and reapply to completely coat the cake. Let the cake cool completely. Slice and serve. Wrapped in plastic wrap, the cake can be stored at room temperature for up to 3 days.

Jam Pocket Pies

I call these pocket pies instead of hand pies because when my kids were little, they would stick one in their pocket, put another one in their hand, and head back outside to play. Such sweet memories of sticky pockets and busy kids. Use your homemade jams to make these easy weekday treats. These days I'm making new memories by using my Blueberry Basil Lilac Spread (page 49).

MAKES 6 MINI PIES

Flour, for rolling

½ (14.1-ounce) package (1 sheet) refrigerated pie dough or ½ recipe Grandma's Pie Dough (page 340)

¼ cup strawberry or raspberry jam, preferably homemade

1 large egg white, beaten with 1 teaspoon water

Turbinado, demerara, or raw sugar

1 · Preheat the oven to 375°F. Line a rimmed baking sheet with parchment paper.

2 · On a lightly floured work surface, roll out the dough until about ⅛-inch thick. Using a 4-inch round cookie cutter, cut out 12 rounds. Using a ½-inch round cookie cutter, cut out and discard the centers from 6 rounds to make the tops of the mini pies.

3 · For each pie, spoon 2 teaspoons jam in the center of a dough round. Brush the edge of the round with the egg wash. Center the tops over the bottoms and press the edges together with the tines of a fork. Brush the tops with the egg wash and give them a generous sprinkle of turbinado sugar. Transfer to the prepared sheet.

4 · Bake until golden brown, 12 to 15 minutes. Cool on the pan for 5 minutes, then transfer to a wire cooling rack and let cool completely.

VARIATION

Cranberry Pocket Pies: Substitute Orange Spice Cranberry Sauce (page 304) for the jam.

Sweet Tooth

Blueberry Basil Lilac Crumb Pie

My Blueberry Basil Lilac Spread doubles as a delicious pie filling. The crumb topping makes it extra special.

MAKES 8 SERVINGS

Flour, for rolling

½ recipe Grandma's Pie Dough (page 340)

Double batch Blueberry Basil Lilac Spread (page 49)

Crumb Topping

⅔ cup all-purpose flour

⅓ cup unsalted butter cold, cut into chunks

⅓ cup light brown sugar

1 tablespoon lilac-infused sugar (see page 216)

1 · Preheat the oven to 400°F.

2 · On a lightly floured work surface, roll out the dough into a round about ⅛-inch thick. Transfer to a 9-inch pie pan, fit the dough into the corners, and cut off the excess dough, leaving a 1-inch overhang. Shape the edges. Spread the prepared filling in the pie crust.

3 · Make the crumb topping: In a food processor, combine the flour, butter, brown sugar, and infused sugar and pulse until combined. Remove the blade. Grab a handful of the crumb topping, squeezing it in your hand to create a few larger clumps, and sprinkle over the filling. Repeat until the pie is evenly covered and the crumb topping is used.

4 · Loosely cover the pie edge with a silicone pie ring or strips of aluminum foil.

5 · Bake until the filling is bubbling and the crumble topping is golden brown, 40 to 45 minutes. Transfer to a cooling rack and cool completely. Slice and serve.

Peach Slab Pie

Frozen peaches are the star of this dish. Thaw just enough to easily cut. Serve this comforting flavor combination warm or at room temperature.

MAKES 8 SERVINGS

2 pounds frozen peaches, slightly thawed and cut into ½-inch pieces

¾ cup light brown sugar

3 tablespoons cornstarch

1 tablespoon lemon juice

1 teaspoon vanilla extract

1 teaspoon ground cinnamon

¼ teaspoon ground nutmeg

1 (14.1-ounce) package refrigerated pie crusts (2 crusts) or 1 recipe Grandma's Pie Dough (page 340)

Milk, for brushing crust

Turbinado sugar (optional)

1 · Preheat the oven to 400°F. In a large bowl, combine the peaches, brown sugar, cornstarch, lemon juice, vanilla, cinnamon, and nutmeg, stirring until the peaches are coated. Let stand.

2 · On a lightly floured surface, roll out one crust in a 10-by-14-inch rectangle. Place into a 7-by-11-inch (2-quart) baking dish, leaving an overhang. Add the peach filling and spread evenly.

3 · Roll out the second dough into an 8-by-12-inch rectangle and lay on top of the filling.

4 · Gather the bottom and top edges, tuck under, and crimp together to seal.

5 · Cut 4 or 5 slits into the top crust, or a few shapes, to vent. Lightly brush the edges and top with milk and sprinkle with turbinado sugar, if desired.

6 · Bake for 40 to 45 minutes, or until the crust is golden and the filling is bubbly. Serve warm.

Grandma's Pie Dough

Grandma's never-fail recipe always works, making homemade pie truly "easy as pie." What makes this dough special are a few "secret" ingredients: Baking powder is insurance for a flaky crust, the egg helps the dough hold together, and the vinegar reacts with the flour for extra tenderness. Also, this makes plenty of dough. If you're like me and enjoy decorating pies with cutouts, you will love playing with the additional pastry.

MAKES ENOUGH DOUGH FOR ONE 9-INCH DOUBLE-CRUST PIE OR TWO SINGLE-CRUST PIES

3¼ cups all-purpose flour

1 tablespoon sugar

1 teaspoon baking powder

1 teaspoon salt

1¼ cups shortening, cut into 1- to 2-inch chunks

5 tablespoons water

1 large egg, beaten

1 tablespoon white vinegar

1 · Sift the flour, sugar, baking powder, and salt together into a large bowl. Add the shortening, turning until coated. Using a pastry blender, cut in the shortening until the mixture mostly resembles coarse breadcrumbs, with pea-sized pieces of shortening. Make a well in the middle of mixture.

2 · In a small bowl or cup, mix the water, egg, and vinegar together. Measure 8 tablespoons of the liquid and add to the well. Stir until the dough clumps together. Finish shaping the dough with your hands.

3 · Divide the dough into two portions. Shape each portion into a thick disk. Wrap each disk tightly in plastic wrap and chill for at least 30 minutes or up to 1 week. To freeze, place the wrapped dough in a resealable freezer bag, pressing out as much air as possible, and freeze for up to 2 months. Thaw overnight in the refrigerator before using. Let the chilled dough stand at room temperature for about 10 minutes before rolling.

VARIATIONS

Herb Pie Crust: This dough is delicious for pot pies and quiche. Stir 2 teaspoons Herbes de Provence Seasoning Blend (page 109) or Italian Seasoning Blend (page 110) into the sifted dry ingredients.

Floral Pie Crust: Stir 2 teaspoons Flower-fetti (page 110) or 1 tablespoon fresh petals into the sifted dry ingredients.

Acknowledgments

Like so many things, writing a cookbook is a journey. Parts of the path are thorny and full of weeds, not always easy to travel. But with the support of others, the journey can be a beautiful adventure with twists and turns of excitement and possibility. Because of the people mentioned here, my journey to becoming a published author was a beautiful, life-changing experience, and I will forever be grateful to all of them.

To my husband, Kevin, my partner and best friend. Look what we did! Who would have imagined two kids choosing the hard road would end up three decades later sharing with the world their passion for a simple, joyful life, built together? Thank you for taking this leap of faith with me. It's the greatest gift to be growing up and growing old with you.

To my kids, Katlyn, Cole, Jack, Ryan, Sidnee, and Violet. You are the reason I do these projects. You are the reason I breathe. Choosing not to go back to a full-time job and instead focusing on writing this book came with many sacrifices for our family. Yet through it all you remained supportive, interested, and encouraging. I am so proud of all of you.

To my editor, Doris Cooper, you've changed my life in the most amazing ways. I will be forever grateful for this opportunity you've given me.

To the Simon & Schuster and Simon Element families, thank you to all who touched this book one way or another. With every pass and every conversation, the book bloomed and grew in the most magical ways. I'm so thankful to all of you. A special acknowledgment to Jen Wang, Maria Espinosa, Katie McClimon, Laura Jarrett, Madelyn Rodriguez, Allison Har-zvi, and Richard Rhorer.

To Kim O' Donnel, thank you for helping me put the puzzle together and for hearing me all along the way. You not only helped to bring this book to life, but you also did it with excitement, honesty, and intention. I couldn't have finished this without you.

Thank you to Rick Rodgers, for your guidance. To my photography team: Michael Shay (owner/photographer), Jeremy Dunham (photographer), Muffy Kruger (studio manager), Darcy Henderson (photography stylist extraordinaire), Erika Von Trapp (chef/food stylist), Stephen Dean (photography assistant and master latte maker), and Aiden Vetterlien (photography assistant) at Polara Studio. What a pleasure it was to work with all of you on this project. One of my favorite parts of this whole process was styling and shooting the photos with you. Not only did I walk away with the most beautiful photographs for my book, I walked away with a wealth of knowledge and more important, new friends for life. I appreciate you all so much.

Thank you to my brother, Benjamin Bankhardt, for keeping my kitchen running when I needed it the most. I love you, Ben.

To my extended family and sweet friends. Your continued support, encouragement and positive energy was my fuel to keep going when things seemed overwhelming. Thank you for always challenging me to reach higher, stay true to myself, and dream big.

Thank you to God, my heavenly grandmothers, and my dog Gram (or the G's, as I call them) for being by my side for every step of the way of this project. I deeply felt my Grandma Bonnie and Grandma Naomi guiding me in the kitchen, almost like we wrote this book together. Gram was often just a few feet away keeping me company while loving me unconditionally, and God is always with me, giving me strength and peace. I'm so grateful for my G's.

Last but far from least, thank you to my @BigFamilyLiving online community for making it possible for this to even happen. Your follows, likes, comments, reshares, and saves literally changed my life. I wouldn't be here without them. I wrote this book with you always top of mind. My goal was to create a timeless cookbook that will inspire, teach, and support you on your own beautiful journey. I hope it becomes a treasure in your cookbook collection.

With love and gratitude always,

Holly Capelle

Journal Pages

Index

NOTE: Page references in *italics* refer to photos of recipes and food preparation; page references in **bold** refer to charts.

altitude, 65–66, **67**
anise hyssop tea, 172
apples, 21, 72, 119, 142–44
    Apple Cinnamon Oatmeal, 250
    applesauce, about, 144, 152
    Applesauce, Apple Pie, 80
    Apple Spice Tea, 178
apricots, 21–22, 72, 122, 144
artichokes, 26–27
asparagus, 27, 123, 146
Avocado Garden Toast, *252*, 253
avocados, about, 144

baby food, 152
Baked Lavender Orange French Toast, 251
bananas, 22, 120, 144, 152
    Banana Bread, 311
    Chocolate, Tahini, and Banana Muffins, *312*, 313
Barbecue Sauce, 303
Basic Fruit Leather Recipe, 131
Basic Quick-Pickled Fruit, 59
Basic Quick-Pickled Vegetables, 59
basil
    Blackberry Basil Bars, 325
    Blueberry, Lemon, and Basil Garden Cooler, 162
    Blueberry, Pear, and Basil Fruit Leathers, 132
    Blueberry Basil Lilac Crumb Pie, 338
    Blueberry Basil Lilac Spread, 49
    Blueberry Basil Mocktail, 238
    Blueberry Basil Simple Syrup, 225, *227*
    holy basil tea, 174
    Purple Basil Salt, 207
    Purple Basil Vinegar, 187
    Raspberry Basil Vinaigrette, 281
    Tomato Basil Crackers, 245
    Tomato Basil Pasta Salad, 296–97
Bath Salts, Botanical, 209

beans, 27, 123, 149, 152
    Slow-Cooked Dried Beans, 290
    Vegetable and Bean Dried Soup Mix, 136
    Vegetable and Bean Soup, 263
bee balm/bergamot tea, 172
Beet Chips, Oven-Roasted Dried, 137
beets, about, 27, 123, 146
berries, 22, *23*, 72, 120, 144. *See also* blackberries; blueberries; elderberries; raspberries; strawberries
    Berry Blast Oven Fruit Rolls, 133
    Berry Good Freezer Smoothie Cubes, *40*, 41
    Berry Quick Cheesecake, 329
    Cranberry Pocket Pies, 337
    Cranberry Sauce, Orange Spice, 304
    Hibiscus Berry Tea, 179
    Homestead Berry Syrup, 84
    juniper berries tea, 174
beverages, 236–41. *See also* water infusions
    Blueberry Basil Mocktail, 238
    Botanical Water, *164*, 165
    Concord Grape Juice, 81
    Easy Homemade Soda, 238
    Garden Coolers, 162
    North Pole Hot Chocolate with Whipped Toppers, 240
    Strawberry, Lime, and Thyme Cooler, 239
    Summer Sunset Champagne Cocktail, 239
    Summer Sunset Mocktail, 239
    Sunshine Mocktail, 236
    Tequila Sunset Cocktail, 239
    Whipped Toppers, 240, *241*
blackberries
    Blackberry, Orange, and Rosemary Garden Cooler, 162
    Blackberry Basil Bars, 325
    Scented Blackberry Sauce, 329
    Spiced Blackberry Vinegar, 188

Black Pepper Plum Jam, 50
blanching, 18
blueberries, 144
    Blueberry, Lemon, and Basil Garden Cooler, 162
    Blueberry, Pear, and Basil Fruit Leathers, 132
    Blueberry Basil Lilac Crumb Pie, 338
    Blueberry Basil Lilac Spread, 49
    Blueberry Basil Mocktail, 238
    Blueberry Basil Simple Syrup, 225, *227*
    blueberry tea, 172
    Spiced Blueberry Simple Syrup, 229
boiling water canning, 62–85
    about, 63, 64, 66–67, 68, 76
    altitude and, 65–66, **67**
    Apple Pie Applesauce, 80
    Concord Grape Juice, 81
    Dandelion Jelly, 82
    for fruit, 72–75
    Homestead Berry Syrup, 84
    Homestyle Pickles, 85, *85*
    jams and jellies, 76
    Mint Jelly, 83
    packing methods for, 65
    preparation for, 65
    Refrigerator Jelly, 82
    Rose Jelly, 83, *83*
    Spiced Raspberry Jam, 79
    syrups for, 65, **66**
    tools for, 64–65
    troubleshooting, **70–71**
    Wild Violet Jelly, 82
Botanical Bath Salts, 209
Botanical Candy Bars, *326*, 327
Botanical Graham Crackers, 322, *323*
botanical teas (tisanes), 171–75
Botanical Water, *164*, 165
breads, 305–17
    Banana Bread, 311
    Calendula Cornbread, 308

Chocolate, Tahini, and Banana Muffins, *312*, 313
Herb and Cheddar Biscuits, 314, *315*
Lavender Cornbread, 308, *309*
Lavender Scones, 310
Lemon, Lilac, and Poppy Seed Bread, *306*, 307
Quick Honey Wheat Bread, 305
Rosemary Baguettes, *316*, 317
Rose Scones, 310
breakfast, 248–61
   Apple Cinnamon Oatmeal, 250
   Avocado Garden Toast, *252*, 253
   Ham and Cheese Garden Quiche, 254, *255*
   Lavender Granola, 257
   Lavender Orange French Toast, 251
   Lavender Orange French Toast, Baked, 251
   Lemon Lilac Doughnuts, 248–49, *249*
   Make-Ahead Oatmeal, 251
   Pumpkin Spice Pancakes, 250
   Smart Start Smoothie, 258, *259*
   Sweet Garden Toast, 253, *253*
   Tickled Pink Smoothie Bowl, 261
   Tropical Dreams Smoothie, *260*, 261
broccoli, 27, 125, 152
Brussels sprouts, 27, 146–48
butter, infused, 198, **199**
   Garden Butter Log, *199*, 200, 201
   Holiday Butter Balls, *202*, 203
   Homestyle Butter, 203
Butterfly Pea Flower Simple Syrup, 225, *226*
butterfly pea flower tea, 172

cabbage, 123, 148
Calendula and Thyme Finishing Salt, 208
Calendula Cornbread, 308
Candied Bacon Chicken Sandwich, 268
Candy Bars, Botanical, *326*, 327
Capelle, Holly, 9–10
carrots, about, 29, 125, 148, 152
Carrots, Glazed, 288, *288*
Carrots, Quick-Pickled Lavender, 60
cauliflower, 29, 125, 148
celery, 125, 148
celery salt, homemade, 148
Chamomile Honey, 215
Chamomile Honey, Melon Ball Salad with, *282*, 283
chamomile tea, 172
Champagne Cocktail, Summer Sunset, 239
charts
   altitude adjustments for boiling water canning, **67**
   compound butter mix-and-match menu, **199**
   culinary herbs, **90–93**
   edible flowers, **99–103**
   fancy pants ice menu, **166**
   flavored simple syrup menu, **224**

   fruit and vegetable pickle prep, **56–57**
   infused honey flavoring menu, **213**
   infused oil flavoring menu, **191**
   infused salt flavoring menu, **205**
   infused vinegars mix-and-match menu, **186**
   quick pickle partners, **54–55**
   syrups for canning, **66**
   syrups for light packs, **19**
   troubleshooting freeze-dried foods, **153**
   troubleshooting home canning, **70–71**
   troubleshooting home freezing, **37**
Cheddar Cheese Ball, 242
Cheesy Tomato Dipping Oil, 195
cherries, 22–24, 73, 120, 145
Chile Hot Sauce, Dried, 111
chiles, about, *104*, 105–6
Chili Powder, *108*, 111
Chili Sauce, Garden Wraps with Sweet, 274–75, *275*
Chili Sauce, Sweet, *275*, 276
Chive Blossom Vinaigrette, 280
Chive Blossom Vinegar, 187
Chive Blossom Zucchini Chips, 136
chocolate
   Chocolate, Tahini, and Banana Muffins, *312*, 313
   Chocolate Raspberry Truffles, 328
   Chocolate Zucchini Bundt Cake, 332
   Fresh Mint Chocolate Chip Ice Cream, *42*, 43
   Garden Mint Chocolate Ganache, 333
   North Pole Hot Chocolate with Whipped Toppers, 240
   Strawberry Chocolate Chunk Ice Cream, 39
citrus, about, 25, 120, 145. *See also* lemons; oranges
Citrus Bundt Cake with Orange Glaze, Rosemary, 334, *335*
cocktails. *See* beverages
Cold Infusion, 165
Colorful Fruit Ice Cubes, 169
compound butter, 198. *See also* butter, infused
Concord Grape Juice, 81
condiments, 303–4
coneflower tea, 172
corn, about, 29, 125
Cornbread, Calendula, 308
Cornbread, Lavender, 308, *309*
Crab Cakes, Pacific Northwest, 284
cranberries, about, 24
Cranberry Pocket Pies, 337
Cranberry Sauce, Orange Spice, 304
Creamy Garlic Scape Sauce, 299
Creamy Roasted Tomato Soup, 262
cucumber
   Cucumber Body Mist, 165
   Cucumber Rose Garden Salad, *278*, 279
   Strawberry, Cucumber, and Mint Garden Cooler, 162

culinary powders, about, 113
curing, of alliums, 105–6

Dandelion Jelly, 82
decoction, 171. *See also* water infusions
dehydrating, 114–37
   about, 115, 116
   Basic Fruit Leather Recipe, 131
   Berry Blast Oven Fruit Rolls, 133
   Blueberry, Pear, and Basil Fruit Leathers, 132
   Chive Blossom Zucchini Chips, 136
   culinary powders, 113
   Floral Fruit Chips, 134
   Fruit Chips, 134
   Fruit Punch Chips, 134
   fruits, 116–17, *118*, 119–22, *121*, *124*
   herbs and flowers, 128–31, *129*
   Oven-Roasted Dried Beet Chips, 137
   Peach and Mango Oven Fruit Rolls, 133
   rehydrating, 119
   Spiced-Up Fruit Chips, 134
   Vegetable and Bean Dried Soup Mix, 136
   vegetables, 117–19, *118*, 123–28, *124*
desserts, 318–40
   Berry Quick Cheesecake, 329
   Blackberry Basil Bars, 325
   Blueberry Basil Lilac Crumb Pie, 338
   Botanical Candy Bars, *326*, 327
   Botanical Graham Crackers, 322
   Chocolate Raspberry Truffles, 328
   Chocolate Zucchini Bundt Cake, 332
   Cranberry Pocket Pies, 337
   Floral Pie Crust, 340
   Floral Sugar Cookies, 318, *319*
   Fruity Jelly Candies, 331
   Garden Mint Chocolate Ganache, 333
   Grandma's Pie Dough, 340
   Herb Pie Crust, 340
   Homemade Elderberry Candies, *330*, 331
   Ice Cream Sandwiches with Botanical Graham Crackers, 322, *323*
   Jam Pocket Pies, *336*, 337
   Peach Slab Pie, 339
   Raspberry Jam Thumbprint Cookies, 324
   Raspberry Sauce, 329
   Rosemary Citrus Bundt Cake with Orange Glaze, 334, *335*
   Scented Blackberry Sauce, 329
   Strawberry Thyme Bars, 325
Deviled Eggs, Pretty in Pink, 246, *247*
dinner, 284–302
   Creamy Garlic Scape Sauce, 299
   Garden Focaccia, 302, *302*
   Glazed Carrots, 288, *288*
   Go-To Spice Rub, 289
   Herby Pizza Dough, 300
   Homemade Herb Pasta, *292*, 293, *294*, 295
   Homestead Tartar Sauce, 285
   Honey-Glazed Pork Loin, 289
   Pacific Northwest Crab Cakes, 284
   Pantry Tomato Sauce, 296

Index

dinner (cont.)
    Pizza Assembly and Baking, 301
    Pizza Sauce, 301
    Potato Roses, 286, *287*
    Rainbow Rice, 291
    Roasted Marinara Sauce, 297
    Scalloped Potatoes, 291
    Slow-Cooked Dried Beans, 290
    Spinach Parm Pasta, *298*, 299
    Stuffed Zucchini, 285
    Tomato Basil Pasta Salad, 296–97
    Vegetable Rice, 290
dog food, 152
drying, 86–113. *See also* dehydrating; freeze-drying
    about, 87
    of chiles, *104*, 105–6
    Chili Powder, *108*, 111
    culinary powders and, 113
    curing of alliums, 105–6
    Dried Chile Hot Sauce, 112
    Flower-fetti, *108*, 110
    of flowers, *94–96, 95, 97, 98,* **99–103**
    Greek Seasoning Blend, *108*, 109
    Herbes de Provence Seasoning Blend, *108*, 109
    of herbs, 88–89, **90–93**
    Italian Seasoning Blend, *108*, 110
    Mild Taco Seasoning, *108*, 111

Easy Homemade Soda, 238
eggplants, 29–30, 148
Eggs, Pretty in Pink Deviled, 246, *247*
elderberries, 120, 173, 231
    Elderberry Syrup, 231
    elderberry tea, 173
    Homemade Elderberry Candies, *330*, 331
elderflower tea, 173

fancy pants ice, 166, **166**
Farro Soup, Vegetable, Beef, and, *266*, 267
figs, 24
flowers. *See also* charts; *individual names of flowers*
    culinary powders, about, 113
    dehydrating, 128, *129*
    drying, *94–96, 95, 97, 98,* **99–103**
    Floral Fruit Chips, 134
    Floral Ice Cubes, 169
    Floral Iced Tea, 178
    Floral Pie Crust, 340
    Floral Sugar Cookies, *318*, 319
    Floral Teas, 178
    Flower-fetti, *108*, 110
    Flower Pasta, 293
    freeze-drying, 152
    freezing, 29, *36*
    Garden Butter Log, *199, 200,* 201
    types of, for botanical teas, 171–75
freeze-drying, 138–57
    about, 139, 140–42
    for baby food, 152

culinary powders, 113
    for dog food, 152
    flowers, 152
    foods to avoid freeze-drying, 153
    Freeze-Dried Vegetable Chips, 156, *157*
    Freeze-Dried Yogurt Drops, *154,* 155
    fruits, 142–46, *147,* 151
    Raspberry Vanilla Drops, 155
    rehydrating, 142
    tools for, 141–42
    troubleshooting, **153**
    vegetables, *143,* 146–53, *147,* 151
freezing, 14–43
    about, 15, 17
    Berry Good Freezer Smoothie Cubes, *40,* 41
    checklist, 21
    of fresh fruit, 21–26
    Fresh Mint Chocolate Chip Ice Cream, *42,* 43
    of fresh vegetables, herbs, flowers, 26–35
    Garden Yogurt Pops, 38
    Lavender Ice Cream, 43
    packing and preparing, 17–21
    Strawberry Chocolate Chunk Ice Cream, 39
    Strawberry Patch Ice Cream, 39
    Strawberry Rose Sorbet, 39
    tools for, 17
    troubleshooting, **37**
Fresh Mint Chocolate Chip Ice Cream, *42,* 43
Fresh Pea Soup, 264, *265*
fruits. *See also* charts; *individual names of fruits*
    Basic Fruit Leather Recipe, *130,* 131
    Basic Quick-Pickled Fruit, 59
    boiling water canning, 72–75
    Colorful Fruit Ice Cubes, 169
    culinary powders, about, 113
    dehydrating, 116–17, *118,* 119–22, *121, 124,* 128–34
    Floral Fruit Chips, 134
    freeze-drying, 142–46, *147,* 151
    freezing, 21–26
    Fruit Chips, 134
    Fruit Chips, Spiced-Up, 134
    Fruit Punch Chips, 134
    Fruits and Flowers Tea Blend, *176,* 177
    Fruity Jelly Candies, 331
    Fruity Sugar, 218
    quick pickle partners/preparation for, **55, 56**

Garden Butter Log, *199, 200,* 201
Garden Coolers, 162
Garden Focaccia, 302, *302*
Garden Mint Chocolate Ganache, 333
Garden Wraps with Sweet Chili Sauce, 274–75, *275*
Garden Yogurt Pops, 38

garlic, 54, 105–6, *107,* 125–26, 148–49
    curing of alliums, 105–6
    Garlic and Herb Marinade, 196
    garlic scapes, about, 106, 126
    Garlic Scape Sauce, Creamy, 299
    Garlic Scape Vinaigrette, 280
    Rustic Herb and Garlic Crackers, *244,* 245
Glazed Carrots, 288, *288*
goldenrod tea, 173
Go-To Spice Rub, 289
Graham Crackers, Botanical, 322, *323*
Grandma's Pie Dough, 340
Grandma's Raspberry Freezer Jam, 47
grapefruit, 25
Grape Juice, Concord, 81
grapes, about, 24, 122, 145
Greek Seasoning Blend, *108,* 109
greens. *See* spinach

Ham and Cheese Garden Quiche, 254, *255*
hawthorn tea, 173
headspace, defined, 19
health-care products, 11
    Botanical Bath Salts, 209
    Cucumber Body Mist, 165
    Rose Sugar Body Scrub, 222
herbs. *See also* charts; *individual names of herbs*
    Calendula and Thyme Finishing Salt, 208
    Calendula Cornbread, 308
    dehydrating, 128, *129*
    drying, 88–89, **90–93**
    freeze-drying, 149
    freezing, 29–30
    Garden Butter Log, *199, 200,* 201
    Garlic and Herb Marinade, 196
    Herbal Whipped Cream, 180
    Herb and Cheddar Biscuits, 314, *315*
    Herb and Dried Tomato Cheese Log, 243
    Herb and Dried Tomato Cheese Spread, 243, *244*
    Herb Croutons, 279
    Herbes de Provence Dipping Oil, 195
    Herbes de Provence Seasoning Blend, *108,* 109
    Herb Garden Vinegar, 187
    Herb Infused Olive Oil, *192,* 193
    Herb Pie Crust, 340
    Herby Pizza Dough, 300
    Homemade Herb Pasta, *292, 293, 294,* 295
    quick pickle partners/flavors for, **54–55**
    Rustic Herb and Garlic Crackers, *244,* 245
    types of, for botanical teas, 171–75
Hibiscus Berry Tea, 179
hibiscus tea, about, 173
Holiday Butter Balls, *202,* 203
Holiday Ice Cubes, *168,* 169
holy basil/tulsi tea, 174
Homemade Elderberry Candies, *330,* 331
Homemade Herb Pasta, *292, 293, 294,* 295

Homemade Tomato Paste, 113
Homestead Berry Syrup, 84
Homestead Tartar Sauce, 285
Homestyle Butter, 203
Homestyle Pickles, 85, *85*
honey, infused, 211, *212*, **213**, 213–14
    Chamomile Honey, 215
    in Honey-Glazed Pork Loin, 289
    Lilac Honey, 215
    in Melon Ball Salad with Chamomile Honey, *282*, 283
    in Quick Honey Wheat Bread, 305
    Spiced Honey, 215

ice and ice cubes. *See* water infusions
ice box recipes. *See* freezing
Ice Cream Sandwiches with Botanical Graham Crackers, 322, *323*
Infused Sugar Shapes, *220*, 221
infusions, 159–231
    savory, 182–209
    sweet, 210–31
    water, 160–80
Italian Seasoning Blend, *108*, 110

Jam Pocket Pies, *336*, 337
jams, no-can, 44–51
    about, 45, 46, 76
    Black Pepper Plum Jam, 50
    Blueberry Basil Lilac Spread, 49
    cooked vs. no-cook, 46
    Grandma's Raspberry Freezer Jam, 47
    Nectarine Jam, 51
    Peaches and Cream Jam, 51
    Quick Rhubarb Jam, 48
    Strawberry Rose Jam, 47
    tools for, 46
jasmine tea, 174
jellies, 76. *See also* jams, no-can
    Dandelion Jelly, 82
    Fruity Jelly Candies, 331
    Mint Jelly, 83
    Refrigerator Jelly, 82
    Rose Jelly, 83, *83*
    Wild Violet Jelly, 82
Jerk Vibes Marinade, 197
juniper berries tea, 174

Kickin' Ketchup, 304
kohlrabi, 30

labeling, 19–21
lavender
    Baked Lavender Orange French Toast, 251
    Lavender Cornbread, 308, *309*
    Lavender Granola, 257
    Lavender Ice Cream, 43
    Lavender Orange French Toast, 251
    Lavender Scones, 310
    Lavender Vinegar, 187
    Quick-Pickled Lavender Carrots, 60, *61*

leeks, 126
lemon balm/lemon verbena/lemongrass tea, 174
lemons
    Blueberry, Lemon, and Basil Garden Coolers, 162
    Lemon, Lilac, and Poppy Seed Bread, *306*, 307
    Lemonade Ice Cubes, 169
    lemon juice, bottled, 76
    Lemon Lilac Doughnuts, 248–49, *249*
    Lemon Lilac Marinade, 197
lilac
    Blueberry Basil Lilac Crumb Pie, 338
    Blueberry Basil Lilac Spread, 49
    Lemon, Lilac, and Poppy Seed Bread, *306*, 307
    Lemon Lilac Doughnuts, 248–49, *249*
    Lemon Lilac Marinade, 197
    Lilac Honey, 215

Make-Ahead Oatmeal, 251
mangoes, 24–25, 145
marinades, 196–97
Mediterranean Dipping Oil, 195
Mediterranean Vibes Tea Blend, 177
Melon Ball Salad with Chamomile Honey, *282*, 283
melons, about, 145
Mild Taco Seasoning, *108*, 111
Mint Jelly, 83
mint tea, 174–75
Minty Strawberry-Orange Sauce, 311
mocktails. *See* beverages
mushrooms, 126, 149

Nectarine Jam, 51
nectarines, about, 73, 122, 145
North Pole Hot Chocolate with Whipped Toppers, 240

Oatmeal, Apple Cinnamon, 250
Oatmeal, Make-Ahead, 251
oils, dipping, 194
    Cheesy Tomato Dipping Oil, 195
    Herbes de Provence Dipping Oil, 195
    Mediterranean Dipping Oil, 195
oils, infused, 190, **191**
    Herb Infused Olive Oil, *192*, 193
    Rosemary Peppercorn Infused Olive Oil, 193
onions, 30, 105–6, 126–27, 149
oranges, 25
    Blackberry, Orange, and Rosemary Garden Cooler, 162
    Lavender Orange French Toast, 251
    Lavender Orange French Toast, Baked, 251
    Minty Strawberry-Orange Sauce, 311
    Orange Spice Cranberry Sauce, 304
    Rosemary Citrus Bundt Cake with Orange Glaze, 334, *335*

Oregano Salt, 207
Oswego (bee balm/bergamot) tea, 172
Oven-Roasted Dried Beet Chips, 137

Pacific Northwest Crab Cakes, 284
packing methods, 18–19, 53, 65. *See also individual names of foods*
Pancakes, Pumpkin Spice, 250
Pansy and Rosemary Salt, 207
Pantry Tomato Sauce, 296
parsnips, 35, 125
peaches, 25, 73, 122, 145
    Peach and Mango Oven Fruit Rolls, 133
    Peaches and Cream Jam, 51
    Peach Slab Pie, 339
pears
    about, 25, 73, 122, 145
    Blueberry, Pear, and Basil Fruit Leathers, 132
peas, about, 30–32, 127, 149–50, 152
Pea Soup, Fresh, 264, *265*
pepper(s)
    Black Pepper Plum Jam, 50
    Chile Hot Sauce, Dried, 111
    chiles, drying, *104*, 105–6
    Chili Powder, *108*, 110
    Chili Sauce, Sweet, *275*, 276
    Garden Wraps with Sweet Chili Sauce, 274–75, *275*
    hot/sweet, about, 32, 127, 150
    Rosemary Peppercorn Infused Olive Oil, 193
    Wild Violet Peppercorn Vinaigrette, 281
perfuming, 171. *See also* water infusions
pickles, quick, 53–61
    Basic Quick-Pickled Fruit, 59
    Basic Quick-Pickled Vegetables, 59
    packing and storage for, 53
    partners/flavors for, **54–55**
    preparation for, 53, **56–57**
    Quick-Pickled Garlic Scapes, 60
    Quick-Pickled Lavender Carrots, 60, *61*
    tools for, 53
Picnic Potato Salad, 283
Pie Dough, Grandma's, 340
pineapples, 73–74, 122, 146
Pizza Assembly and Baking, 301
Pizza Dough, Herby, 300
Pizza Sauce, 301
Plum Jam, Black Pepper, 50
plums, 25–26, 74, 122, 146
potatoes, 32, 127, 150
    Picnic Potato Salad, 283
    Potato Roses, 286, *287*
    Scalloped Potatoes, 291
potatoes, sweet (yams), 32, 127, 150, 153
Powder Pasta, 293
preserving, 9–10. *See also* infusions; saving of foods
Pretty in Pink Deviled Eggs, 246, *247*
Pumpkin Spice Pancakes, 250

Index

Purple Basil Salt, 207
Purple Basil Vinegar, 187

Quick Honey Wheat Bread, 305
Quick Rhubarb Jam, 48

radishes, 127, 150
Rainbow Rice, 291
raspberries
   Chocolate Raspberry Truffles, 328
   Grandma's Raspberry Freezer Jam, 47
   Raspberry Basil Vinaigrette, 281
   Raspberry Jam Thumbprint Cookies, 324
   Raspberry Sauce, 329
   Raspberry Simple Syrup, *226*, 228
   raspberry tea, 175
   Raspberry Vanilla Drops, 155
   Raspberry Vinegar, 189
   Spiced Raspberry Jam, 79
   Spiced Raspberry Syrup, 228
red clover tea, 175
Refrigerator Jelly, 82
rehydrating, 119, 142. *See also* dehydrating;
   freeze-drying
rhubarb, about, 26, 74
Rhubarb Jam, Quick, 48
Rhubarb Simple Syrup, *227*, 229
Rice, Rainbow, 291
Rice, Vegetable, 290
Roasted Marinara Sauce, 297
Rose Jelly, 83, *83*
rosemary
   Blackberry, Orange, and Rosemary
      Garden Coolers, 162
   Pansy and Rosemary Salt, 207
   Rosemary Baguettes, *316*, 317
   Rosemary Candied Bacon, *270*, 271
   Rosemary Citrus Bundt Cake with
      Orange Glaze, 334, *335*
   Rosemary Peppercorn Infused Olive Oil,
      193
roses
   Rose Jelly, 83, *83*
   Rose Salt, 207
   Rose Scones, 310
   Rose Sugar, 218
   Rose Sugar Body Scrub, 222
   Rose Tea Latte, 180
   Rose-Vanilla Tea, 178
   Rose Vinegar, 187
   Strawberry Rose Jam, 47
   Strawberry Rose Sorbet, 39
Rustic Herb and Garlic Crackers, *244*, 245

safety
   of boiling water canning, 64, 68
   of elderberries, 120, 173, 231
   of jasmine, 174
salads, 274–83
   Cucumber Rose Garden Salad, *278*, 279
   Garden Wraps with Sweet Chili Sauce,
      274–75, *275*

Garlic Scape Vinaigrette, 280
Herb Croutons, 279
Melon Ball Salad with Chamomile Honey,
   282, 283
Picnic Potato Salad, 283
Raspberry Basil Vinaigrette, 281
Sweet Chili Sauce, *275*, 276
Wild Violet Peppercorn Vinaigrette, 281
salt, infused, 198, *204*, 205, 205–6
   Botanical Bath Salts, 209
   Calendula and Thyme Finishing Salt, 208
   Oregano Salt, 207
   Pansy and Rosemary Salt, 207
   Purple Basil Salt, 207
   Rose Salt, 207
   Spicy Finishing Salt, 209
sandwiches. *See* soups & sandwiches
saving of foods, 14–157
   boiling water canning, 62–85
   dehydrating, 114–37
   drying, 86–113
   freeze-drying, 138–57
   freezing, 14–43
   no-can jams & quick pickles, 44–61
savory infusions, 182–209. *See also* butter,
   infused; oils, dipping; oils, infused; salt,
   infused; vinegars, infused
Scalloped Potatoes, 291
serving the seasons. *See* beverages; bread;
   breakfast; desserts; dinner; salads;
   snacks; soups & sandwiches
Simple Syrup Glaze, 230
Simple Syrup Snow Cones, 228
Slow-Cooked Dried Beans, 290
Smoothie, Smart Start, 258, *259*
Smoothie, Tropical Dreams, *260*, 261
Smoothie Bowl, Tickled Pink, 261
snacks, 242–47
   Cheddar Cheese Ball, 242
   Herb and Dried Tomato Cheese Log, 243
   Herb and Dried Tomato Cheese Spread,
      243, *244*
   Pretty in Pink Deviled Eggs, 246, *247*
   Rustic Herb and Garlic Crackers, *244*,
      245
   Tomato Basil Crackers, 245
   Totally Twisted Yogurt, *256*, 257
soups & sandwiches, 262–73
   Candied Bacon Chicken Sandwich, 268
   Chive Blossom Vinaigrette, 280
   Creamy Roasted Tomato Soup, 262
   Fresh Pea Soup, 264, 265
   Rosemary Candied Bacon, *270*, 271
   Teatime Sandwiches, 268, *269*
   Turkey-Stuffed Lettuce Wraps, *272*, 273
   Vegetable, Beef, and Farro Soup, *266*,
      267
   Vegetable and Bean Soup, 263
Spiced Blackberry Vinegar, 188
Spiced Blueberry Simple Syrup, 229
Spiced Honey, 215
Spiced Raspberry Jam, 79

Spiced Raspberry Syrup, 228
Spiced-Up Fruit Chips, 134
Spicy Finishing Salt, 209
spinach, about, 33, *34*, 126, 149
Spinach Parm Pasta, *298*, 299
squash, 33, 128, 150–51
   squash potato bites, 153
   Zucchini, Stuffed, 285
   Zucchini Bundt Cake, Chocolate, 332
   Zucchini Chips, Chive Blossom, 136
strawberries, 26, 122, 146
   Minty Strawberry-Orange Sauce, 311
   Strawberry, Cucumber, and Mint Garden
      Cooler, 162
   Strawberry, Lime, and Thyme Cooler,
      239
   Strawberry Chocolate Chunk Ice Cream,
      39
   Strawberry Patch Ice Cream, 39
   Strawberry Rose Jam, 47
   Strawberry Rose Sorbet, 39
   strawberry tea, 175
   Strawberry Thyme Bars, 325
   Strawberry Thyme Simple Syrup, 230
   Strawberry Top Simple Syrup, 230
Stuffed Zucchini, 285
sugar. *See also* honey, infused
   Fruity Sugar, 218
   Infused Sugar Shapes, *220*, 221
   infusing, 211, 216, 217
   in jams and jellies, 75
   Rose Sugar, 218
   Rose Sugar Body Scrub, 222
   Sugar Cookies, Floral, 318, *319*
   Sugared Botanicals, 222
Summer Sunset Champagne Cocktail, 239
Summer Sunset Mocktail, 239
Sunshine Mocktail, 236
Sweet Chili Sauce, *275*, 276
Sweet Garden Toast, 253, *253*
sweet infusions, 210–31. *See also* honey,
   infused; sugar; syrups
sweet potato bites, 153
syrups
   Blueberry Basil Simple Syrup, 225, *227*
   for boiling water canning, 65, **66**
   Butterfly Pea Flower Simple Syrup, 225,
      226
   Elderberry Syrup, 231
   flavored, about, 224, **224**
   Raspberry Simple Syrup, *226*, 228
   Rhubarb Simple Syrup, *227*, 229
   saving fruit with liquid packs, **19**
   Simple Syrup Glaze, 230
   Simple Syrup Snow Cones, 228
   Spiced Blueberry Simple Syrup, 229
   Spiced Raspberry Syrup, 228
   Strawberry Thyme Simple Syrup, 230
   Strawberry Top Simple Syrup, 230

Tartar Sauce, Homestead, 285
Teatime Sandwiches, 268, *269*

Tequila Sunset Cocktail, 239
Tickled Pink Smoothie Bowl, 261
tisanes (botanical teas), 171–75
tomatoes, 33–35, 74–75, 128, 151–52
    Cheesy Tomato Dipping Oil, 195
    Creamy Roasted Tomato Soup, 262
    Herb and Dried Tomato Cheese Log, 243
    Herb and Dried Tomato Cheese Spread, 243, *244*
    Homemade Tomato Paste, 113
    Pantry Tomato Sauce, 296
    Roasted Marinara Sauce, 297
    Tomato Basil Crackers, 245
    Tomato Basil Pasta Salad, 296–97
tools. *See* boiling water canning; dehydrating; drying; freeze-drying; freezing; jams, no-can; pickles, quick; *individual recipes*
Totally Twisted Yogurt, *256*, 257
Tropical Dreams Smoothie, *260*, 261
troubleshooting, **37, 70–71, 153**
tulsi (holy basil) tea, 174
Turkey-Stuffed Lettuce Wraps, *272*, 273
turnips, 35

vegetables. *See also* charts; *individual names of vegetables*
    Basic Quick-Pickled Vegetables, 59
    culinary powders, about, 113
    dehydrating, 117–19, *118*, 123–28, *124*
    Freeze-Dried Vegetable Chips, 156, *157*
    freeze-drying, *143*, 146–53, *147*, *151*
    freezing, 26–35
    quick pickle partners/preparation for, **54, 57**
    Vegetable, Beef, and Farro Soup, *266*, 267
    Vegetable and Bean Dried Soup Mix, 136
    Vegetable and Bean Soup, 263
    Vegetable Rice, 290
    veggie balls, 153
    Veggie Pasta, 293
    Zero-Waste Vegetable Broth, 163
vinegars, infused, *184*, 185, **186**
    Chive Blossom Vinegar, 187
    Herb Garden Vinegar, 187
    Lavender Vinegar, 187
    Purple Basil Vinegar, 187
    Raspberry Vinegar, 189
    Rose Vinegar, 187
    Spiced Blackberry Vinegar, 188
    Wild Violet Vinegar, 187

water infusions, 160–80
    about, 161
    Apple Spice Tea, 178
    botanical teas, 171–75
    Botanical Water, *164*, 165
    Cold Infusion, 165
    Colorful Fruit Ice Cubes, 169
    Cucumber Body Mist, 165
    fancy pants ice, 166, **166**
    Floral Ice Cubes, 169
    Floral Iced Tea, 178
    Floral Teas, 178
    Fruits and Flowers Tea Blend, *176*, 177
    Garden Coolers, 162
    Herbal Whipped Cream, 180
    Hibiscus Berry Tea, 179
    Holiday Ice Cubes, *168*, 169
    Lemonade Ice Cubes, 169
    Mediterranean Vibes Tea Blend, 177
    Rose Tea Latte, 180
    Rose-Vanilla Tea, 178
    Zero-Waste Vegetable Broth, 163
Whipped Cream, Herbal, 180
Whipped Toppers, 240, *241*
wild violets
    Wild Violet Jelly, 82
    Wild Violet Peppercorn Vinaigrette, 281
    wild violet tea, 175
    Wild Violet Vinegar, 187

yams, 32, 127, 150, 153
Yogurt, Totally Twisted, *256*, 257
Yogurt Drops, Freeze-Dried, *154*, 155
Yogurt Pops, Garden, 38

Zero Waste Alerts, about, 11
Zero-Waste Vegetable Broth, 163
zucchini. *See* squash

About the Author

Holly Capelle is a passionate home cook, dedicated food preservationist, and advocate for sustainable living. She is the founder of @BigFamilyLiving, an online community for people who like to preserve, create, cook, and garden. With more than three decades of culinary experience, Holly Capelle has mastered the art of combining traditional preservation techniques with modern-day practicality. Together with her husband, Kevin, and their six children, she has transformed their suburban home into a thriving mini-homestead, where they grow, harvest, and preserve their own food. She lives just outside Portland, Oregon.

SIMON ELEMENT

An Imprint of Simon & Schuster, LLC
1230 Avenue of the Americas
New York, NY 10020

For more than 100 years, Simon & Schuster has championed authors and the stories they create. By respecting the copyright of an author's intellectual property, you enable Simon & Schuster and the author to continue publishing exceptional books for years to come. We thank you for supporting the author's copyright by purchasing an authorized edition of this book.

No amount of this book may be reproduced or stored in any format, nor may it be uploaded to any website, database, language-learning model, or other repository, retrieval, or artificial intelligence system without express permission. All rights reserved. Inquiries may be directed to Simon & Schuster, 1230 Avenue of the Americas, New York, NY 10020 or permissions@simonandschuster.com.

Copyright © 2025 by Holly Capelle

All rights reserved, including the right to reproduce this book or portions thereof in any form whatsoever. For information, address Simon Element Subsidiary Rights Department, 1230 Avenue of the Americas, New York, NY 10020.

First Simon Element trade paperback edition July 2025

SIMON ELEMENT is a trademark of Simon & Schuster, LLC

Simon & Schuster strongly believes in freedom of expression and stands against censorship in all its forms. For more information, visit BooksBelong.com.

For information about special discounts for bulk purchases, please contact Simon & Schuster Special Sales at 1-866-506-1949 or business@simonandschuster.com.

The Simon & Schuster Speakers Bureau can bring authors to your live event. For more information or to book an event, contact the Simon & Schuster Speakers Bureau at 1-866-248-3049 or visit our website at www.simonspeakers.com.

Interior design by Jen Wang

Photography by Polara Studio: Michael Shay, Jeremy Dunham
Photography on the following pages was provided by Holly Capelle: 78, 168, 249, 252, 302, 309, and 319

Manufactured in China

10 9 8 7 6 5 4 3 2 1

Library of Congress Cataloging-in-Publication Data has been applied for.

ISBN 978-1-6680-2629-8
ISBN 978-1-6680-2630-4 (ebook)